If you want to be challenged and encouraged for your assignment in the marketplace, you will want to read this book! It will give you perspective and help you "stay the course" in whatever you face in your Monday through Friday work.   JAMES BARNETT
President, DaySpring

Richard Blackaby brings a wealth of experience interacting and training countless number of leaders, many who run our nation's largest and most well-known corporations. As a corporate CEO, it was my privilege to sit under his teaching. His keen understanding of the business leader's world and of the Bible and its lessons are invaluable. Richard has captured the essence and true source of inspiration for us all. Regardless of your career position, this book is a must read.   RON F. WAGLEY
Chairman, CEO and President Transamerica Insurance (retired)
Author of, *Finding Strength in Tough Times*

The Inspired Leader is a great book because it is written by exceptional leaders! Richard Blackaby's keen insight into business history combines with life lessons from several outstanding modern-day CEOs. All who aspire to serve God in the marketplace will find this devotional to be a compelling, instructive, and uplifting companion.

JOHN D. BECKETT
Chairman, The Beckett Companies
Author of, *Loving Monday* and *Mastering Monday*

Richard Blackaby's book accomplishes two important things. First, it encourages Christian leaders to take a good look at their own lives and motivations—but not for too long. Second, and more importantly, it helps them take that attention off of themselves, and turn their gaze heavenward.
JIM DALY
President, Focus on the Family

If you are seeking a collection of devotions written for business leaders who need a spiritual boost while seeking to bring glory to God, this devotion will inspire and encourage you.

TERENCE CHATMON
President and CEO, FCCI,
Fellowship of Companies for Christ International

What I especially like about Richard Blackaby's new book is that we, the readers, are both challenged and inspired. The questions at the end of each chapter challenge us to get serious about living out our faith in the workplace. The stories inspire us to live our lives at the highest level possible. This is one of those books that we will read and reread!   TIM IRWIN

Author of, *DeRailed: Five Lessons Learned from Catastrophic Failures of Leadership*

Richard Blackaby's new book makes it possible to learn a new devotional thought each day that will accelerate your career as a leader or person of influence. Knowing Richard's character and devotion I am pleased to recommend his new book: *The Inspired Leader.*

WES CANTRELL
Chairman and CEO Lanier Worldwide (retired)

Richard uniquely uses an engaging style of humor and personal experiences to teach scriptural truth and this has had an enormous impact on my life and those around me. I am forever grateful for our friendship and for the incredible wisdom and truth that the Lord has imparted to me through Richard. Read *The Inspired Leader* and be blessed!   DAVE DUNKEL
Chairman and CEO, KForce, Inc. (Faithful Priest)

I have been with Dr. Blackaby for 20 intense days of study over the last three years. He provided a unique bridge between my Christian life and my business world revealing how each day I can be involved in God's activity in my business. He is a great storyteller and teacher and you will be blessed by reading this book.   JOHN HAMPTON
Chairman and CEO, First Western Bank

Richard Blackaby has influenced my life by his powerful, biblically inspired speaking and writing. His biblically based wisdom brings transformation in the Board Room, to the shop floor, and to the home.

ROBERT VERMEER
Chairman, Vermeer Corporation

In a world where the Christian life can seem so complicated, this collection of devotionals provides clear-cut insight on what it means to be a business leader who is alive with Christ.   BERRY CARTER
President, S&B Filters

In *The Inspired Leader* Richard Blackaby masterfully weaves and intermingles key spiritual principles from Scripture with compelling lessons from the lives of famous historical leaders to create a beautiful tapestry and a powerful, enduring masterpiece. I strongly endorse and highly recommend this book to leaders everywhere. It will encourage, equip and empower you to inspire others. DR. BRUCE COOK

Founder & President, VentureAdvisers Inc.,
Kingdom House Publishing, Kingdom Economic Yearly Summit (KEYS)

Each devotion is thought provoking and character building for anyone who desires to bring the light of Christ into the marketplace. JEFF COORS

Chairman, Fiskeby Holdings US LLC.

Richard Blackaby is a tremendous blessing to Christian business leaders. Over the years, I have enjoyed learning from one of God's great teachers. I am so grateful that he has created a collection of these inspirational devotionals from which we can draw strength as we join God's where he is working in our businesses and in the marketplace.

JOE CRAFTON

President / Partner CROSSMARK, Inc.

Richard has blessed us with *The Inspired Leader*. Once again he has shown how God is using business leaders in the marketplace to impact the world. This devotional is a must read for those in the marketplace…

ED KOBEL

President and COO, DeBartolo Development

Inspiration helps me refocus on what is important. Thanks to Richard and the CEOs who contributed to this book. There are wonderful stories and examples from leaders trying to fight the good fight. May God inspire you as He did me! JACK ALEXANDER

Vice Chairman and Partner, Rainmaker Group Holdings

Richard Blackaby is keenly aware of the challenges that everyone faces as they participate in today's business environment, and has dedicated much of his energy preparing others to rise above them. By recounting the power, wisdom, and love of the Lord, *The Inspired Leader* will encourage and inspire readers to take full advantage of the promises of the Lord.

LOU GIULIANO

Chairman, CEO and President ITT Corp (retired)

Dr. Blackaby is uniquely equipped to meld God's truth with the workplace issues that most of us face each day. His passion for history, leadership, and God's word has inspired me on my spiritual journey.

MIKE MULCAHY, CFA

President, Bridgeway Capital Management, Inc.

Dr. Blackaby has done an exceptional job in providing a handbook for Christian businesspersons. I only wish that every working person in America would read it. It would completely change our culture.

CORT RANDELL
President, Corporate Media Services, Inc.

The Inspired Leader is a profoundly valuable collection of devotionals. The penetrating questions that accompany these devotionals challenge us to focus on the critical reflection that is so important to maintaining a healthy perspective of ourselves and our circumstances in light of the activity of God in our lives.   EDWARD BJURSTROM
Pharmaceutical Executive and Founder of CompassioNow

Richard Blackaby is clearly qualified to author a book on leadership. He comes from the unique perspective of personally bearing such responsibility for a church and seminary, and also interacting with hundreds of business leaders in the course of his work at Blackaby Ministries International. He has taught, counseled, and listened to the testimonies and concerns of CEOs of some of the world's major corporations.

Richard understands this and the obstacles business leaders face in grasping, applying, and implementing biblical truths and insights in the complex and diffuse world of business organizations. The reader who applies this book to their life and work is in for a real blessing.

LAWRENCE COLLETT
Chairman, Cass Information Systems, Inc.

Richard has a God given gift for using historically famous businesspeople and working their lives into spiritually edifying lessons for current times.

LEO F. WELLS
President, Wells Real Estate Funds

The
INSPIRED
LEADER

101 BIBLICAL REFLECTIONS FOR
BECOMING A PERSON OF INFLUENCE

Richard Blackaby

RUSSELL MEDIA

Boise, Idaho

Published in Boise, Idaho by Russell Media
Web: http://www.russell-media.com

Cover and Text Design by Woohoo Ink, LLC

This book may be purchased in bulk for educational, business, ministry, or promotional use.

For information please email info@russell-media.com.

ISBN (print): 978-1-937498-07-8
ISBN (e-book): 978-1-937498-08-5

Printed in the United States of America

CONTENTS

SECTION SIX

SECTION SEVEN

SECTION EIGHT

SECTION NINE

SECTION TEN

OVER THE PAST several years, members of the CEO Forum and I have been privileged to sit under Richard Blackaby's teaching of the Scriptures at the Forum's Spiritual Leadership Institute. God has uniquely gifted Richard with an ability to apply Scripture to real-life situations in the workplace in ways that cause his listeners (or readers) to "get it"—that we not only *should*, but we *can* use Scripture as the basis for our personal and our work lives.

Richard served as president of a seminary for 13 years. In that arena, he faced many of the pressures that corporate leaders face: having to fire executives, meeting budget, addressing immorality in the workplace, facing critical press. So he speaks and writes from a backdrop of personal business experience, but his perspective is also that of a man whose life is steeped in the truth and the power of God's word.

In *The Inspired Leader: 101 Biblical Reflections for Becoming a Person of Influence*, Richard provides wisdom, encouragement, challenge, and hope for Christian business leaders working in secular environments. Following each reflection, which he has taken from his own devotional writings produced for the CEO Forum and from those of other Forum members, he invites us to "Reflect for a moment," asking ourselves—and God—how we can apply what we've read to truly become persons of influence for His kingdom.

I'm honored to count Richard Blackaby not only as a teacher and spiritual mentor, but also as a friend and trusted colleague. I wholeheartedly recommend *The Inspired Leader* to you.

DAVID "MAC" MCQUISTON
President and CEO, CEO Forum, Inc.

As an eighteen-year-old, first-year university student, I had an unforgettable encounter with God. When it was over, I knew I'd be spending the remainder of my life serving Him. As might be expected for an on-fire Christian of my vintage, I began preparing myself to go to seminary upon graduation from college, and then becoming a pastor of a church. Sure enough, after some eventful moments in university and a prolonged stay at seminary, I launched my ministry career as the senior pastor of Friendship Baptist Church, in Winnipeg (affectionately dubbed "Winterpeg" by its frigid inhabitants) Canada.

My ministry at the church would be considered a success by most standards. Numbers rose significantly. Debts were paid off early. Enthusiasm became widespread. But something changed during my fledgling years as a minister. I always worked hard, arriving at the office generally by 6:30 a.m. Each week I would diligently prepare my sermons, perform various administrative duties, meet with staff, and conduct my correspondence. Everything I did anticipated the coming Sunday, the big day. My success as a minister hinged largely on how well Sunday went. Did we have a good attendance? A sizeable offering? Good music? Enthusiastic response? Were there visitors? Did people laugh at my jokes?

After a year or two, I had the church functioning like a well-oiled machine. But something seemed to be missing. It dawned on me that while I sat ensconced in my church office day after day, waiting for Sunday to return, my congregants were marching off to work each morning, living out their lives in the midst of the marketplace. I began to realize that the "action" was not so much what happened for an hour or two at the church building on Sunday morning, but what my people were experiencing at their workplaces and in their neighborhoods, Monday through Friday.

I began paying visits to my members where they worked. For the vast majority of them, it was the first time a minister had ever been to their office or shop floor. To say it was eye-opening is an understatement. I had no idea what they dealt with each week! Some faced enormous pressure from their overbearing boss to compromise their moral convictions. Others carried the burden of responsibility for hundreds of employees. Several faced the constant scrutiny of government regulations. Others worked in hospitals and with people suffering from psychological issues that left them emotionally fatigued. Still others labored for companies in financial crisis, unsure if they would still have a job the following week. I also saw that many of my church members were highly regarded and appreciated by their colleagues. The people in my church were engaged in spiritual battles every day, and I had just learned where the front line was!

I learned some important lessons as a young minister. For one, church services on Sundays were not the primary work. That is where we met with God corporately so we could prepare for our task. The mission for God's people occurs once they leave the church building and go out into the world. My job as a pastor was not to enlist laypeople to help me to have a successful church. My calling was to equip the people to be salt and light when they went to work. Finally, I learned that it can be tough practicing your faith in a secular environment that is often hostile to your beliefs.

Since that time, I have found myself investing myself in undergirding and equipping those who enter a hostile mission field each day as they go to work. I have also been privileged to work with a number of outstanding Christian organizations whose purpose is to minister to the marketplace. The ministry I have been most involved with is the CEO Forum. This organization ministers to Christian CEOs in corporate America as well as in Asia. Through it I have been privileged to get to know outstanding, talented, and dedicated Christian business leaders who are purposefully and successfully impacting their world for Christ. I have also worked with organizations such as the Fellowship of Christian Companies International that is helping business leaders be on God's agenda in their business.

If you were to ask me where I see God at work today, I would tell you, "In the marketplace." That is the forum in which God has always worked. And, it is where He has gathered many of His most talented and dedicated servants. If you work in a secular job, this book is for you. It is a collection of devotionals written for people who need a spiritual boost as they go to work each day while seeking to bring glory to God.

ACKNOWLEDGEMENTS

Thank you to my wife Lisa.
Every year I think I could not possibly grow
to love her any more than I already do,
and then I always discover I was wrong!

Thanks to my children: Mike, Daniel, and Carrie.
They make me have hope for the future!

Thanks also to Mac McQuiston and the CEO Forum
for the privilege of investing in some amazing
men and women of God who are serving their Lord
in extraordinary ways in the marketplace.

THE HUMAN BODY craves water. Our bodies use two to four liters daily. People can only live three to five days without it. Without proper amounts, our bodies soon begin suffering the debilitating effects of dehydration. Certain conditions such as cold or hot temperatures or physical exercise cause us to require greater amounts of water. Physically, we have all experienced this and innately know it to be true.

What can catch us by surprise, however, is that our souls require continuous replenishing as well. Without it, we soon begin to suffer the effects of spiritual dehydration. Depending on the condition of our environment, our spirit dries up at varying rates. The business world can quickly parch our spiritual vitality. It regularly bombards us with materialistic attitudes. The love of money is widespread. Greed, corruption, selfishness are ubiquitous. Non-Christian colleagues and people who are critical of our faith can drain our spiritual vibrancy. As we progress through the week, the spiritual "high" we experienced on Sunday can quickly morph into a desolate wilderness by Friday. If we are not careful, our souls become parched and barren.

The psalmist David lamented: "*O God, you are my God; early will I seek You; my soul thirsts for You; my flesh longs for You in a dry and thirsty land where there is no water*" (Psalm 63:1). David recognized that the only remedy for a withered soul was spending time in God's presence. One way to do that was to worship God in the tabernacle. David said, "*So I have looked for You in the sanctuary, to see Your power and Your glory*" (Psalm 63:2). David could also obtain spiritual nourishment by spending personal time with the Good Shepherd who invariably led him beside still waters (Psalm 23:2).

That is the purpose of this book. It is designed to provide

you some tranquil moments beside still waters where you can refresh your soul before getting back to work. Today's marketplace is stressful. It is often antagonistic to your faith, and draining to your soul. The following pages are designed to provide a spiritual oasis. Let the truths contained in them refresh, challenge, and prepare you for what God knows is coming next in your life.

I originally wrote many of these devotions for an amazing group of Christian CEOs of major American companies. This book also contains devotions written by some of those CEOs as they share the spiritual lessons God taught them on shop floors and in boardrooms. They live where you do and they have experienced the practical difference Christ makes in their work life. God has used these words to encourage and inspire top business leaders across America as well as in Asia. My prayer is that you will allow the truths contained in the following pages to speak to your heart and to revive your spirit.

God's Call on Your Life

DAVID EVENTUALLY BECAME immensely wealthy. More than a few people who knew him as a youth would have been surprised at how his life ultimately turned out. David grew up as a simple shepherd boy, the youngest of eight brothers. Later he was appointed chief harpist for the king when the monarch needed his jittery nerves calmed. He rose to become his nation's most renowned warrior and Philistine slayer. Unfortunately, David subsequently topped the government's "most wanted" list as a homeless fugitive with a price on his head. Despite seemingly insurmountable odds, he eventually rose to become king and lived in a palace in the City of David. His is truly a "rags to riches" story. If David lived in our day, he might write a book on *How To Leverage Your Shepherd's Staff into a King's Scepter* and make the rounds on the morning talk show circuit. But notice what David asked God:

"Lord, make me to know my end, and what is the measure of my days, that I may know how frail I am. Indeed, You have made my days as handbreadths, and my age is as nothing before You; certainly every man at best is but a vapor. Surely every man walks about like a shadow; surely they busy themselves in vain; he heaps up riches and he does not know who will gather them. And now, Lord, what do I wait for? My hope is in you".   PSALM 39:4-7

Success didn't go to David's head! He had a healthy perspective on his life. He knew that all good things come to an end, even being the top CEO in the nation. We don't hear of David feverishly collecting and building palaces. He did not hide in his treasury greedily counting gold coins, nor did he invest his nation's resources building grandiose monuments to perpetuate his legacy. Instead, David placed his trust in God. His aspirations were for eternal life. He sought to live his life with purpose and joy. David realized that accumulating wealth, power, or fame was fleeting at best, completely dissatisfying at worst.

Consider for a moment that God has determined your life's purpose, just as He did for David. He knows to the exact second how long your life will be. He is aware of how your life can exert its maximum impact and how you can experience the most joy. The only way for *you* to know these things is to relate to Him, closely. You only get to live your life *once.* So develop a close, vibrant, growing walk with Christ and let Him reveal to you His purposes for your life. Then live that life with abandon.

Your Life's Dream

JON HAMMOND SAGELY noted: "The early bird may get the worm, but the second mouse gets the cheese." Many people dream of obtaining the "cheese" in life. However, not everyone is successful.

As a young man, John Rockefeller envisioned being worth $100,000 one day. He spent the remainder of his life far surpassing that youthful ambition. In the eleventh grade Bill Gates predicted that by the age of 30 he'd be a millionaire. In fact, by age 31 he was worth a billion. Warren Buffet claimed that he'd reach one million in net worth by the age of 35. The rest, of course, is history.

Some people set goals that are perpetually out of their reach. As a young man, George Washington tried to join the British Navy but was thwarted. He grew up dreaming of becoming an officer in the British Army. Some speculate that his future animosity toward the British stemmed in part from the fact that colonials were prohibited from serving as officers in the British Army. Washington eventually recalibrated his aspirations and experienced stellar success.

Some people achieve or surpass their youthful goals only to discover that their dreams were not worth their life's investment. As a young man, Paul had a compelling vision for his life. He aspired to be a prominent national leader who

21

dominated its religious scene. Yet one day he came face to face with the risen Christ. God gave Paul a new purpose for his life: to take the Gospel to the Gentiles across the known world. His life dream was upgraded! Now it originated from heaven rather than his self-righteous ego. At the close of Paul's life he declared, *"I was not disobedient to the heavenly vision"* (Acts 26:19).

In Shakespeare's *Tempest,* the aged Prospero announced,

> *Our revels now are ended. These our actors,*
> *as I foretold you, were all spirits, and are melted into air,*
> *into thin air: And like the baseless fabric of this vision,*
>
> *The cloud-capp'd tow'rs, the gorgeous palaces,*
>
> *The solemn temples, the great globe itself,*
>
> *Yea, all which it inherit, shall dissolve,*
>
> *And, like this insubstantial pageant faded, leave not a*
> *rack behind.*
>
> *We are such stuff as dreams are made on;*
> *and our little life is rounded with a sleep.*

Your life's dream will ultimately define your life. It may be to attain a certain position or to enjoy prosperity or to make the world a better place. Perhaps you are purposing to enjoy your family or to build a great company. You may be intentionally investing your life in extending God's kingdom. Life is, indeed, the stuff of dreams. The question is: is your dream worth the investment of your life?

> *For in the multitude of dreams and many words*
> *there is also vanity. But fear God*
>
> ECCLESIASTES 5:7

REFLECT FOR A MOMENT

1. *What is driving your career? Is it simply to earn a living? Become rich? Pay off your debts? Or is it to fulfill God's purpose for your life?*

2. *Do you know what God's will is for you? Would you recognize God's voice if He was communicating it to you?*

3. *Take a few moments to pray and ask God to clearly reveal His will for your life. Start a journal and write down everything you sense the Holy Spirit says to you over the next couple of months as you read your Bible, pray, attend Bible studies and church, listen to Christian music, and read books. Keep your spiritual senses alert to what He communicates to you.*

Positioned by God

WHEN GOD LAUNCHED His magnificent work to provide salvation for all humanity, He called Abraham, one of the most successful businessmen of his day (Genesis 24:35). Abraham's son Isaac also prospered in the marketplace (Genesis 26:12-14). Likewise, Isaac's son Jacob became wealthy through his business acumen (Genesis 30:43). These were the Patriarchs of God's people. They were not priests, pastors, or missionaries, but businesspeople. Amos was not a prophet, nor the son of a prophet but a sheep breeder and a tender of sycamore fruit (Amos 7:14). Jesus would later follow this pattern when He called fishermen and businesspeople as His disciples (Mark 1:16-20). The patriarchs were trained, not in religious schools, but in the marketplace. It was as they surrendered their lives, skills, and abilities to their Lord that they dramatically impacted their world.

Then there was Joseph. He, too, had youthful dreams of what his life could achieve (Genesis 37:5-11). However, his career was unlike those of his prosperous ancestors. He lost his mother when he was young. His ten older brothers hated him and treacherously sold him into slavery after first contemplating murder. He was unjustly imprisoned by his master and forgotten by his friends. At this point in his life, had Joseph written an autobiography entitled *Success in the*

Marketplace, it would not have been a bestseller!

When he later reviewed his career with his brothers, Joseph concluded, *"But as for you, you meant evil against me; but God meant it for good, in order to bring it about as it is this day, to save many people alive"* (Genesis 50:20). Viewing Joseph's life from a human perspective, you would naturally focus on how people betrayed and injured him throughout his life. You would notice the numerous disappointments he suffered. But Joseph viewed his life from God's perspective. God knew a world crisis was looming. He wanted one of His servants to be positioned to make a significant difference internationally when calamity struck. God used a circuitous route to place Joseph as the CEO controlling the Egyptian economy, raising him up out of a squalid prison to achieve his nation's second most influential post. Significantly, when God chose Joseph to impact his world, God didn't make him a general or a minister; He elevated him to be an influential administrator involved in business. To serve God, Joseph didn't need theological or military training. Instead, he had to understand grain storage, commerce, and government finance. Because God strategically positioned His servant, thousands of lives were spared, God's name was glorified, and God's purposes advanced.

From your vantage point, you could trace how you achieved your current position: a good education, hard work, superior job performance, and some lucky breaks. But how does God view your career? Could your previous experiences be preparatory for God's great assignment for your life? Our world is in dangerous and critical times. God is positioning His servants in crucial roles throughout the marketplace so they can impact peoples' lives globally, change their world, and uplift His name. God placed you where you are for a purpose. Do you know what it is? You may have plans for your career and for your company, but God has one too. Whose plans are you following?

REFLECT FOR A MOMENT

1. *Has God led you to develop certain skills that could be beneficial to His kingdom? If so, what are they and how is God presently using them?*

2. *Have you experienced some difficult times in your career? How might God use those experiences for His purposes?*

3. *People view your life and career from one perspective. How might God's perspective on your life be different from what people see? Why is that important?*

Drudgery or Calling?

WHEN A *USA Today* online poll asked people, "If you won the lottery, would you quit your job?" 45.4% replied "definitely." Another 18.9% said "probably." Only 10.9% claimed they definitely would not retire. It is perhaps telling that two-thirds of the respondents would abandon their work without hesitation. Apparently vast numbers of people are working from necessity but not out of a sense of calling. If people typically enter the workforce at age 20 and retire at age 65, they will generally work 40 hours per week, 2,000 hours per year, and 90,000 hours over a lifetime. That's a lot of time to spend doing one thing when you would rather be doing another.

God designed people to work. Even in the perfect Garden of Eden people had jobs to do. God commanded the first people, *"Be fruitful and multiply; fill the earth, and subdue it, have dominion over the fish of the sea, over the birds of the air, and over every living thing that moves on the earth"* (Genesis 1:28). After God gave people their assignments, He declared that everything He had done was "good" (Genesis 1:31). God has a purpose for our work lives.

It was because of sin that work God designed to be noble was transformed into toil and drudgery (Genesis 3:17-19). Now, instead of honoring God through their labor, people count down the minutes (or years) until their job is over. But life is meant to be far more than merely putting in time until retirement affords people the "good life." Life is a calling—an opportunity for people to fulfill God's purposes.

Just as Jesus called businesspeople to follow Him and to become fishers of men (Mark 1:16-20), so Christ beckons us to follow Him as we work each day. Our life's purpose involves far more than merely earning a living or paying our bills. It stems from our calling to follow Christ and to serve Him wherever He leads.

Burl Cain accepted the job as warden at Angola state prison in 1995. At the time, Angola was the most violent and dangerous prison in America. Louisiana's state laws ensured that a life sentence meant life—no chance for parole, period. With 3,700 serving life sentences and the remaining 1,500 sentenced to an average of 91 years, the men had nothing to lose, no incentive for good behavior. Angola was a house of darkness, the abode of the hopeless. Enter Warden Cain.

For Cain, going to work each day could have been a sentence, if he had not viewed his job as a divine calling. He began teaching the course *Experiencing God* to the inmates. Hundreds of the prisoners were converted and many of those felt God call them into ministry and some even to missions. Violent crimes in the prison declined by 73%. Other prisons requested some of Cain's prisoners, so dozens of "missionaries" were sent out in groups of two. One prison saw violence decrease by 48% only six months after receiving two of Angola's inmates. Cain introduced numerous novel programs into Angola to minister to the inmates and their families. He loves his job and believes God called him to it for a reason. The inmates are effusive in their praise for him and the difference he has made in their lives.

What about you? Are you counting the days until you can retire and finally do what you want to do? Or are you counting the ways your world is becoming a better place and lives are being transformed because God called you to your career? God gave you gifts and an aptitude that has made you successful. Do you know why? Are you using your skills and influence for Him?

REFLECT FOR A MOMENT

1. *Do you feel invigorated by your job or is it drudgery? Why is that?*

2. *Do you have a sense that God has called you to your present job? If so, what is the evidence? How is the world becoming better because of what God is doing through your life?*

3. *What would need to change for you to be more excited about your work? Do you need to change jobs or gain a new perspective on your current one?*

Spiritual Incubation

BILL GATES WAS a child prodigy. While enrolled at a private boys' school named Lakeside, he was introduced to his first computer and was instantly smitten. As a teenager, Gates spent every moment he could working on computers and writing programs. He and some teenage friends formed a technology company. Then in 1973, during his senior year of high school, the giant defense contractor TRW hired Gates along with his friend Paul Allen, to debug one of its software programs. Gates took three months off from his senior year in high school and moved into an apartment with Allen to take on his first-full time job (earning $165/week). He returned home in time to graduate. The only calculus class he attended that year was the final, which he aced. He set aside his dream of forming a software company to honor his parents' wishes for him to attend university. He once told a friend he had gone to Harvard University to learn from people who were smarter than he was… and left disappointed. Two years later, in 1975, Gates dropped out of Harvard to launch the Microsoft Company, along with his high school friend, Paul Allen. The dream birthed in Gates as a high school student had become a reality at last.

The greatest achievements in our lives don't usually occur instantaneously, but over time, and often after much hard work. The seeds of your eventual success may be planted in your life years before they reach fruition.

The greatest achievement of Mary's life occurred after an angelic messenger informed her, *"And behold, you will conceive in your womb and bring forth a Son, and shall call His name Jesus. He will be great, and will be called the Son of the Highest; and the Lord God will give Him the throne of His father David"* (Luke 1:31-32). God's answer for the deliverance of His people was not a full-grown adult, but a baby. God had done this before. He also sent Moses, Samson, Samuel, and John as babies to people in need of deliverance.

Imagine what it must have been like for Mary to be raising a child from infancy that she knew was God's answer to her peoples' prayers. For years Mary would have taught and nurtured and cared for her child as He matured and gradually prepared for His divine role. What went through Mary's mind as she heard her people crying out to God for deliverance while she knew the Deliverer was playing childhood games with His friends?

At times God will give birth to a dream in your heart. Perhaps it is a company He inspires you to start. Maybe it is a new ministry He intends to do through your life. He may speak to you about writing a book. But the time is not yet. The vision God gave you needs to mature and grow. It must be nurtured and developed over time. Can God trust you to nurture a divine work in your life until it is full grown?

Some people never experience the mighty work God intended to do in and through their life because they don't have the patience to allow God to bring His work to maturity. They want to act *now.* They want deliverance *now.* They don't want to wait for God's work to be nurtured and cared for until its time has come. As a result, they never experience what could have been. What is God currently preparing to do in and through your life? Are you faithfully waiting and preparing?

REFLECT FOR A MOMENT

1. *Has God placed a dream in your heart? If so, what is it?*

2. *Are you presently waiting for God to accomplish some things in your life or to provide something for you? How are you waiting? Have you remained patient? Faithful? Believing? Other?*

3. *Do you sense God wants to do more through your life than He presently is? If so, what must happen in you, before you are prepared for God's new work? Based on how you have followed God so far, does your track record demonstrate you can handle more from God?*

Just as He Pleased

FOR DECADES, TRUETT Cathy, founder of the popular fast-food chain, Chick-fil-A, found time each Sunday to teach a fifth grade boys' Sunday School class at First Baptist Church, Jonesboro, Georgia. Numerous businessmen would later testify to having had the chicken sandwich tycoon as their Sunday School teacher. Likewise, John Rockefeller taught Sunday School at his church for many years. It seemed an oddity to many that the wealthiest man in America would take time every Sunday to attend church and to teach Bible stories to children. Yet while Rockefeller's business ethics might be questioned at times, his devotion to his church was legendary.

Wise businesspeople understand that, regardless of their corporate commitments, they have a higher calling. Sir Thomas More rose to the highest office under the intimidating Henry VIII. As the king's chancellor, he administered much of the kingdom for his sovereign. One day while in church, More kept receiving urgent messages that the king needed him at once. Undeterred, More remained in the worship service. He finally sent a message to Henry that he would come shortly, but only after he had paid homage "to a higher king." Even though he worked under one of the most demanding, and notorious, CEOs in history, More always maintained his love for Christ and His Church.

Scripture teaches that we do not choose the church we attend based on our tastes in music or our appreciation of particular preaching styles. Rather, "*God has set the members, each one of them, in the body just as He pleased*" (1 Corinthians 12:18). God has a unique purpose for every congregation. To properly equip each church for its assignment, Christ adds particular members to that body. The members bring unique skills, passions, and experience with them that can equip their church to fulfill its divine assignment.

Businesspeople have unique skills. They are often entrepreneurial. They solve problems. They understand marketing. They generally have good people skills. They have a practical, pragmatic outlook. As you feel drawn to a particular church, you must ask, "Why is Christ adding me to this congregation? What is it God has placed in my life that He knows my church needs?" Sometimes we see problems in our church. Such occasions are not opportunities to criticize or to leave, but to let Christ use our lives to be a part of His solution. If you are presently in a church that is suffering difficulties, could it be that Christ added you to your congregation for such a time as this?

Scripture also teaches that "*if one member suffers, all the members suffer with it; or if one member is honored, all the members rejoice with it*" (1 Corinthians 12:26). When Christ assembles a congregation, members do not suffer or rejoice alone. They are interconnected.

It's easy for people to become so consumed with their business commitments that their involvement in their church languishes. Businesspeople can invest their best efforts and skills into making their business successful and then offer little to make their church more effective. We must remember that Christ is the Head of our church (Colossians 1:18). We owe Him our ultimate loyalty. If He placed you into a particular congregation, He had a purpose. Are you presently investing yourself fully into the church body Christ assigned you?

REFLECT FOR A MOMENT

1. *Presently, are you actively involved in a local congregation? Rate your involvement on a scale of 1-10, with 10 being the most involved.*

2. *Why do you think God led you to the church He did? How is He leveraging your skills and resources to bless your church?*

3. *What adjustments might you make so you do more to bless your church in the future? What is preventing you from making those adjustments now?*

Opportunities

WINSTON CHURCHILL SPENT most of his life in politics. His career encompassed numerous failures and disappointments. His father, Sir Randolph Churchill, never believed his son would make much of himself, despite his continual effort to do so. Winston later confessed that his father had told him he should join the army. This was not, as Winston first supposed, because he showed an aptitude for the service, but because he demonstrated no promise for law. Winston lost office and switched political parties more than once. He repeatedly teetered on the brink of bankruptcy. Yet on May 10, 1940, he finally became Prime Minister of Britain. He was 66 years old. It would not be until he was a senior citizen that Winston Churchill achieved the position he had coveted his entire life.

Harry Truman's early life was, like Churchill's, filled with disappointment. He suffered bankruptcy. Being a plainspoken, ordinary man, he was often overlooked. He was usually the underdog in elections in which he ran. He was the third vice president to serve under Franklin Roosevelt. His presidency, beginning when he was 61, was much like Churchill's role as prime minister, largely unexpected. In each case, the men served with distinction and changed the course of history.

Moses was 80 years old when God gave him the assignment of his life. Everything he had done previously was preparatory to the task the octogenarian would undertake for the enslaved Israelites. When God first told Moses of His plans, the shepherd was filled with excuses why he could not do what God was asking. Yet God was far from finished with Moses. In fact, his best days were still ahead of him.

In youth we are generally blessed with vigor and vision. We feel as if anything is possible. As we get older, we tend to become more conservative and careful. Rather than a vision for the future, we begin to play it safe and count the years until retirement. Yet with God, we can't rest on our laurels. We never reach an expiry date on our usefulness to Him. With God there can always be a new opportunity for us to serve Him, regardless of our age or previous success. That is what makes walking with God so exciting. There is always a fresh opportunity looming, if we are faithful.

Some people become the victims of their previous success. They have achieved much in the past so they begin to think their best days are behind them. They glory in their fruitful past rather than anticipating what God will do through their lives next. Others are victims of their past. They may have failed in previous efforts. Perhaps people have dismissed them as being of no further usefulness. As a result, they are not even looking for what God might have for them next.

This is not to say that we will achieve our greatest roles later in life, as Churchill and Truman did. But it does mean there can always be a new undertaking that challenges us afresh and calls upon everything we previously learned in life. With God, there are limitless possibilities!

How are you living? Are you winding down, coasting,

living in the past, or expectantly embracing life, knowing that God is never finished with you and that He always has one more thing for you to do and to become?

REFLECT FOR A MOMENT

1. *Are you living your life with a continual sense of expectation? Or, have you become pessimistic about your future? Why?*

2. *Is your life characterized by exciting new adventures or by focusing on what happened in the past? Has your past history encouraged you or discouraged you? How is your past affecting your present outlook on life?*

3. *Do you truly believe that with God ALL things are possible? If so, how does the way you are living reflect that belief?*

Alert Expectancy

Lou Giuliano

Chairman and CEO ITT CORP, retired. Workforce Ministries

OVER THE LAST several years I have had the privilege of mentoring a number of businessmen in significant leadership positions who have a strong desire to follow the Lord. As I reflect on our conversations, they eventually revolve around career issues. Most people I talk with express dissatisfaction with where they are or they are facing job transitions that are raising vexing concerns. Of course, I don't have answers for them, just more questions. God has you in your job for a reason. What do you think that is? Is God using your current position to open doors to new opportunities? Most often the answer is, "I don't know," which suggests the need for more prayer, Bible study, and patience.

God provides practical guidance to us in the Scriptures. Unless we remain closely connected to Him, we can do nothing (John 15:5). Our first task is to continue to build our relationship with Him. Throughout our questioning and decision-making, He must remain at the center of our thoughts. Henry Blackaby puts it succinctly: "Find out where God is working and join Him." We need to be "aggressive responders" to the Lord's direction.

But this is entirely foreign to what most business leaders are accustomed to doing! We are much more comfortable taking the lead, planning ahead, and making things happen. The idea of responding to another's plan, rather than carrying out our own doesn't fit with our training, experiences, or aptitude! As usual, this is the complete opposite of what the world has trained us to do. I have come to expect that if an approach does *not* run contrary to popular thinking, it probably is not coming from God!

Abraham is a great example of God working in a manner that ran contrary to commonly held assumptions. God revealed His unusual plan to Abraham. Abraham believed and obeyed. The result: *"We call Abraham 'father' not because he got God's attention by living like a saint, but because God made something out of Abraham when he was a nobody."* (Romans 4:17 *The Message*). *God's plan often requires patience and character, but if we are willing to remain faithful and in a state of "alert expectancy," we are never left shortchanged* (Romans 5:3-5 *The Message*).

Alert expectancy. What an exciting way to look at things! Our faith in Christ gives us the opportunity to live in a state of alert expectancy; patiently waiting for what God will do next. People who choose this path will one day look back in amazement at what God did.

In one instance a man chose to leave a good, long-term employer for family reasons, and accept a staff role in a new company. His friends all said moving from a P & L responsibility to a staff job was a mistake—a step backwards for his career. He was violating conventional wisdom. But he sought to put his family's needs first, responding as he thought the Lord was leading him to. He not only enjoyed the new position, but within two years he was back in a P & L slot and within the next few years, he unexpectedly found himself as the CEO of this Fortune 500 company. It is amazing to watch God do through us what we could never accomplish on our own. It is comforting to know we have a God who is, always faithful, desires more for us than we could imagine, and perfectly capable of doing the impossible.

If you are presently facing significant challenges in your life, trust in the Lord! Be an aggressive responder who lives with alert expectancy!

Godspeed.

REFLECT FOR A MOMENT

1. *Would you describe the style of your Christian life as, "alert expectancy"? Do you assume God will show you what to do next?*

2. *Are you an "aggressive responder"? When God speaks, are you quick to respond?*

3. *How attached are you to your plan? Could you relinquish it for God's? Have you?*

Starched Collars and Black Robes

David L. Dunkel
Chairman and CEO, KForce, Inc.

Last Mother's Day my wife and I had the opportunity to visit my 84-year-old widowed mother who lives 1,200 miles away. As we talked and caught up, I found myself excitedly relaying all that God was doing in my life and as my passion increased, my mom stopped me and said, "You know, I always thought you would be a priest." Our family has a long history in the Catholic faith (including my years as an altar boy), so our image of a priest was white starched collars and black robes. There are many references to priests (1 Peter 2:5) throughout Scripture but especially important to me is 1 Samuel 2:35: *"Then I will raise up for Myself a faithful priest who shall do according to what is in My heart and in My mind. I will build him a sure house, and he shall walk before My anointed forever."*

As we grow in our faith and understanding of what it means to be called by God, it can be intimidating to consider that *we* are the priests He is referring to in the above passage. In fact, we know that priests and pastors are not restricted to clerics ministering in church buildings adorned with crosses. A defining moment in the life of a committed follower of Jesus

Christ occurs with the realization that we *are* priests, and that as priests we hold a special responsibility to be "faithful" in carrying out what is on the Lord's heart and mind.

We, of course, are not capable in and of ourselves of the faithfulness God asks of us. Fortunately, the High Priest, Jesus Christ, lives in us through the Holy Spirit (Galatians 2: 20; Colossians 1: 27). As the High Priest, He commissions, guides, and empowers us to be "faithful" and to execute what is on His heart. Our role is to accept this commission and diligently seek Him with all our heart, mind, and souls—hearing His voice and being obedient to His priestly assignments.

The rewards of obedience to what is on the Lord's heart and mind are clearly stated: *"I will build him a sure house and he shall walk before My anointed forever."* In our role as "faithful" priest, God has given us a confidence built upon His firm foundation so that our walk is along the path that He has ordained uniquely for us. The significance of this promise should not be overlooked and any risk taken or effort required pales in comparison to the promised reward. So, "Lord, I come before You in humility and awe and ask that You work through Your servant to do what is on Your heart and on Your mind; so that I may be Your faithful priest in the assignment You have given me for Your plans and purposes in the marketplace. I love You Lord and trust in Your promise of a sure house and to walk before Your Anointed forever."

By the way, I answered my mom promptly and directly, "I am, Mom. I am a priest and I am serving the Lord in His ministry field in business." Thankfully I don't have to wear a starched collar or black robe.

REFLECT FOR A MOMENT

1. *Do you see yourself as a priest? If so, how? If not, why not?*

2. *Are you confident you know what is on God's heart and mind? If so, list some of those things.*

3. *Take a few moments to spend time with God and ask Him to lay over your heart what is on His.*

Thy Kingdom Come... Now!

Lawrence A. Collett
Chairman of the Board, Cass Information Systems, Inc.

WE UTTER THIS statement every time we repeat the Lord's Prayer. It is accompanied by the connecting phrase "*on earth as it is in heaven*." In making this request we are generally focused on some future event. We visualize an "end time" period when God will transform the earth, as we know it. His Kingdom will then be present and its rule effective on this planet.

Biblical reality, however, places the kingdom within our grasp *now*. We can, and should, expect to see the many facets of the kingdom expressed in our lives, daily. What prohibits us from doing so?

In addition to deferring this reality to a future event, we also have a tendency to limit the performance of the kingdom to an earthly framework. That is, we reduce kingdom activity and results to what we see and experience in our earthly lives. Our expectations and plans correlate to what our reason and logic perceive.

In doing so, we miss the enormous impact kingdom resources can have on our lives, our work, and the world. Our thoughts and expectations are defined by the "normal" rather than the "supernatural." We settle for less and miss the awesome experience of kingdom power and growth. We also miss the "blessing." That is, seeing the glory of God become reality and experiencing the fullness of His being during our time on earth.

One of the many things Jesus accomplished on earth was to make the kingdom a present reality that can be expressed in our work and daily activities. We can, and should, expect to see kingdom results in all that we put our hand to. This certainly has applications for our business endeavors.

How do we react to challenges that may have a detrimental effect on operational or financial performance? Do we limit ourselves to MBA teachings and methods or allow the kingdom to impact the situation?

In the kingdom, we think bigger than normal. We expect a global impact that affects future generations. We allow ourselves freedom to pursue and expect what seems otherwise impossible. We broaden our scope because we have access to kingdom resources. We are unwilling to settle for worldly activities and results. We expect to overcome, create, exceed, and pursue the unthinkable, the impossible, and the seemingly unobtainable.

When the kingdom comes, we can expect to see the fruit of its activity. We have full access now! What are we waiting for?

REFLECT FOR A MOMENT

1. *How are you presently seeking the kingdom of God as a top priority in your life?*

2. *In what areas of your life, such as work, family, church, do see opportunities for God's kingdom to be advanced?*

God's "Big" Assignments

Greg King
Principal of GCK Ventures, LLC

MOST OF US work or have worked in jobs where we are able to influence a lot of people. Whether it's with employees, analysts, investors, or the media, we have an opportunity daily to serve the Lord in a significant way. I was in just such a position as President of Valero Energy Corporation for many years and I enjoyed this aspect of my job more and more over time. After all, I was serving the Lord in a big way and it felt good.

As a result I tended to focus on certain words of Jesus such as *"the one who has been entrusted with much, much more will be asked"* from Luke 12:48 and *"I will put you in charge of many things"* from Matthew 25:21NIV. I wanted to be a "five talent" guy for the Lord and I thought the best way to do this was to serve the largest number of people He placed in my path.

What I didn't realize until recently is that I had other "bigger" assignments that I either ignored or neglected. I knew that the role of husband and father was a higher priority than those work assignments, but was I living that way each day? What about opportunities at my church or my relationships with extended family and friends? Those were important, but did I view them as important to God as shepherding thousands of employees at my company?

God revealed to me that I was trapped—the big assignments at work were constantly pressing me to work harder, which took away my energy to invest in family, church, or other important relationships. The validation at work fed my ego and gave me significance. I sought the affirmation of man rather than God's affirmation—an easy trap to fall into when you lead an organization of any size. I had become too focused on the world's view of big assignments, but God wanted me to see things from His point of view as He makes clear in Isaiah 55:8, *"For my thoughts are not your thoughts, neither are your ways my ways."* I needed to change my "measuring stick" from the world's perspective to God's perspective.

My definition of a big assignment is changing. It is now much easier for me to obey God when the Spirit nudges me to take a walk with my wife, spend time with a friend in need or write a note to my mother-in-law! The world does not applaud or affirm me, but I know that God is smiling. These are big assignments in His eyes.

This is not to say that being in a position to influence large numbers of people is bad or is not an assignment from God. But what is our motivation? Obedience or our needs? God's smile or the world's temporary pat on the back? This transformation has been significant for me. I now embrace each day, waiting for the Lord to reveal His plans for me instead of asking Him to bless my plans.

Are you more focused on the assignments from God that ultimately feed your ego, give you more power/prestige or add to your bank account? My challenge to you is to ask God to reveal any assignments that you have been neglecting or ignoring and that you would instead embrace them with passion, joy, and gratitude regardless of what others think. God's smile awaits us as we obey Him.

REFLECT FOR A MOMENT

1. *What is your definition of a "big" assignment?*

2. *How has your view of big or important assignments changed over the years?*

3. *How might God evaluate your life and job differently than the way the Harvard Business School might evaluate it? Whose evaluation matters most to you?*

Your Character, Forged in the Marketplace

Peter, Andrew, James, and John were in the midst of their daily routine at work, when Jesus suddenly passed by their fishing boats. *"Follow Me, and I will make you become..."* (Mark 1:17) Jesus said. You can't truly follow Jesus without becoming more like Him. The longer you are with Him, the more you will view circumstances from His point of view. He will place His love for people over your heart. His confidence in the Father will become your attitude. Following Jesus will inevitably change you.

Paul claimed that when you become a Christian, it is no longer you who directs your life, but Christ, who lives out His life in you (Galatians 2:20). In time, Jesus' character becomes your character (Galatians 5:22-23). What a blessed thought! Regardless of how selfish or greedy or hard-hearted we may have been when we commenced following Jesus, we can one day act, and think, and approach life the same way He does.

We must be mindful that God accomplishes His divine work in our lives not once a week as we attend church services, but every day as we go to work. As we interact with difficult clients or troublesome colleagues, Christ will be transforming us into His likeness. Our successes as well as our failures become God's instruments for our character transformation. Every circumstance and relationship becomes a divine tool. What can appear to be a hardship may in fact be God's vehicle for accomplishing His greatest work in our life.

What are your life goals? To be promoted into the CEO office? To become wealthy? To own your own company? To become like Jesus? How far along are you in your quest toward Christlikeness? Are you cooperating in that divine endeavor with the only One who can get you there?

A Higher Standard

IN RECENT YEARS America has been scandalized by a parade of prominent business leaders caught abusing their authority. Due to the public nature of their position, the potential for executives to cause widespread damage is enormous. Accordingly, the media has vigorously condemned them while the courts have levied hefty fines and protracted prison sentences. Bernie Madoff, one of the most notorious of the fallen CEOs, ran a $65 billion Ponzi scheme. He was sentenced to 150 years in prison and ordered to forfeit $17.179 billion in assets. Jeffrey Skilling, one-time CEO of Enron was convicted of fraud and conspiracy. His punishment: a $45 million fine and a 24-year jail sentence. Former WorldCom CEO Bernie Ebbers was sentenced to 25 years of incarceration for securities fraud, conspiracy, and filing false reports with regulators. For misappropriation of Tyco International's corporate funds, Dennis Kozlowski was sent to prison for up to 25 years. The penalty for corruption of a high leadership position is severe in the business world. If anything, it is even more so in the spiritual realm.

The apostle James warned that those holding positions of influence would face greater accountability (James 3:1). The Old Testament backs up James' assertion. Moses was a businessman for 40 years before he became a national leader. After faithfully guiding the Israelites on their exhausting and tumultuous journey, he was on the brink of finally delivering them into the Promised Land. Then, in a moment of frustration, Moses publicly dishonored God. The Lord ordered him to speak to a rock and bring forth water for the thirsty people (Numbers 20:8-13). Instead, Moses angrily struck the stone and spoke as though the glory was as much his as God's. Moses would pay dearly for that blatant, arrogant act. God barred him from achieving the greatest dream of his life, and Moses had to humbly explain to his people, "*The Lord was angry with me for your sakes, and swore that I would not cross over the Jordan, and that I would not enter the good land...*" (Deuteronomy 4:21).

Why was the cost so great for that one transgression? Because Moses was a spiritual leader and an entire nation was watching his relationship with God, ready to take their cue from him. The Bible warns, *"To whom much has been given, much is required"* (Luke 12:48). Conversely, leaders have the privilege of blessing people. God elevated Solomon to the throne so he could uplift his nation. The Queen of Sheba declared of Solomon *"Blessed be the Lord your God, who delighted in you, setting you on the throne of Israel! Because the Lord has loved Israel forever, therefore He made you king, to do justice and righteousness"* (1 Kings 10:9).

Whether it is business, family, politics, or spiritual matters, a leader's conduct *always* affects others. Because of their influence, leaders who betray their office or who disgrace God's name will be held to a high standard of accountability. It matters not who you are. If you dishonor God, it will cost you. The reverse is also true. God will honor you, if you honor Him (1 Samuel 2:30). Consider your current role: Through it are you honoring God and blessing people?

REFLECT FOR A MOMENT

1. *Are you going to work each day with a keen sense that your conduct is a direct reflection on how people will think about God? How does that affect the way you are living?*

2. *Do you have habits or behaviors that are reflecting poorly on Christ? If so, what should you do about them?*

3. *Has God given you much? If He has, how are you using what God gave you to honor Him in return?*

Strengths or Weaknesses?

EVERYONE HAS STRENGTHS and weaknesses. A hotly debated issue for businesspeople is which of those two areas should receive the majority of their attention. In 2001, Marcus Buckingham and Donald Clifton wrote, *Now Discover Your Strengths* in which they claimed people should not waste time trying to improve on their weaknesses but should instead play to their strengths. In a survey of 1.7 million employees globally, only 20% said they were able to engage in activities they were good at during their normal working day. In addition, the higher the people's position in the corporate hierarchy, the less the employee worked in areas of his or her strength. Buckingham and Clifton argue that productivity would dramatically improve if employees and management focused on what they do best.

In 2009, Robert A. Kaiser edited the book, *The Perils of Accentuating the Positive,* in which he and other authors challenged the popular strengths-based view. Kaiser noted, "therein lies the problem: when practiced with single minded focus, the strengths approach can become an exercise in self-indulgence. It emphasizes what comes easy for managers and what they enjoy doing. What is ignored is what the organization needs from the position that the person's job is designed to provide. It is a case of putting the needs of the individual above the needs of the organization." The authors contend that people are naturally drawn to do what comes easily and wins accolades. Few people want to put in the hard work required to strengthen their weaknesses. The problem for those in upper management is that the skills that earned them their corner office are not necessarily the same abilities necessary for their executive duties. Yet most people are reluctant to shift away from that which has traditionally brought them success. If you have always been good with a hammer, when you reach management you continue wanting to hit things with your trusty tool! Furthermore, leaders going 90 mph in their strengths, rarely take time to address their weaknesses. One day, these one-dimensional leaders come crashing down when their neglected weaknesses bring them to ruin.

How do businesspeople who are committed to Jesus Christ address their deficiencies? Certainly they can do as Walt Disney did and hire to their weaknesses. Disney was a creative visionary but unskilled in administration, so he brought his brother Roy on board to handle logistics. When God looks at us, He sees our potential. He is undaunted at addressing our weaknesses, especially if they make us vulnerable or if they reflect poorly on Him. Despite all that Moses accomplished for the nation of Israel, God did not excuse his weaknesses in delegating or anger management (Exodus 18; Numbers 20:1-13). Likewise Jesus knew that Peter had a penchant for boasting and overconfidence (Matthew 26:33-35). Jesus might have ignored Peter's swagger in light of his other strengths, but he did not. Even after Peter failed miserably, Jesus walked with his humbled disciple until he had decisively addressed his weakness (John 21:15-19). Jesus didn't condemn Peter but neither did he excuse or ignore his behavior.

As a business leader, you have strengths that no doubt got you where you are today. What about your weaknesses? Have you been avoiding or excusing them? Are they limiting you? Are others suffering because of them? Why not trust in God's grace to help you overcome them today?

REFLECT FOR A MOMENT

1. *What is one of your strengths? How are you managing it? Is it glorifying God? Are you using it too much? Is it making you overly confident?*

2. *What is one of your weaknesses? How are you addressing it? How has it limited you in the past? What does God want to do about it?*

3. *Have you become a lopsided person? Do you overuse your strengths and avoid your weaknesses? How might you be more effective if you addressed your weaknesses? Have you been hiding behind excuses?*

Our Professional Image

SOME PROFESSIONS PROVIDE ample fodder for stand-up comedians and cartoonists. Politicians have long provided a tempting target for humorists. Mark Twain quipped, "Suppose you were an idiot and suppose you were a member of Congress. But I repeat myself." Will Rogers mused, "I don't make jokes. I just watch the government and report the facts." He also intoned, "Be thankful we're not getting all the government we're paying for" and "This country has come to feel the same when Congress is in session as when the baby gets hold of a hammer."

Recently, along with politicians and attorneys, corporate CEOs have increasingly found themselves in the spotlight of public scrutiny and skepticism. In the June 2009 Rasmussen survey, only 25% of adults surveyed held a favorable view of corporate CEOs. Adding insult to injury, members of Congress were viewed favorably by 30% of adults (*USA Today*, 22 June 2009). To make matters even worse, the public relations tumble by corporate executives has affected their golfing. In an era of massive layoffs and misappropriated company funds, CEOs are apparently wary of being observed golfing while the economy languishes. NetApp CEO Dan Warmenhoven was one of four people who paid $660,000 in 2001 at a charity auction to play a round of golf with Tiger

Woods using Warren Buffet as a caddy. But he later had to curtail his golfing habits. "It's a byproduct of bad economic times" said Warmenhoven (*USA Today,* 22 June 2009). *Golf Digest* magazine publishes a biannual issue rating the top corporate CEO golfers. Interestingly, golf's alleged therapeutic qualities have not always translated into success in the bottom line. Of the top twelve CEO golfers rated by *Golf Digest* in 2006, seven were no longer with the same company in 2009. Of the remaining five, only one CEO's corporation was outperforming the market.

What should business leaders who are followers of Jesus be known for? Their golf scores? Their stock options? Their excessive lifestyles? Or should there be something noticeably different, even admirable, about business people who are committed to following and emulating Christ? Jesus' disciples were known for various behaviors during the skeptical, pagan First Century. In Jerusalem they were recognized as having *"been with Jesus"* (Acts 4:13). In Thessalonica, they were identified as people *"who have turned the world upside down"* (Acts 17:6). In Antioch, they became known as *"Christ-ians"*, or, "belonging to or identified by Christ." In fact, the only three instances where the word "Christian" is used in the New Testament is when non-Christians made observations about the followers of Jesus (Acts 26:28; 1 Peter 4:16).

Business people who profess to follow Christ must recognize that they are under a public microscope. Hopefully they become known as persons of integrity, humility, generosity, and genuine concern for others. In these challenging days, some business leaders are choosing to be more discreet about their personal habits while they are under public scrutiny. What adjustments might you need to make so when people watch your behavior in and out of the workplace, they identify you as someone who clearly shares the heart and priorities of Christ?

REFLECT FOR A MOMENT

1. *What are you known for at work? Are you pleased with your reputation or do you wish it was different? What might you do to change it?*

2. *Do people at your workplace know you are a Christian? If they do, what does the way you conduct yourself lead people to think about Christ?*

3. *Are you focused on issues and behaviors that are important? Or are you known primarily for your hobbies or recreational interests? What are the first things that come to people's minds when they think of you?*

Size Matters!

Malcom Gladwell, in his book *Blink,* relates a survey he took of CEOs of Fortune 500 companies. At the time of his study, the vast majority of CEOs were white males. The average height of the CEOs he studied was just under six feet tall. In contrast, the average height of American men was five feet nine inches. While 14.5% of American men were six feet or taller, among CEOs, the number rose to 58%. In addition, while 3.9% of American men were six feet two or taller, almost 33% of the CEOs he surveyed fell into that category (Malcolm Gladwell, *Blink,* 86-87). Malcolm concluded "Most of us, in ways that we are not entirely aware of, automatically associate leadership ability with imposing physical stature. We have a sense of what a leader is supposed to look like, and that stereotype is so powerful that when someone fits it, we simply become blind to other considerations."

In an earlier age, military might and physical strength were often a prerequisite for leadership, especially in times of warfare (which was often). Being able to wield a sword and stay in your saddle throughout a grueling battle were often as important as your vision for the future and your ability to delegate. People of size and strength automatically gained the loyalty of followers. People who were not tall or particularly muscular or good with a sword or gun were at

a distinct disadvantage. Historians have debated for generations whether the relatively diminutive Napoleon Bonaparte,
standing at five feet six inches was driven as much by an
inferiority complex as he was by his ambition to rule the world.
There is even a syndrome, named the "Napoleon Complex," to
describe people who are driven to prove themselves because
of their small stature.

In one of the most famous biblical expositions on this
issue, the revered judge, Samuel, was looking for Israel's next
king. Having been led to Jesse, of Bethlehem, he naturally
investigated the first-born son. (Eldest children are often
natural leaders and have produced the largest share of U.S.
presidents.) When Samuel looked upon Eliab, the young
man appeared to be everything a leader was expected to be.
But God rejected him. So Jesse ushered his second oldest son,
Abinadab, into the holy man's presence, but to no avail. One
by one Jesse's seven oldest sons were paraded before Samuel
and each one failed to gain God's approval. Jesse hadn't even
thought to summon his youngest son, David, since he did
not seemingly meet the commonly accepted qualifications of
a leader. But, upon seeing him, Samuel knew he had found
God's man. He explained: *"For the Lord does not see as man
sees; for man looks at the outward appearance, but the Lord
looks at the heart"* (1 Samuel 16:7).

While society may not generally place the same value on
one's skill with a battle-axe as it used to, it still prizes attractive,
charismatic, eloquent leaders. The business world values those
with vision and ambition. And, too often, Christian leaders
assume that to succeed, they must conform to the world's
standards. We can spend so much time developing the skills
and appearance the world covets that we neglect areas in our

life that God values. God measures us by our heart. Do we love Him? Do we truly love others? Are we people of faith? If our heart is right with God, there is nothing He cannot do through us. If our hearts are not right, it matters not what secular leadership skills we possess.

REFLECT FOR A MOMENT

1. *Do you fit the stereotype of a worldly leader? Has that been an advantage or disadvantage for you and your career?*

2. *What is it about you that God would focus on if He were looking at you? Would He be as impressed with the qualities that your colleagues notice?*

3. *Where have you spent the bulk of your time and energy: acquiring secular skills valued by society, or developing spiritual and character qualities valued by God? In light of your answer, what adjustments might you need to make?*

Guarding Your Anger

FIELD MARSHAL LORD Allenby was a brilliant World War One commander who led in the overthrow of the Ottoman Empire's stranglehold over the Middle East, liberating both Jerusalem and Damascus. Allenby boasted an illustrious military career, having served in the Second Boer War and later on the Western Front in France during World War One. In 1917, he was given command of the British forces in Palestine with instructions to achieve a breakthrough that forced the Turkish forces to withdraw from the war. The British Army had already suffered two major setbacks before Allenby's arrival. Yet, as one observer noted, "Seldom in the course of military history has the personality of a new commander had such a marked effect on his troops."

Allenby appeared fearless and radiated confidence. He could be relentless in attack. Yet he also had weaknesses. He could lose his temper and, when he did, it was fearsome. He was also a stickler for following rules. If soldiers were expected to have the chinstraps of their helmets in place, Allenby would be furious to find soldiers not following orders. On the Western Front, he once came across the corpse of a soldier who was wearing a cap rather than the mandated steel helmet. Allenby exploded, knowing the man might not have died, had he followed the rules. Perhaps it was this temper that earned the general the nickname "The Bull." His biographer noted that Allenby was never recognized as a great leader, nor was he as popular with his men as one might have supposed, in light of his success. This was due in part because Allenby "lacked a measure of self-control, a little humanity, the power to communicate enthusiasm and to inspire disciples. His sudden explosions of temper, his occasional almost childish petulance, did his reputation the more harm since he never troubled to correct the impression they created" (Archibald Wavell, *Allenby: A Study in Greatness,* 295).

Scripture indicates that "*The Lord is merciful and gracious, slow to anger, and abounding in mercy*" (Psalm 103:8). God is fully aware of our human frailties. He knows only too well how our foolish choices will cost us much grief and heartache. Yet He relates to us graciously. He is *slow* to anger. It is not His automatic response. God seeks to change us rather than to berate us.

People can be extremely frustrating! Their foolish actions can harm your organization and cause you numerous problems. But often your greatness as a leader is not measured by the decibel level you reach as you chew out your colleagues, but by the self-control you demonstrate as you seek a solution. In your encounters with others, do you make them better by what you say?

REFLECT FOR A MOMENT

1. *How well do you handle your anger? Are you known for your temper? How easily do you lose your self-control? If you lose your temper easily, why do you do so?*

2. *What is the greatest character issue that you need to deal with? What is preventing you from addressing it this week?*

3. *Do you tend to focus on others and their need for change, or do you concentrate on what needs to be altered in you? What would God have to change in you for your leadership capacity to be increased?*

Integrity: Is Anyone Asking You the Hard Questions?

J. Michael Perry
EVP Business Development, Williams Financial Group

IF I WERE to ask each of you to describe the values of your organization, I am fairly certain one word would be at the top of that list—Integrity. As leaders of our companies, families, communities, and churches, we all desire to be known as people with honest virtues. And as we all know, this pursuit of integrity in any organization begins with the leadership. As for myself, when I am living a life of integrity, my words and deeds are in sync. I am who I am no matter where I go or with whom I am speaking. Integrity is not so much what we do as it is who we are out of love.

Within the last few years we have witnessed several businessmen and businesswomen, politicians and religious leaders fall short of the values they claimed to uphold. Many of these leaders have publicly professed a personal relationship with Jesus, yet their actions fail to be good representations of the love Jesus embodies. Romans 7:15-16 says, "*I do not understand what I do. For what I want to do I do not do, but what I hate I do. And if I do what I do not want to do, I agree that the law is good* (NIV)". Of course the simple answer to this problem is that people are separated from God—living in their own self-deceptive, self-absorbed, self-centered "I love me" world.

As men and women who wake up daily to follow Jesus in our work, families and communities, we ourselves are not immune to these same shortcomings. It may be something small and seemingly insignificant, but the reality is that we—as men and women of Christ—are not always living up fully to the key aspects of honest living. So as we begin a new year, full of fresh beginnings, our hope and desire is to confess our sins and recognize that we are broken men and women before God in order to be completely reliant on Him for all our needs.

If you have not done so already, I would encourage each of you to ask a close friend who truly knows you to begin asking you the hard questions—sharpening and refining the parts of your heart that are struggling to embody the love and integrity shown by Jesus. James 5:16 says, *"Therefore confess your sins to each other and pray for each other so that you may be healed. The prayer of a righteous person is powerful and effective"*(NIV). This will help us to walk steadily with the Lord on a daily basis and allow Him to refine us so that we will be effective leaders to those we love.

So what are these hard questions?

- How are you treating your spouse and children?

- Are you spending time in Scripture?

- Are you making choices at work that are honoring to God?

- Do you have any sins that you have yet to confess?

By having a close confidant ask these simple questions, you will find that your journey with the Lord will be strengthened far beyond what you can do alone. This will transfer into your leadership abilities and enable your words to match your deeds—thus living a fully integrated life.

REFLECT FOR A MOMENT

1. *Do you have people in your life who have the freedom to ask you difficult, personal questions? If so, who are they? If not, why not?*

2. *Are you comfortable with accountability or do you avoid or resent it? What systems of accountability have you built into your life? If you avoid accountability, why do you?*

3. *Think of one or two people who could help hold you accountable to your commitments if you asked them to. Why don't you increase the circle of accountability in your life during the next month and see if it does not help you take your commitments and integrity to a higher level?*

Guarding Our Achilles' Heel

John D. Beckett
Chairman, The Beckett Companies;
Author, *Loving Monday* and *Mastering Monday*

HARRY STONECIPHER OF Boeing. Mark Hurd at HP. Respected, effective CEOs uprooted through moral failure.

Each of us in leadership is vulnerable. A friend once cautioned, "If you think you can't be deceived, you're deceived already." Adam Galinsky, a business school professor at Northwestern says, "Power makes people feel psychologically invincible and psychologically invisible" (*Wall Street Journal*, 16 October 2010).

Solomon was a king with unparalleled wealth and power. He loved the Lord. God gave him *"wisdom and exceedingly great understanding, and largeness of heart like the sand on the seashore"* (1 Kings 4:29).

However Solomon *"loved many foreign women,"* who, in turn, drew his heart away from the Lord. This was his Achilles' heel and precipitated his downfall. *"So the Lord became angry with Solomon and raised up adversaries"* (1 Kings 11:1, 9, 14).

How do we guard ourselves? Lessons from the Scriptures provide robust companions for our risk-laden journeys through the marketplace.

Watch the little foxes. Solomon himself knew "*little foxes that spoil the vines*" (Song of Solomon 2:15). We must intercept and wrestle down problems when they are small—when no one is looking. A financial executive in our company found ways to get his hands in the cookie jar, grew emboldened, and eventually embezzled a quarter-million dollars.

Mind the "big three" which the Apostle John warned about (1 John 2:16).

Lust of the flesh—the inordinate cravings, the things we feel entitled to and must have.

Lust of the eyes. It matters what we look at, and for how long. The progression for all of us, if we're not careful, is to look… linger… lust.

Pride of life, or in one translation, "boasting of what he has and does." Pride, indeed, goes before a fall. The antidote? Humble yourself. "Never miss an opportunity to humble yourself," a good friend once advised.

When we cross a line, repent. Repentance is an act of the will, not merely an emotional response. It means to stop what we're doing and to proceed in a different direction. "*This is the one I esteem: he who is humble and contrite in spirit, and trembles at my word*" (Isaiah 66:2 NIV 1984).

Finally, our greatest safeguard against moral failure is to walk closely with the Lord, heeding the corrective nudges of the Holy Spirit, applying the Scriptures to our circumstances when they bring warnings, and even "crying out to God" when we are tempted and in danger of falling.

Guard your Achilles' heel. Make it your goal to finish strong. Serve your family, friends, and co-workers by being a good and godly example. We'll never fully know how many people are watching us or who will be either repulsed or inspired by our character and conduct.

REFLECT FOR A MOMENT

1. *What is your Achilles' heel? How are you guarding yourself in the areas you are most vulnerable?*

2. *Do you have an area of your life where you have repeatedly stumbled? If so, how have your dealt with it? Have you truly repented to God? Have you asked the forgiveness of those your behavior affected? What steps have you taken to ensure you do not stumble again?*

3. *Do you tend to excuse your sinful behavior? What excuses have you used in the past (I have always been bad at that... That's just the way I am... I have been under a lot of stress lately...)? How might you take greater responsibility for your actions in the future? Some failures carry enormous consequences. How can you make sure you never fall in those areas?*

Flee

Steve Taylor
Former CEO, Fresh Express

BUSINESS LEADERS WILL be tempted in many unique and compelling ways. Success and the acclaim of others can lead to pride. It becomes all about us and our gifts and talents. Financial rewards open the door to many opportunities that foster our desire to acquire still more. To gain more we may be tempted to "fudge the truth" to protect a reputation or to gain or keep a customer. The line that separates good, hard competition and providing goods and services for our customers from abject greed can be easily blurred. How do we differentiate between coveting our competitor's market position and influence, from staying focused on the assignment God has for us?

When tempted—the operative word from God is FLEE! I originally limited this response to sexual temptation, but God has expanded my understanding of this concept to a much broader context.

In 1 Timothy 6:9-11 Paul writes, *"People who want to get rich fall into temptation and a trap and into many foolish and harmful desires that plunge men into ruin and destruction.*

For the love of money is a root of all kinds of evil. Some people, eager for money have wandered from the faith and pierced themselves with many griefs. But you, man of God, FLEE from all this, and pursue righteousness, godliness, faith, love, endurance and gentleness." In 1 Corinthians 10:14 he says, "*FLEE from idolatry.*" In 1 Corinthians 6:18 he expresses God's command to, "*FLEE from sexual immorality*" (NIV 1984).

Each of us has different temptations to which we are particularly vulnerable. God recently revealed an area that I didn't think was a problem for me—pride. When I receive acclamation and praise for something, it is easy for me to say it doesn't matter (possibly a false humility). God revealed to me the truth that I have to flee the praise of others and get to the spot where the "applause of one" is sufficient—completely sufficient—for the assignments He's entrusted to me.

God promises to help us defeat temptation in our lives and gives us a surprising truth. Paul writes in 1 Corinthians 10:13, "*And God is faithful; He will not let you be tempted beyond what you can bear. But when you are tempted, He will also provide a way out so that you can stand up under it*" (NIV 1984). It is critical to note that God's provision still requires a response on our part—FLEE! God says He will provide a way out, but we must avail ourselves of that opportunity. He will not force us or make that decision for us. David had a way out with Bathsheba: avert his eyes… FLEE! He didn't take it.

And God's surprise? It is found in James 4:7. "*Resist the devil and he will FLEE from you.*" (NIV 1984). So as we obey God and resist the devil by fleeing from our temptations, Satan, the tempter, will flee from us.

A final thought—many times we know something is wrong and it is clear that we should flee. At other times we aren't quite so sure. I suggest you flee in these circumstances and figure it out later. When in doubt… FLEE!

REFLECT FOR A MOMENT

1. *What sins are you most susceptible to commit? What have you done to ensure you avoid them?*

2. *How quick are you to flee when temptation comes? Have you been guilty of lingering when you should have fled? What can you build into your life so you do not find yourself in a compromising situation in the future?*

3. *Have you repeatedly committed the same sin? If so, why do you think that is? How do you think God views your behavior?*

Identity

Richard McClure
President, UniGroup, Inc., and
CEO, United Van Lines and Mayflower Transit

OUR HUMAN PERSPECTIVE is enmeshed in our concept of identity. I am the son of Charles and Dorothy McClure, the husband of Sharon, the father of Ryan and Lindsay. Those are family identities for which I am extremely grateful. In the Bible, men and women were frequently identified through a listing of their ancestors and offspring. I am also currently identified by my current job as a CEO.

The danger in some identities, particularly my identity in business leadership, is that I become defined in my mind by my title at work. When I became a CEO, I found that my ideas were suddenly better, my jokes were funnier, and my decisions greeted with more acclaim. Nothing had changed, of course. I had the same flaws I had before the title was given to me. Business leaders live in an environment where deference is prevalent—and if we're not careful, the impact on our identity inflates our ego and ties our self-image even more to the titles we hold temporarily. If my identity becomes defined by my CEO title, then when that title comes to an end, my identity goes with it.

At one point in my career I left an important government post (at least I thought it was important) and took a job in the banking industry. I went from a big job with a big title and a big office in the state capitol to learning the ropes in a new career. It was a great opportunity—but the job, the title, and the office (really a desk in the middle of the floor) were not the same. It was one of the best lessons I ever learned. My identity was not in my temporary government title or in my new job. I needed to learn a healthy perspective about my identity—that the way the work world defines me is not who I am.

The most important identity to which I aspire is as a follower of Jesus of Nazareth. A game we played with our children in the car is called "Who Am I?" The game involved asking questions until you guessed who the questioner was thinking of. That is not a bad question to ask ourselves! Who am I, in the eyes of others? If people playing the "Who Am I" game were asking questions about morals, ethics, values, and Christian character, how long would it take them to identify me? What does my behavior reveal about my character? My identity in Christ, not my job title, is who I aspire to be.

I desire to be known by the grace I have been given in Christ. I want to identify with Christ's sacrifice, His eternal values, and by living a life based on the love He modeled perfectly for me. That is the identity I am seeking. When my identity is based first and foremost on my relationship with Christ, I have my priorities in order. But when my identity is based on my own actions, my character falls far short of God's ideal. Fortunately, there is nothing I can do to earn Christlikeness—it is given based on unmerited favor. His grace, His redemptive mission and His perfect love provide the only eternal framework for my identity. Everything else is temporary at best.

REFLECT FOR A MOMENT

1. *What factors have exerted the most influence on your sense of identity? How important to you is your job in determining your identity?*

2. *How important is your identity in Christ to you? How has your relationship to Christ affected the way you view yourself? How has your relationship to Christ affected the way others view you?*

3. *What has exerted a greater influence on your sense of identity, your job or your relationship to Christ? Why is that? How might your walk with God become a greater influence in the formation of your identity in the future?*

Marching When the Band Is Not Playing

Ron Wagley
Chairman, CEO & President Transamerica Insurance (retired)

THE MARKETPLACE HAS unique pressures and challenges. For many, sitting in the CEO's chair is viewed with admiration and envy, fueled by a distorted and incomplete perception narrowly focused on prestige, perks, and power. Needless to say, there is another side unknown to most.

At no time is this side more evident than today as business leaders struggle to function in the current economic environment. Difficult and unpopular decisions must be made to assure survival. For executives who are committed to Jesus Christ, such actions, in spite of being justified and necessary, are made even more difficult by their need to act and respond in accordance with God's ways. Being difficult has never been an acceptable reason or excuse for the absence of Christ-centered leadership! To the contrary, godly leadership is greatly needed during tough times.

While the factors for determining specific actions are unique for each business, there are two critical questions common to all organizations led by followers of Christ: What role does faith play in leading the organization through this difficult time? And, does God provide help? It's been said, "If your faith doesn't make a difference in the things that make a difference, then what's the difference?" The world watches the actions and reactions of believers in Jesus to life's experiences and wants to know, "Does God make a difference?"

We see this "God difference" in Daniel 6 when Daniel was the victim of a sinister plot that manipulated King Darius into enforcing a law that sent Daniel into a lions' den. Scripture tells us that early the next morning the king hurried to the den calling out a question that still resounds today, "*Daniel, was your God whom you serve able to rescue you?*" (Daniel 6:19-20). As in the days of Daniel, the world is watching Christ-centered businesspeople and asking whether God makes a difference! Does Christianity merely mean we must forfeit our Sunday mornings to church attendance, or does being a Christian noticeably improve our lives? You know the rest of the story as Daniel greeted the king and "*not a scratch was found upon him.*"

Early in my career I learned that I needed to be able to "march when the band was not playing." People follow the CEO's lead and cadence. It is far easier to march during good times; however the test of leadership is to continue to march when things are not so good. I also discovered that as a follower of Jesus, God's band never stops playing and we can continue to march to a different beat—God's beat—and confidently lead while relying upon, being guided by, and trusting in our Lord.

Yes, business is tough but we serve a great God who knows well each and every situation. Contrary to the business naysayers and the media pundits, take comfort in Proverbs 3:5-6, "*Lean on, trust in, and be confident in the Lord with all your heart and mind; and do not rely upon your own insight or understanding; seek His will in all you do and recognize Him in all your ways and acknowledge Him and His guidance and He will direct and show you what to do and which path to take.*" (NASB; NLT; AMPLIFIED combined)

This could be your finest hour! March on! God is with you and, like the popular TV commercial, is shouting above the business turmoil, "Do you hear me now? Do you hear me now?" Stay close and be led by our great God!

REFLECT FOR A MOMENT

1. *What difference has your faith in Christ made in the way you lead and work? Should it have exerted a greater influence than it has? If so, how? How easy has it been for you to incorporate your faith into your business life?*

2. *If you are in a position of leadership, what impact have you had on those you lead? Has it been positive or negative? How might God use your life to exert a greater influence on others?*

3. *How have you felt pressured to compromise your faith at your job? Do you find it difficult to lead when others do not hold the same values and beliefs that you do? What could you build in to your life so your faith plays a greater role in your workplace?*

Human Nature

Jed Burnham
CEO (retired), Vectra Bank

THE FALLEN NATURE of business leaders can be seen today in the news headlines. It is almost a daily occurrence. Bernie Madoff is only one of the most spectacular CEOs to be caught cheating. Rather than revealing the truth about his company's financial circumstances, he lied and covered up the truth, taking money from Peter to pay Paul. Cooking the books at Enron involved the same policy of deception. The frequency and magnitude of these problems has resulted in a general perception by many, if not most, people that American business is corrupt—dominated by evil leaders who will do anything to get and keep what they have. We, of course, know firsthand this is not true. We see honest, hardworking businessmen and businesswomen in our companies and in our suppliers everyday. What should our role be during this time?

In the 10th chapter of Mark, Jesus says, *"It is easier for a camel to go through the eye of a needle than for a rich man to enter the kingdom of God."* The rich man serves as a metaphor for people who are so secure in life that they don't believe they need God or anyone else. This is the ultimate arrogance.

Today we are reminded more than ever how much, as leaders who follow Jesus Christ, we need God. But is our Christlike character obvious to others? Is our humility an observable contrast to the arrogance of the Madoffs?

Earlier in Mark, Jesus returned from the mountain to find His disciples unsuccessfully attempting to drive an evil spirit out of a young boy. Jesus rebuked the spirit and commanded it to come out, which it did. The disciples couldn't understand why they had failed. Jesus told them that such an undertaking required much prayer. It also necessitated that they turn first to God and not merely rely on their own experiences or resources (Mark 9:13-29). How easy it is to be like the disciples and rely solely upon ourselves.

Jesus wants us first to rely on Him. To pray and row the boat as a friend of mine once said. To be disciplined in seeking first the will of God in our lives and in the decisions we make as business leaders. Our focus upon Him will set us apart from the others and will honor God. Our attitude, especially when we make difficult decisions, can demonstrate to others inside the company and beyond that we are different—that it isn't about how much we keep, but about how much we care.

REFLECT FOR A MOMENT

1. *Human nature is naturally sinful. To what degree has the Holy Spirit changed your innate, sinful instincts?*

2. *The Christian life is based on our utter dependency on Christ. Are you living daily in that frame of mind? If not, what would it take for you to become desperate for Him?*

Why Did God Choose Joseph?

Cort Randell
Corporate Media Services, Inc.

WHY DID GOD choose a young carpenter in a small town called Nazareth to be the earthly father of Jesus? Why not choose a highly placed young man with many educational opportunities in Jerusalem for the earthly father of the Savior of the world? Apparently God found six qualities that He wanted in Joseph that He found in no one else.

1. Joseph had an ability to hear from the Lord (Matthew 1:18-21). Can you imagine being engaged, and suddenly noticing that your fiancée is pregnant? She claims it wasn't some other man, instead she says it was the Spirit of the Lord that got her pregnant. You have a choice, one is to stone her as per the custom, or break off the engagement. Being a truly compassionate man, he chose the latter. Suddenly an angel appeared to Joseph to confirm that Mary was telling the truth, the baby would be a boy, and to call him Jesus (meaning Savior or Deliverer).

2. Joseph was obedient even though it was extremely embarrassing for him (Matthew 1:20-24). The angel brought a third alternative, and that was to marry her. Oftentimes the Lord comes with a much better alternative if we will seek His face. Still, this was a very small town. Having to marry while still pregnant in the old Jewish culture would be a stigma and cause everyone to look down on them both.

3. Joseph was patient and disciplined (Matthew 1:25). The angel told Joseph that he could not have sex with his wife until the baby was born. The beds were small, and he had not had any sexual relationship with Mary, his beloved wife. That would take a lot of patience and discipline for any man.

4. Joseph was totally obedient (Matthew 2:13-15). Think of being awakened in the night and being told to pack everything you have that will fit on top of a donkey and leave immediately with your wife and child and go to a foreign country by walking several hundred miles. Fortunately the Lord had provided some gold via the wise men, but they were still young, going by foot, and into a country that spoke Egyptian. How many of us would have been that obedient?

5. Joseph was protective (Matthew 2:19-23). After a couple of years, Joseph was told to go back so they

began the long walk home. Unfortunately, there was now a new murderous king, Archelaus, near Bethlehem, so Joseph led his wife and child to Nazareth, to protect them.

6. Joseph appears to have lived with Jesus for all of His early years, taking Him to the festivals in Jerusalem (Luke 2:51). As the older brother, Jesus helped raise Joseph's large family.

We might assume that Joseph did not have much effect on Jesus, and that He was only taught by the Holy Spirit. But I think that would be a mistake. Joseph was a successful CEO and for many years he taught and modeled godly principles to his sons and daughters. James, Jesus' brother, wrote the most businesslike epistle in the Bible after Jesus' death.

Would God have entrusted you with the raising of His Son? Would you have had the character qualities God was looking for? What changes do we need to make to be more like Joseph?

REFLECT FOR A MOMENT

1. *What character qualities of Joseph most impress you? Do you possess any of those same attributes? How might you enhance those character traits in your life?*

2. *Why do you think God grants assignments based on character? Why is character so important to God?*

3. *List some assignments God has given you. Have you handled them as Joseph dealt with his? If the way you have handled assignments in the past determines what God gives you next, what should you expect from God in the future?*

Spiritual Influence

OUR LIVES ON earth are brief at best. We spend a few decades walking upon the planet before we return to the dust from which we came. We can choose to spend our years vainly pursuing fleeting pleasures and grasping at petty recognitions, or, we can invest ourselves in eternity. We cannot enjoy our money forever, regardless of its amount or the security of its investment. No government or company or building is eternal. But people are. If we are wise, we will invest ourselves into that which lasts.

Some people live lives that make little or no difference to anyone. They come and go in human history and no one suffers loss when they depart. Yet others live in such a way that the world is never the same after they are gone. Paul was such a man. He began his adult life harming people in his frantic quest to achieve power and fame. Yet once he surrendered his life into the hands of Christ, he changed his world. His enemies in Thessalonica claimed, "*These who have turned the world upside down have come here too*" (Acts 17:6). God showed Paul how to spend his life in such a way that people, and human history, were never the same again. Two thousand years later, we are still feeling the impact of what God did through Paul's life.

How are you living your life? Are you investing in what matters? Are you leaving a spiritual legacy? Will you be fondly remembered for good long after you are gone? Will the world be a better place, because you passed through it? Ask God to show you what you must do to become a person of greater spiritual influence.

Good News!

THE HISTORY OF business could be viewed as a series of periodic breakthroughs. There have been moments of discovery and decision that forever changed the marketplace. Commodore Vanderbilt turned his back on his shipping business to invest in the emerging railroad industry, propelling him to become the wealthiest man in America. Henry Ford perfected a means of producing affordable "horseless carriages" for the masses that brought an end to horse-drawn carriages and revolutionized America. Andrew Carnegie utilized a superior method of manufacturing steel that made him one of America's wealthiest tycoons. Rockefeller developed oil refining and transporting processes until he became the undisputed king of the oil industry. Bill Gates left Harvard University without graduating to throw himself into an innovative new software company. In most cases, a discovery of new methods of production or distribution led businesspeople to spectacular heights. Fresh insights can bring enormous success.

In 1900, Milton Hershey sold his caramel business to his chief rival for one million dollars. It was a premium price. Yet it appeared that an aggressive competitor had pushed Hershey out of the market. The fact was that Hershey believed milk chocolate was the candy of the future and he wanted to be at the forefront of the new trend. Hershey built a factory to produce the chocolate and developed an entire city (Hershey, PA) in which his plant and its employees were located. His major problem was that he did not have a workable recipe for milk chocolate! His teams of inventors worked day and night, conducting numerous experiments to master its production, but to no avail. In 1903, after suffering repeated failure, Hershey invited John Schmalbach from his Lancaster plant to come to his home and help him solve the puzzle. That night, Schmalbach managed to "break the code" and Hershey's milk chocolate was birthed. The good news quickly spread throughout Hershey's employees. Everyone realized they once again had hope, and a future.

On a clear night in the Judean countryside, shepherds were on duty through the night, caring for their flocks of sheep. Shepherds were hardened, working people. Few people trusted them. They labored long hours for a meager reward. Life never changed for shepherds. The great decisions made in the major cities of Jerusalem, Caesarea, and Rome meant little to them.

Suddenly the sky lit up with fiery, heavenly messengers. An angel cried out, *"Do not be afraid, for behold, I bring you good tidings of great joy which will be to all people"* (Luke 2:10). The good news of the Gospel brings great joy. Significantly, the first time it was shared, it was presented to people working the night shift! God loves working people and He delights in bringing them good news.

"Angel" means "messenger." It describes someone who delivers a message. Rather than always dispatching winged emissaries from heaven, God may assign us that task. The news of Christ *is* good news and it brings great *joy*. The marketplace is filled with joyless people who desperately need good news. You can be God's ambassador to your workplace with a message that changes peoples' lives and infuses them with hope. The Gospel can bring people the "breakthrough" they are looking for that forever changes their lives. You could be God's dispenser of good news to your colleagues. Who might you share that message with today?

REFLECT FOR A MOMENT

1. *List three of your colleagues whose lives could be dramatically changed for the better if they learned a truth about God. Begin praying (and looking) for an opportunity share those truths with them.*

2. *Have you lost your sense of wonder at the Good News of the Gospel? How faithful have you been to share it with your colleagues and clients?*

3. *Do you view the Gospel as a set of beliefs, a moral standard, or good news of great joy? How has the good news of Christ been bringing you joy?*

God's Method

"MEN ARE GOD'S method. The Church is looking for better methods; God is looking for better men" (E.M. Bounds, *Power through Prayer*). Throughout history, when society was in crisis, God called upon ordinary people through whom He would bring deliverance. When the Egyptians were oppressing the Israelites, God sent Moses. When the Midianites were abusing God's people, God called Gideon. When the Philistines were bullying the Hebrews God raised up Samson, Samuel, and David to defend His people. When Haman plotted to massacre the Jewish people in Persia, God moved Esther to speak out on behalf of her countrymen. When the poor were being exploited, God summoned Amos to plead for justice. When God launched the greatest work of redemption in history, He entrusted the Savior to a teenage, peasant girl named Mary. God could have commissioned a legion of angels every time His people were in need, but He has generally chosen to work through ordinary people.

In 1994, South Africa elected Nelson Mandela as its president. Everyone is familiar with how he promoted reconciliation in a country rife with alienation and successfully led a peaceful transition from minority to majority rule. In the years following his presidency however, South Africa experienced widespread turmoil as housing and job shortages increased. People from all over the continent began pouring in to South Africa, many of them having never heard the Gospel message. As unemployment skyrocketed, so did the crime rate. Clearly a political solution was not enough. The nation also needed to turn to God. In this turbulent time, God raised up an ordinary, unknown farmer named Angus Buchan.

Buchan's life had been challenging. He was a maize and cattle farmer in Zambia until political unrest forced him to relocate to Greytown, KwaZulu-Natal, South Africa. He was an ambitious, hot-tempered man who occasionally neglected his wife and children in his desperate attempts to make his farm successful. Local residents nicknamed him "Nikosaan Italiaan" because they claimed he acted like a mad Italian. In 1979, Angus had a personal encounter with Jesus Christ, and it completely changed his life. He began speaking to groups of men and challenging them to turn their focus away from political unrest and economic uncertainty. Instead, he urged them to trust Christ and to live for Him, regardless of what was happening in their country. Buchan eventually opened his farm to men from across South Africa, inviting them to spend a weekend. He spoke to those who came and challenged them to act and think like mighty men of God. In April 2009, over 200,000 men arrived at his farm. In 2010, over 300,000 came. Buchan took his message throughout the country. Gigantic soccer stadiums overflowed with over 60,000 men in attendance as Buchan challenged people to commit their lives to Christ. His story was told in a book and a later movie entitled *Faith Like Potatoes*. Buchan is an ordinary working man with a meager eighth grade education, yet he is drawing more people to hear him preach than world famous celebrities. Lives are being dramatically transformed at a time when his nation is longing for healing and change.

When society desperately needs to be reformed, God typically raises up someone through whom He will work. Could it be that in these turbulent times in our country, God is calling you? What are the limits to what He could do through your life to dramatically impact your nation and world, for good?

REFLECT FOR A MOMENT

1. *Has God raised you up to accomplish His purposes in some way? If so, what do you think God intends to do through your life?*

2. *Do you tend to look for others to change situations or to solve problems, or do you assume God will use your life? What adjustments might you need to make so you are prepared for God to use your life more powerfully in the future?*

3. *God used Angus Buchan, not because of his education, position, or finances, but because of his heart and passion for God. Do you ever feel that you are too ordinary or untrained or lacking in financial resources to make much difference in God's kingdom? In reality, what are the limits to what almighty God could do with your life, if He chose to? Do you truly believe God can use you life to impact your world? If so, are you living as if you believe it?*

Setting People Free

T.E. LAWRENCE WAS the illegitimate son of Thomas Chapman and Sarah Junner. He stood just over five feet five inches tall and, as a young man, was variously described as "an odd gnome, half cad—with a touch of genius" and "this extraordinary pip-squeak" (Michael Korda, *Hero, 6*). He graduated from Jesus College in Oxford and devoted his early years to archeological digs in the Middle East. When World War One erupted, he was assigned as a liaison to the Arabs, due to his familiarity with their land and culture. Palestine, as well as the Arabian Peninsula, and modern Syria and Lebanon were under the longstanding subjugation of the Ottoman Empire. The Arab peoples, consisting largely of Bedouins, were disorganized with antiquated weapons and inadequate leadership to free themselves from the vicelike-grip of the Turks. In one of the most celebrated stories of World War One, Lieutenant Lawrence, an archeology major, gained the trust of the Arab leaders and helped them unite in the common cause of liberating themselves from their oppressors. Nations exist today that were forged from his efforts. Made famous around the world as "Lawrence of Arabia," he risked his life to liberate people who were entirely different from himself. Lawrence devoted himself to others' freedom.

Jesus claimed, *"And you shall know the truth, and the truth shall make you free"* (John 8:32). Jesus, Himself, is the Truth (John 14:6). He came to earth to set people free. Sin and death held humanity in an inescapable vicelike grip that propelled people toward eternal destruction. Yet when Jesus came, many people rejected Him (John 1:5). Throughout human history, sin has worked its evil to blind people and to keep them in bondage. Nevertheless, the light of Christ continues to shine, dispelling the darkness and setting people free (John 1:9-12).

Jesus told His disciples that they were to be lights in a darkened world (Matthew 5:14-16). Rather than keeping His followers at a safe and comfortable distance from spiritual darkness, Christ strategically positions His disciples where their light can dispel the darkness around them and set people free.

At times you may wonder why a colleague seems captivated by money or promotions or earning bonuses. You may be shocked to learn of colleagues who are addicted to alcohol, drugs, or pornography. It can be bewildering to see intelligent people forfeit their marriage or family or reputations for momentary pleasures and foolish choices. But the reason is simple: they are in bondage. They need to be set free. Why do people waste their life? Why do they harm other people? Why do they pursue fleeting pleasures and accumulate guilt and regret? They are captives to sin and deception.

Every time you encounter someone who is in bondage to something, ask yourself, What truth of God could set this person free? For every form of human bondage, God has a remedy. There is a truth in God's word that, if believed and embraced, would set every enslaved person free. The great privilege of Jesus' disciples is to be entrusted with His truth. Every time we encounter people in bondage, we can share divine truth with them that has the power to free them from their servitude. Of course, you cannot force truth on anyone. Neither can you believe on someone else's behalf. But you can share what you know. (Conversely, you can't share what you don't know!)

How familiar are you with God's truth? If you entered a conversation with someone suffering from addiction, what truth would you share? If you met someone in bondage to fear, what Scripture would you point him to? If you encountered someone in bondage to guilt or greed or anger, what Scripture passage would you reach for? All the truth in the world will do no good if you are unprepared to share it. As you enter the workplace, arm yourself with truth. Then keep your spiritual eyes and ears alert for someone you can share it with today. Remember, truth is amazingly powerful. It *can* set people free.

REFLECT FOR A MOMENT

1. *How well do you know the truths found in the Bible? Do you know God's word well enough to share it with those who need to experience it?*

2. *Think about the people you work with. Are some of them in bondage to something? Consider a truth from God's word that, if believed, could set them free. Now look for an opportunity to share those truths.*

Prayer Warriors

ON OCTOBER 15, 1892, John Hyde and five other Presbyterian missionaries set sail from America for India. Hyde found a letter in his cabin from a dear friend. The man promised he would pray for Hyde every day until he was filled with the Spirit. At first Hyde was offended at the suggestion that he, a devout Christian, and a seminary-trained missionary lacked any qualification. But as Hyde searched his heart, he realized that without the full measure of the Holy Spirit in his life, He would fail in his undertaking.

Hyde became a fervent prayer warrior for the millions of people in India. Every day he cried out to God for the salvation of the people with whom he worked. In 1908, Hyde felt led to pray that God would allow him to personally lead one person to faith in Christ, *each day.* Hyde continually watched for the person God had for him to share Christ with that day. Hyde was famous for beginning conversations with people while riding the train. When he arrived at his stop, he would often be so deeply engaged in conversation with someone that he rode past his destination. He would eventually lead the man to faith in Christ. Upon boarding a train going the opposite direction, however, he would become involved in another conversation and again, he would bypass his stop to see that person born again. One day this happened four times. By the time he finally arrived at the convention meeting he was to attend, it was over, but four people had entered into God's family. In 1909, Hyde felt impressed to ask God for two converts a day, and, by year's end, God had granted twice as many converts to Hyde as in the previous year. In 1910, Hyde boldly asked God for four converts per day. Once again, God granted his request. Hyde would often pray throughout the night for those he would encounter the following day. So fervent was his praying that it was claimed that upon examination by a physician in 1911, Hyde's heart had moved from the left to the right side of his chest. One man demonstrated what impassioned prayer could do to impact a nation for Christ.

The apostle James exhorted Christians, saying, "*The effective, fervent prayer of a righteous man avails much. Elijah was a man with a nature like ours, and he prayed earnestly that it would not rain; and it did not rain on the land for three years and six months*" (James 5:16-17). Scripture reminds us that Elijah was not a spiritual superhero with extraordinary abilities in communing with God. He was an ordinary person, like us, who believed God and prayed fervently. His prayers shook his nation. Mary, Queen of Scots allegedly said of the fiery preacher, John Knox, "I fear the prayers of John Knox more than the assembled armies of Europe." Prayer is a powerful instrument in the hands of a child of God!

God has strategically placed you in the marketplace. Every day you encounter colleagues, employees, customers, and vendors who desperately need to experience a life-changing encounter with Christ. There may be times when you can share a clear witness that helps them find Christ. At other times such a testimony may be impossible. But you can always pray. Your colleagues may not understand why they are being inexorably drawn toward Christ, but you will know. They may not realize why you are filled with peace when everyone else is anxious, but you will understand. God intends to use your life to be a bastion of intercession for those in your workplace. Pray fervently, then watch and see who God brings across your path next.

REFLECT FOR A MOMENT

1. *On a scale of 1 to 10, rate your current prayer life. If it is not what you think it ought to be, what are three things you could do to improve it?*

2. *Make a list of the people with whom you work most closely. Beside each name, list one or two things you believe God wants to do in his or her life. Take time each week to pray for those things. Don't give up until you witness God's will accomplished in each person.*

3. *Have you witnessed any answers to your prayers in your workplace? Ask God to show you what to be praying for. Then keep your spiritual senses alert to God's activity in response to your prayers.*

Catalysts for Revival

THROUGHOUT THE BOOK of Judges, a cycle of apostasy and revival repeatedly occurs. God's people neglect their relationship with God and embrace sin. God disciplines His people until they repent and return to Him. God forgives His people and uses them once again to exert a godly influence on their land. But inevitably God's people turn away from Him again and the cycle repeats itself (Judges 2:10-11). Each time God's people departed from Him, He called upon someone through whom He could draw His people back to Himself. These people become catalysts for revival.

The same pattern occurs throughout church history that we find in Scripture. During the 1720s and '30s, God used preachers such as Jonathan Edwards and George Whitefield to turn people back to God. During the early 1800s, God used Charles Finney to bring revival to America. While visiting a factory in New York Mills in 1826, Finney passed through a large room filled with women working at looms and spinning jennies. Some of the women recognized him and began talking among themselves. Soon several women became agitated and could no longer keep working. A powerful sense of conviction for their sin gripped people throughout the factory. Finally the manager, who was not a believer in Christ, called everyone together and invited

Finney to speak. Revival had entered the factory as God's man walked through it! In 1857-8, God used a businessman named Jeremiah Lamphier to spark a citywide revival in Manhattan that ultimately saw one million people converted across the nation. In 1904-5, God used a former coal miner named Evan Roberts to bring revival to Wales. In six months, 100,000 people were converted. God also used a Scotsman named Duncan Campbell. On one occasion, Campbell was to speak at the Hamilton Avenue Presbyterian Church for an annual convention meeting. Suddenly he sensed God placing the small island of Berneray on his heart. The divine impulse was so strong that he did not remain to preach the next morning as scheduled, but flew to the Isle of Harris. There he took a ferry to the small island of Berneray. He knew no one there and had told no one he was coming. Upon his arrival, however, he discovered that an elder in the local church had already prepared a room for him and announced there would be a meeting at 9:00 p.m. in which Campbell would speak. Revival came to that little island.

God declared, "*So I sought for a man among them who would make a wall, and stand in the gap before Me on behalf of the land, so that I should not destroy it; but I found no one. Therefore I have poured out My indignation on them; I have consumed them with the fire of My wrath; and I have recompensed their deeds on their own heads, says the Lord God*" (Ezekiel 22:30-31). When God seeks to revive his peoples' spiritual lives, He looks for someone through whom He can work. God often utilizes business people as sparkplugs for revival in their churches and nations. In fact, the marketplace is an excellent venue for revival to spread throughout America. It is interconnected with people from every denomination.

If God revived the hearts of His people in the business world, it would not take long to impact every church and denomination in America. America is in dire need of revival once more. God is looking for people willing to stand in the gap as His holy instruments of renewal. Will you be one?

REFLECT FOR A MOMENT

1. *Do the people you work with need a fresh encounter with God? If so, could God have placed you at your company so you could be a catalyst for revival? How might God use you to refresh the spiritual lives of your colleagues?*

2. *Is your heart ready to be used by God in revival? The people God has often used may have been ordinary, but they were passionate about God. What might God need to do to revive you first, before He uses you to revive others?*

3. *Revival always comes after people repent of their sin. If God is going to use your life to bring revival to others, are there sins you need to repent of and turn away from, before you are in a position to be of use to God? Make a list of sins in your life and then repent of them to God. Get your heart ready for the work God is preparing to do through your life, where you work and where you go to church.*

Glorifying God

During the 2011-12 National Football League season, Tim Tebow, the rookie quarterback for the Denver Broncos, became a national sensation by routinely praying on the field and for giving God the credit for his success when he was interviewed on television. His actions created a stir among Christians and non-Christians alike concerning the appropriateness of so blatantly using every public opportunity to point people to Christ. Many Christians were delighted with a professional athlete who would take such a bold and public stand for his faith. Others claimed it was overkill. It highlighted a dilemma that many Christians face in the workplace: How publicly can or should I practice my faith? Is the office an appropriate place to verbally thank God for my success? Is the boardroom a proper venue for praying for God's guidance? Is it right to seemingly impose my faith on colleagues who may not be believers?

Scripture exhorts us: *"Therefore, whether you eat or drink, or whatever you do, do all to the glory of God"* (1 Corinthians 10:31). Clearly in even the most basic matters of life, such as eating and drinking, there are ways to honor God. If our life's purpose is to glorify God, then certainly we cannot set aside the bulk of our workdays as being off limits for our sacred task. Yet the next verse offers this caution: *"Give no offense, either to the Jews or to the Greeks, or to the church of God, just as I also please all men in all things, not seeking my own profit, but the profit of many, that they may be saved"* (1 Corinthians 10:32-33). Paul urged Christians to avoid offending people with their actions. Instead they were to behave in ways that drew people to Christ.

Jesus cautioned His followers, *"Do not give what is holy to dogs; nor cast your pearls before swine, lest they trample them under their feet, and turn and tear you to pieces"* (Matthew 7:6). It is important to use wisdom when we share what is precious. In some settings, declaring our faith will merely subject it to the ridicule and derision of others, without attracting them to embrace it themselves. Perhaps Daniel is a helpful example. He served as a top executive in a pagan organization. He walked a fine line, for his boss, and most of his colleagues, rejected his faith and held views contrary to his. We do not hear of Daniel chastising his colleagues for their pagan beliefs or even asking his associates to practice his religious routines. Yet people knew he was a man of prayer and a believer in the true God. He never hid his faith or compromised it before others. This caused him to have enemies, but that was because of their own unbelief and sin, not because of Daniel's offensive behavior. Ultimately God vindicated Daniel for his integrity, as well as his gracious spirit (Daniel 6).

As Jesus commissioned His disciples, He declared, *"Behold, I send you out as sheep in the midst of wolves. Therefore, be wise as serpents and harmless as doves"* (Matthew 10:16). We live in an age when the Christian faith is under attack. There are many who violently oppose it. We must be careful. At the same time, we live in day that calls for us to shine our light for Christ fearlessly and unashamedly. As with so many areas of life, there is no direct, unequivocal teaching on what we should do. We must seek the Spirit's guidance for our particular situation. Let God show you how He wants you to express your faith where you work.

REFLECT FOR A MOMENT

1. *Have you struggled to know how openly to express your faith at work? What are some areas where you are unsure about how openly to talk about your Christian beliefs? Take a moment right now to pray and ask God to guide you.*

2. *Are you presently being the witness God wants you to be at work? Have you allowed your boss or unbelievers to intimidate you from openly declaring your beliefs? How might you take a bolder stand for Christ in the future? Ask other believers to pray for you as you do.*

3. *Have you been too confrontational or outspoken about your faith at work? Could you have inadvertently offended people, rather than attracting them to Christ? Seek God's guidance in how directly He wants you to present your faith and the Gospel at this time.*

Salt or Light?

ON JANUARY 5, 1914, Henry Ford and James Couzens announced the startling news that the Ford Motor Company was doubling factory workers' wages to the unheard of level of $5.00 per day. Because Ford assumed that many of these laborers had never possessed such plentiful income before, he also established a sociological department at his company to teach employees how to properly handle their finances. To be eligible for the raise in pay, employees had to demonstrate that they did not drink alcohol, did not physically mistreat their family, did not keep boarders in their home, maintained a clean house, demonstrated good moral character, and regularly deposited money into their savings account. Ford told Reverend Samuel Marquis, who would lead the sociological department, "I want you, Mark, to put Jesus Christ into my factory" (Stephen Watts, *The Peoples' Tycoon,* 208). However, by 1920 it became apparent to Ford that his attempt to transform the moral character of his employees had failed.

President Richard Nixon also sought to use his powerful position to influence the moral fiber of the nation. His personal goal for 1971-2 was, "President as moral leader..." (Richard Reeves, *President Nixon,* 278). This initiative would self-destruct spectacularly!

Jesus expects His followers to exert a godly influence on those around them. He identified two major ways to impact others (Matthew 5:13-16). One is to act as *light* in the midst of the surrounding darkness. The presence of light is unmistakable. Light draws attention to itself. Darkness cannot remain in light's presence. Individuals in the workplace who are committed to Jesus Christ should behave in a way that dispels darkness and reflects Christ's light. John Beckett, as president of R.W. Beckett Corporation, chose to lead his company in an unmistakably Christlike manner. The result led to an interview on ABC's prime time news broadcast in which Beckett declared on national television, "My main mission in life is to know the will of God and do it" (John D. Beckett, *Loving Monday*, 23). Beckett shed the light of Christ on his company before a watching world.

Sometimes, however, business leaders do not have the freedom to openly practice their Christian beliefs. To begin a meeting in prayer or lead a Bible study in the boardroom could draw reprisals or even lead to job loss. However, Jesus also commanded His followers to be *salt*. Salt does not dramatically announce its presence or draw attention to itself. However, over time, proximity to salt can lead to drastic changes! There are times when wisdom will lead us to behave like salt in our workplace. We may pray for colleagues and be Christlike in our conduct but wait for the opportune moment to overtly talk about our relationship with Christ. We can bide our time and be sensitive to how and when to talk about our faith with colleagues. God will give you unique opportunities to glorify Him at work.

Are you exerting a Christlike influence on your workplace? Jesus commanded believers to be both salt and light. Salt enriches and preserves; light illuminates and guides. For some, we have been salt too long and need to boldly shine our light before others. For others, we have let our light shine brightly but the response may have discouraged us. God will give us the wisdom to discern whether to behave like salt or light in any given situation. What does God want you to be today?

REFLECT FOR A MOMENT

1. *What are some ways God wants you to be "light" in your workplace? Do you need to expose darkness where you work? Are there moral or ethical issues that need to be spoken against? Do you need to make it clear that your Christian values are clearly different from certain beliefs being expressed at work?*

2. *What are ways you could act as "salt" in your workplace? Do you need to exert a gradual, unobtrusive influence? Are there ways your example or attitude can gradually make a positive difference where you work?*

3. *Light boldly stands out. Salt gradually exerts an influence. Pray for wisdom to know which one God wants you to be in each situation.*

Tearing Down High Places

HIGH PLACES ARE seductive (Genesis 11:4). Before the Israelites entered the land of Canaan, the pagan religions built altars on hilltops to worship idols. These man-made shrines honored such gods as Baal the storm god who allegedly brought rain and wealth, Ashtoreth the fertility goddess, and Molech a detestable god to whom people sacrificed their children. These religions often provided prostitutes as a part of their depraved "worship." Such hedonistic religion appealed to people's base senses of greed and sensuality.

No wonder God commanded Joshua to obliterate the Canaanites. Yet despite Joshua's victories, remnants of the pagan peoples stubbornly remained (Joshua 17:12; Judges 1:27). Pagan worship centers continued to blight the nation's hilltops. Appealing to people's carnal nature, the high places were always popular (Judges 2:12-13, 17; 1 Kings 14:22-24).

Tragically, it was Israel's leaders who allowed the despicable practices to continue. King Solomon actually built high places for gods such as Ashtoreth, Milcom, and Chemosh (1 Kings 11:6-7). King Jeroboam established high places in Bethel and Dan so the northern tribes would not travel to Jerusalem to worship the true God (1 Kings 12:25-33). Every leader in Israel and Judah had to decide what his approach to the high places would be. Some evil kings like Ahaz and Manasseh enthusiastically supported the high places and even made sacrifices to idols (2 Kings 16:4; 2 Kings 21:1-3). Few people matched Elijah's courage in challenging King Ahab's false religion on the top of Mount Carmel (1 Kings 18).

Perhaps most disappointing were kings such as Rehoboam (1 Kings 14:22-23), Asa (1 Kings 15:14), Jehoshaphat (1 Kings 22:43), Jehoash (2 Kings 12:2-3), Jehoahaz (2 Kings 13:6), Amaziah (2 Kings 14:4), Azariah (2 Kings 15:3-4), and Jotham (2 Kings 15:34-35). These monarchs generally sought to rule righteously, but they stopped short of tearing down the high places. However, Judah's two godliest leaders did have the courage to actively demolish the bastions of wickedness in their land: Hezekiah (2 Kings 18:4), and Josiah (2 Kings 23:4-20).

Ultimately God destroyed the nation of Israel for its debauched worship at its pagan altars and the depravity that ensued (2 Kings 17:9-18). Scripture concludes, *"Therefore the Lord was very angry with Israel, and removed them from His sight"* (2 Kings 17:18). Likewise, the nation of Judah became so perforated with centers of evil that even the righteous King Josiah could not dissuade God's wrath and the destruction of his nation (2 Kings 23:26-27).

What are the high places of America today? They are the people, organizations, and centers that promote sinful attitudes and carnal practices. They are the groups that mock God and His word, and promote falsehood. Tearing down a nation's high places is not easy. William Wilberforce recognized that many Christians were unconcerned or ignorant of the depravity their society embraced with the slave trade. After losing a critical vote in the Commons, Wilberforce lamented that there were enough Christian MP's at the opera that evening to have deposed the slave trade had they cared enough to show up.

As a business leader today, are you satisfied, as were most of the leaders in Israel's history, to merely mind your own business? Or, will you allow God to use your life and influence to bring the high places of your day crashing down?

REFLECT FOR A MOMENT

1. *Consider for a moment where the "high places" are in your community and workplace. What are the centers from which ungodly influences are spewing into society?*

2. *Prayerfully consider how God might use your life and fellow Christians to "bring down" the centers of evil in your community. Don't assume there is nothing you can do. God knows how to defeat evil. Talk with other believers about what God might have you do.*

3. *Take a Saturday or an evening and prayer walk with other believers through your community and ask the Lord to show you what is happening where you live. Allow God to place His heart for your community over your heart and to help you see the people and establishments in your neighborhood the way He views them.*

All Authority Is from God

ON OCTOBER 12, 1960, Lorenzo Sumulong from the Philippines delivered a speech at the 902nd plenary meeting of the United Nations General Assembly. Nikita Khrushchev, leader of the Soviet Union, had earlier denounced the imperialism of western nations. However, when Sumulong challenged Khrushchev to give freedom to nations in Eastern Europe, the Soviet leader grew incensed. Khrushchev removed the shoe from his right foot and waved it menacingly toward Sumulong. Then he began pounding it on his desk more and more loudly until the entire assembly was transfixed at the spectacle of the leader of the world's second most powerful nation defying the world.

On October 16, 1962, President John F. Kennedy was informed that the Soviet Union, at Khrushchev's direction, was installing medium range missiles in Cuba, only 90 miles from the United States border. On October 22, in a nationally televised speech, Kennedy informed his nation of the looming crisis. It appeared the two superpowers were racing toward a cataclysmic nuclear exchange. The American navy blockaded Cuba to intercept Soviet ships transporting weapons to there. Americans across the country nervously braced themselves for the coming holocaust. Bomb shelters were prepared, food supplies were stored, and air raid drills held. People around the world feared the worst. The fate of civilization hinged on how the volatile Soviet leader chose to act. Then on October 27th Khrushchev communicated with Kennedy his terms for the removal of the missiles and the crisis quickly abated. One man had pushed the world to the brink of oblivion.

Khrushchev received a call on October 12, 1964, at his villa on the Black Sea while he was on vacation. It was his lieutenant, Leonid Brezhnev, requesting his immediate return to Moscow to discuss urgent matters at a special meeting of the Presidium. On October 13, Khrushchev's subordinates harangued him mercilessly, forcing him to resign from office. The fallen leader was cast aside for the remainder of his life, living on a small pension in obscurity. Khrushchev suffered from depression in his retirement and had to be prescribed sleeping pills and tranquilizers. Nevertheless, when one of his grandsons was asked what the ex-premier was doing in retirement, the boy replied, "Grandfather cries." After he died on September 11, 1971, he was denied a state funeral while *Pravda* announced his demise in one sentence. The dacha where he spent most of his final years was leveled to prevent it from becoming a shrine.

The psalmist declared, *"Why do the nations rage, and the people plot a vain thing? The kings of the earth set themselves, and the rulers of the earth take counsel together, against the Lord and against His Anointed, saying 'Let us break Their bonds in pieces and cast away Their cords from us.' He who sits in the heavens shall laugh; The Lord shall hold them in derision. Then He shall speak to them in His wrath, and distress them in His deep displeasure"* (Psalm 2:1-5).

Government leaders may oppose God and His purposes.

They may make headlines and issue bold pronouncements. But they rule solely at God's discretion (Romans 13:1). He appoints and removes them at His pleasure. Ultimately, rulers will give an account of their leadership to Him. To whom much has been given, much will be required (Luke 12:48). This should cause leaders to tremble.

REFLECT FOR A MOMENT

1. *This evening, watch the national and international news. As you see what world leaders are doing and threatening to do, prayerfully ask the Lord for His perspective on your world. People may boast and strut across the world stage, but their every breath depends upon the grace of almighty God.*

2. *Do you find yourself being intimidated by secular authorities? At times we can fear people more than we fear God. Take an inventory of your life. Have you allowed people in authority to make you compromise what you know are God's standards?*

3. *Do you pray regularly for your government leaders? Make a list of the government officials over you and regularly pray for them as Scripture instructs you to. Ask God to show you how to be a citizen who makes a positive difference in your nation.*

Knowing the Times

In his book *Outliers*, Malcolm Gladwell, author of *The Tipping Point* and *Blink*, explores the roots of one of today's most popular subjects: success. He suggests that while qualities such as intelligence, physical skill, and tenacity obviously contribute to high achievement, other less evident factors also play a significant role. For example, he notes that more National Hockey League players have birthdays in January than in any other month. The cut off age for little league hockey is December 31, so those born in January are as much as eleven months older than many of the peers against whom they compete for elite teams and coaching. For little league baseball, the cutoff date is July 31. Not surprisingly, more major league baseball players are born in August than any other date. Likewise, Gladwell studied the seventy-five wealthiest people in history and discovered that fourteen of them were Americans, born within nine years of each other (*Outliers*, 61). The 1860s and '70s saw the American economy skyrocket so rapidly that it produced a new aristocracy of extremely wealthy businesspeople. Those born in the 1820s were too old to capitalize on the Gilded Age and people born in the 1840s were too young. Significantly, fourteen of the wealthiest people in history were Americans born between 1831 and 1839. January 1975 was the dawn of the personal computer age. To capitalize on this technology and dominate the new industry, people would not want to be too old in 1975 to adjust their careers to the new possibilities nor too young to enter the business world.

Gladwell suggests that being born around 1954 or 1955 would put you at a perfect age to rapidly adjust to the cyberspace age. Bill Gates was born on October 28, 1955. Steve Jobs, February 24, 1955. Both brilliant men, but they were also born at the optimal time to dominate the cyberspace industry.

What's the point? It's futile to bemoan the fact you aren't working in the Gilded Age or during a booming economy. It has been said that if you long for the "good old days," just turn off your air conditioning! What *is* important is to understand the age in which you live. Scripture speaks of the sons of Issachar "*who had understanding of the times, to know what Israel ought to do*" (1 Chronicles 12:32). Those who make a positive difference in their world are not the ones pining away for better days, or waiting idly by for the tides of fortune to change, but those who boldly face the unique challenges and opportunities of their own generation.

Spiritual leaders recognize the possibilities that their day offers for the expansion of God's kingdom. What advanced technologies are available? What new methodologies, alliances, and political realities are uniquely at play now that previous Christians could never have imagined? Vibrant economies offer many opportunities; so do depressed ones.

It was said of King David, "*For David, after he had served his own generation by the will of God, fell asleep, was buried with his fathers, and saw corruption*" (Acts 13:36). David took what was given to him, understood the times in which he lived, and faithfully served his own generation by the will of God. Of all the ages throughout history you *could* have lived, why did God allow you to be born at this time? Are you discerning the days in which you are alive? Do you recognize the unique possibilities that lie before you? Seize the opportunities God has provided and fully live the one life you have to the glory of God.

REFLECT FOR A MOMENT

1. *Take a moment and list characteristics of your day that are unique in history. Prayerfully ask the Lord why He chose to put you in the family, city, nation, and time in history that He did. What purpose did God have for placing you on the earth at such a time as this?*

2. *Make a list of the technologies and opportunities unique to your day that could be used to advance God's kingdom. Today's Christians have means at their disposal to spread the Gospel that earlier believers did not have. What tools has God made available to you and your company that could be used uniquely for God's purposes?*

3. *Are you carefully observing your world? How do you stay informed of world events? Do you know where Christianity is advancing in the world today? Do you know where Christianity is under attack (especially in your own country)? What might you do to become better informed about the spiritual condition of the world in which you live?*

Our Companies Are Platforms for Jesus

Clyde Lear
Former Chairman, CEO, and Founder (now retired),
Learfield Communications, Inc.

*You are the salt of the earth; but if the salt has
lost its taste, how shall its saltiness be restored?
...You are the light of the world. A city set on a hill
cannot be hidden... Let your light so shine before
others, so that they may see your good works and
give glory to your Father who is in heaven.*
MATTHEW 5:13-16 (ESV)

RECENTLY I WAS riding with one of our sales executives in
Indianapolis. As he drove us between calls, I engaged him
about his personal life: recent college grad, did sales for a
minor league team, then joined Learfield; loves his work.

"Have a girlfriend?" I inquired.

"I'm living with a lady now," he said.

So I pushed him gingerly, "any intentions of buying a ring
soon?"

To which he stammered: "Nah, I don't think so. I just
don't—you know—think she's—you know—the girl for me."

I didn't think I'd earned the right just yet to play the Jesus card, so instead I offered something more secular, "Well, that's interesting, but I gotta tell you that I think what you're doing isn't the gentlemanly thing to do. In the first place it isn't fair to her if you're leading her on, is it? Moreover, my friend, the bottom line is that she's only a sexual convenience. Am I right?"

It was quiet, really quiet, for a while until we got to the next call. On the way back to the office, I offered up Jesus in a way he could understand, "I tell you these truths only because I care about you. Please know I'm not judging and what we've discussed today will have nothing to do with your work here. You're such a wonderful young man and I care very much. That's all. The God of the universe loves you so much and wants the very best for you. And, so do I."

A week later the lad called me and told me he'd moved out.

Our companies are platforms for Jesus. We should use them as such. We need to boldly proclaim God's truth at every opportunity. Yet, we must be sensitive to the hearer and respect where he is spiritually. Otherwise we risk alienation. Being insensitive to others is offensive, ineffective and isn't of Jesus.

People desire truth in their lives. Yet they won't listen to their parents; "friends" give credence and usually encouragement to errant decisions; most employers refrain entirely from getting involved in the personnel lives of their staff.

As Chairman of my company I think I've earned the right to boldly engage people. I can be most effective when I judge each circumstance, pray about it, hear His instructions, and then ACT. Rarely is inaction the Lord's methodology.

REFLECT FOR A MOMENT

1. *Your workplace is your platform. How have you been using it?*

2. *Encounters you have with people throughout your day may in fact be divinely orchestrated. Reflect on the people you have talked with this week. Could any of those meetings have been opportunities for God to work through you?*

3. *If you are uncomfortable speaking about matters of faith with people you meet at work, consider taking a class or seminar on sharing your faith. You may be missing some amazing opportunities.*

What Is a Warrior?

Jeff D. Reeter
Managing Partner, The Texas Financial Group, LP

In Exodus 15:3 Moses leads the Israelites in singing, "*The Lord is a warrior, Yahweh is his name*" (NLV). This insight into God's nature was born out of Moses' abiding relationship with God in which honest communication flowed. This was not just a concept he thought about; this was an experience he lived.

One summer at our ranch in Washington County, Texas, we had a group of young men working in what we call Warrior Weeks. These young men (college and high school age) would rise early in the morning, have a daily quiet time to feed their intimate, personal relationship with Jesus, work up to nine hours a day in the Texas summer heat, and memorize Scripture throughout the day. These athletes lift weights, drink protein shakes, hog and varmint hunt at night, and have the time of their lives. Throughout their bunkhouse are poster boards with Scripture and "iron sharpens iron" words of encouragement.

The Warrior Weeks (W^2) program was first inspired by Scripture that jumped off the page of a daily quiet time. The Scripture is found in Joel 3.

> *Say to the nation: Get ready for war! Train up*
> *your BEST warriors. Let all your fighting men*
> *advance for attack. Hammer your plowshares*
> *into swords and your pruning hooks into spears.*
> *Train even your weak ones to be warriors.*

Our world needs more warriors. What does becoming a warrior mean to you? What are we doing to prepare ourselves for battle? So much that is happening in our world today suggests that the conflict is between good and evil, the visible and the invisible, truth and lies, the way of the Lord and the way of the world, life in the fast lane, and journeying on His road less traveled.

Joel 2 describes a keen vision of God's army.

> *They charge like warriors; they scale walls like*
> *soldiers. They all march inline, not swerving from*
> *their course. They do not jostle each other; each*
> *marches straight ahead... they move forward*
> *without breaking rank... The LORD thunders at*
> *the head of his arm... and mighty is the army that*
> *obeys his command.*

I'm convinced that men and women in leadership positions who are following Christ can better join together in pursuit of battle worthiness, becoming warriors alongside the Greatest Warrior of all. Our quiet times must be more authentic and life transforming. We must hide God's word in our hearts that we may obey Him. We must connect with each other in an "iron sharpens iron" environment where walking in the light and in the truth and being real are courageously happening. We must model to our world a work life similar to that of Moses, Joseph, David, Daniel, Esther, and others who learned to abide in their relationship with God and to repent whenever they acted independently of Him. Let us passionately pursue life as a warrior, set apart, distinctive, moving forth in His calling and power and thus being available for Him to work through us as He sees fit.

REFLECT FOR A MOMENT

1. *Have you ever viewed yourself as a spiritual "warrior"? How might God want to use your life in that way?*

2. *Are you presently prepared for the spiritual battles you may face? Have you been defeated recently in spiritual conflicts? If so, how?*

3. *How do you tend to view God? Have you seen Him as a warrior? If not, how might that viewpoint of God help you as you enter the marketplace?*

Facing Crises and Opposition at Work

EVERYONE EXPERIENCES STORMS in their lives. We cannot prevent them. We can only prepare for them. The 12 disciples had just experienced the greatest accomplishment of their lives thus far. With only a handful of loaves and fishes, Jesus had fed 5,000 men and their families. The disciples were exhausted after dispersing the ample food to the crowd and then collecting 12 baskets of leftovers. This was one of the most astounding miracles in history. Wearily they climbed into a boat and set out across the Sea of Galilee for a much needed respite. Then the storm struck. While they were exhausted, defenseless, and unprepared, the wind and waves viciously assaulted them. So fierce was the storm that even the seasoned fishermen feared for their lives.

Suddenly Jesus appeared. And, as He always did, He had the exact words to speak that changed everything. "*Be of good cheer! It is I; do not be afraid*" (Mark 6:50). Be of good cheer? They were about to die! How can anyone be happy in the midst of a life-threatening storm? Jesus affirmed several important truths that apply in any crisis. First, He claimed there was no reason to fear, even when facing a life-threatening circumstance. Second, they could have joy, even though everything seemed to be going against them. Why? Because Christ was *with* them. As long as Jesus was present, every resource of heaven was available to them. How could they not be courageous and joyful in light of that reality?

As you go to work each week, storms will inevitably arise. Some you can foresee, others will catch you by surprise. The one constant will be Christ's presence with you. Do you know how to experience heavenly joy even in the midst of life's fiercest storms?

If the Foundations Are Destroyed

JOHN ROCKEFELLER WAS one of the most brilliant businessmen in American history. His colossal company, Standard Oil, became the envy or the nemesis of countless people. To overcome federal laws prohibiting companies from conducting business across state lines, Rockefeller developed an elaborate system of trusts whereby Standard Oil extended its interests across North America and the world. For years government agencies sought to curb the excessive power and influence of Standard Oil but despite efforts by critics, U.S. presidents, and various government agencies, Rockefeller's company continued to prosper. Then in 1911, the Supreme Court finally ruled against Standard Oil's antitrust violations and Chief Justice White instructed Standard Oil to be dismembered and the stock of the resultant companies to be publicly traded on the stock exchange, something Rockefeller had always avoided.

Initially this appeared to be a devastating blow for America's most famous businessman. His massive empire would be subdivided into 34 independent companies. Rockefeller's critics were initially ecstatic at his dramatic downfall. His enemies had caused his life's work to be destroyed. Yet what appeared to be a devastating defeat became in reality an enormous windfall. Rockefeller owned roughly 25% of

Standard Oil so, with its division, he now owned 25% of the 34 new companies. When these companies began to be publicly traded, investors were so eager to buy into Rockefeller's companies that stock prices soared. At the time of the court's ruling in 1911, Rockefeller was worth 300 million dollars. By 1913, his assets reached 900 million dollars, almost making him the world's first billionaire. It has been estimated that the equivalent amount of wealth in 1996 would have been 13 billion dollars. The foundations of Rockefeller's world had been shaken and he had come out stronger than ever.

In Psalm 11 King David, CEO of Israel, once asked: *"If the foundations are destroyed, what can the righteous do?"* (vs 3). He wondered this at a time when his enemies were aggressively pursuing his downfall (vs 2). His friends were urging him to flee. It appeared as if he could lose everything. Yet David chose to evaluate his situation from this starting point: *"In the Lord I put my trust"* (vs 1). Every decision he made concerning his future was based on his unwavering faith in God. David understood that God allows difficult times to come. For the wicked, these trials are forms of divine judgment (vs 5-6), but for the righteous they are times of testing (vs 4-5). David passed the test! He concluded: *"For the Lord is righteous, He loves righteousness; His countenance beholds the upright"* (vs 7).

David began his psalm by contemplating running from his problems and trying to save himself. He ended by basking in God's presence. David's hope was not that all he had lost would be restored, or that circumstances would return to the way they once were, or that like Rockefeller, he would prosper through his adversity. David's thoughts rose higher. He realized that God's presence was all he needed.

For David, God was enough. Some Christians want God PLUS success, or wealth, or victory, or... David found such joy, satisfaction, and peace in the divine presence, everything else was secondary. In these days in which the foundations are being shaken, how are you facing the test?

REFLECT FOR A MOMENT

1. *Make a list of the crises you have faced recently. Review the list. Have they shaken the "foundations" of your life? Which adversity has been the most difficult for you to endure? Why is that?*

2. *How has Christ's presence in your life made a difference as you endured crises? Have you sensed His presence? Have you experienced His peace and joy in the midst of what you have been going through?*

3. *What have others witnessed as they watched you undergo difficulty? Has it demonstrated to people the profound difference Christ makes in people's lives? Has God been glorified by how you handled your crises? If not, what does God want to teach you before the next problem inevitably comes?*

Resurrection Power

IN OCTOBER 1907, America plunged into a massive financial crisis. Banks and brokerage houses were failing by the dozens. On October 19, 70-year-old J.P. Morgan returned to New York to try to save the situation. Crowds of terrified businesspeople waited outside 23 Wall Street, desperately hoping to gain Morgan's help. When Charles Barney of Knickerbocker Trust was denied admission to see Morgan, he committed suicide. Other suicides followed. Morgan saved New York City from bankruptcy. He summoned bank presidents and collected $25 million in 15 minutes to rescue the New York Stock Exchange. He instructed religious leaders what to preach on Sunday. The White House made an additional $25 million in Federal money available to Morgan to stem the tide of the financial panic. Though many businesses failed to survive, the crisis was averted. Subsequently, the Federal Reserve System was developed for, as Senator Nelson Aldrich declared, "Something has got to be done. We may not always have Pierpont Morgan with us to meet a banking crisis."

Business leaders expect to deal with challenges and crises. Throughout history people have occasionally risen to Olympian heights to save their business as well as others from ruin. Yet at times, even the most famous executives experienced grievous failure. Morgan's marriage was riddled with infidelity. He was addicted to purchasing expensive works of art that left his finances in precarious condition. His only son was terrified of him. Human saviors inevitably have feet of clay.

The apostle Paul urged people to trust in the one Savior whose power was always sufficient for every problem. He prayed that they might know "*what is the exceeding greatness of His power toward us who believe, according to the working of His mighty power which He worked in Christ when He raised Him from the dead and seated Him at His right hand in the heavenly places*" (Ephesians 1:19-20).

No one ever faced the magnitude of crises that Jesus did. Satan hurled every demon and weapon of evil against Him. Death had always proven invincible to its doomed captives until it attempted to restrain Christ. We cannot begin to comprehend the weight of sin that Jesus bore. Consider if every sin YOU ever committed were piled into your mind and conscience and you were forced to carry the burden for them yourself. Now imagine if the guilt for every person's sin *throughout history* was placed upon your conscience and you had to carry that load. We'll never know the depths of evil Jesus faced as He bore humanity's sins upon His shoulders. The power of wickedness, death, and sin were fiercely determined to destroy Jesus and His work. Yet Christ overwhelmingly conquered them!

Why do we celebrate Easter? Because it reminds us that the same power that overcame humanity's most insurmountable problems is now resident within every believer. There is *nothing* you can face in your life or business that God's power cannot decisively overcome. Trust in Christ and live daily in His power.

But take heart! I have overcome the world.

JOHN 16:33b

REFLECT FOR A MOMENT

1. *Think of the three greatest challenges you are presently facing at work or in your personal life. Consider their complexity and difficulty in being resolved. Now imagine the power required to raise Jesus from the dead when Satan and all of his evil hordes, Death, that had never been defeated, and Sin, that had ravaged humanity throughout history, were desperately trying to keep Jesus in the grave. In light of that, do you think God can handle your problems?*

2. *Consider for a moment that the same power God used to defeat Sin, Death, and Satan is constantly at your disposal to enable you to live a life that glorifies Christ. What is one example of that power being exercised in your life this week? Would a non-Christian be attracted to Christ if he watched your life and looked for the powerful difference Christ makes in you?*

3. *Are you presently living in defeat in some area of your life? Why not take your discouragement to Christ and let Him show you what He can do with it?*

Loss

IN 1858, NINETEEN-YEAR-OLD Samuel Clemens was living his boyhood dream, working in the pilothouse of the *Pennsylvania* riverboat as it ferried passengers up and down the Mississippi River. He had encouraged his favorite brother, Henry, to join up as a ship's hand. They had taken six trips together. One day the pilot, William Brown, became furious at Henry Clemens and began to physically assault him. Samuel quickly came to his younger brother's aid and proceeded to pummel Brown for several minutes until the ship, pilotless, came dangerously close to a collision. The animosity between the two men was so fierce that Samuel had to be transferred to a different ship to restore order to the crew. On June 11, Henry Clemens departed from New Orleans aboard the *Pennsylvania* with his older brother Samuel scheduled to follow two days later aboard the *Lacey*. At 6:00 a.m. on June 13, a boiler exploded, obliterating the *Pennsylvania*. Over 250 people were killed in one of the worst steamboat disasters in American history. Henry was sleeping above the boilers. The blast propelled him into the sky on a jet of steam. Henry fought for his life for several days, but his scalded and broken body was beyond the restorative powers of the physicians.

Clemens' biographer notes, that "Henry's death closed

a door in Samuel Clemens's heart for the rest of his life" (Ron Powers, *Mark Twain: A Life,* 89). He notes, "Now his skepticism regarding the Christian faith hardened into non-belief, and he embarked on a lifetime of guilt over his role in guiding his brother toward his doom, a guilt compounded by the excruciating luck of his own survival." Though he became a popular humorist, sorrow always lay just below the surface throughout Clemens' life.

One of life's great certainties, widely ignored or defiantly denied, is that every person you meet, including yourself, will one day die. Indeed, every day of life we enjoy is a gift from our Creator (Psalm 139:16). The biblical character Job had a realistic perspective on life, "*Naked I came from my mother's womb, and naked I shall return there. The Lord gave, and the Lord has taken away; blessed be the name of the Lord*" (Job 1:21). Job understood that each day of life, and each relationship we enjoy, are gifts from God. Nevertheless, everything eventually comes to an end. As the writer of Ecclesiastes notes, "*To everything there is a season, a time for every purpose under heaven: a time to be born, and a time to die*" (Ecclesiastes 3:1-2). Life has its seasons when relationships and activities in our life are birthed, and other seasons when they draw to an end. Such are the seasons of life.

So how do we live our lives? With gusto! We embrace each day as if it is our last. We savor relationships, never knowing if we will have a further opportunity in this life to enjoy them. We seek to invest our lives in eternity, because it is only those investments that will follow us to heaven.

Samuel Clemens became fixated on the loss of his brother, rather than on the gift of his family. He continually asked why God had taken, without rejoicing that God had first given. He also refused to surrender his soul to the God who would one day draw all of history to a close and gather every saint together to enjoy eternal bliss. Clemens chose to judge God from his own human perspective, rather than seeking to understand the ways of God.

Some people squander great portions of their lives, mourning what they have lost. It could be a position, or an investment, or a relationship, or an opportunity. They can't let it go. It haunts them and saps their joy. Others accept the hardships of life along with the good. In times of loss they weep. But then they enthusiastically embrace the next opportunity or relationship or activity that God brings along. Life is far too brief to waste it wondering what might have been! Life does have hardships. But they are in part what make its joys so sweet. So how are you living your life? Plan to get the absolute most out of today, and each day that follows.

REFLECT FOR A MOMENT

1. *How have you handled death and loss? Have they made you bitter? Have they tempted you to question God? Or, have they caused you to appreciate life and what God has given, even more?*

2. *Are you carrying any bitterness or cynicism with you from the past? Have you allowed previous experiences to rob you of your joy? Do you need to do as the apostle Paul and "forget" what lies behind, and press on to what God has for you in the future? Take an inventory of your life to see*

if anything in your past is harming your present. Then ask the Lord to set you free from it.

3. *Are you living your life with gusto? Do you savor each day God grants you? Or, are you living with resentment and sadness? Take time with God to consider the amazing gift that each day of life is. Reflect on what God has given you, rather than on what has been lost. Make a list of things in your life for which you are (or should be) grateful. Take time to thank God for His goodness, today.*

Unprepared for Battle

USA Today REPORTED that the percentage of American soldiers unfit for active combat had risen sharply (*USA Today,* 3 March 2010). In 2008, up to 16% of the soldiers in some brigades were considered ineligible for battle. Between 2006 and 2008, bad backs, strained knees, and other ailments increased from 1.4 million to 1.9 million. Cases involving mental health rose from 657,144 to 1.1 million. Today, when a unit is deployed into a combat zone, many of its soldiers are left behind or relegated to non-combative tasks. An army with the illusion of possessing the necessary assets to properly engage the enemy may in fact have insufficient field strength to conduct critical operations. How frustrating it is for a general to issue marching orders only to be informed that 16% of his troops are unfit for battle!

In a notorious encounter during WWII the not-so-politically correct General George S. Patton visited a field hospital in Italy. He encountered a serviceman who had no bandages or obvious physical wounds. When Patton asked the soldier why he was hospitalized, he was told it was for battle fatigue. The famous general flew into one of his infamous rages, cursing the patient for choosing the safe comfort of a hospital while his comrades were facing enemy bullets. Patton was severely reprimanded for his breach in protocol, to say nothing of his blatant lack of bedside manner. Patton had no patience for those he suspected of avoiding battle. He knew such conduct could cost others.

We are called by God to serve on a spiritual battlefield. The apostle Paul used an extended military metaphor as he exhorted the faithful in Jesus Christ to ready themselves for warfare against the forces of darkness (Ephesians 6:10-18). The *belt of truth* encircles a warrior and holds the armor in place. The *breastplate of righteousness* covers the heart. The Bible repeatedly warns us to guard our heart—leaving it vulnerable is lethal. Our feet are to be shod with the *Gospel of peace.* Too many of Christ's soldiers have gone lame and are unprepared for deployment.

The *shield of faith* protects us from enemy blows. Roman shields often functioned in an interlocking manner, so as soldiers stood in rank with their shields locked together, arrows and missiles could not find an opening to hit their mark. Believers in the marketplace can find themselves in a fierce, take-no-prisoners spiritual conflict. Only by linking their shields of faith with other believers can they withstand the enemy's barrage. When our faith grows weak, others protect our flank. The *helmet of salvation* protects the head. From the moment of salvation, as a new creation, you no longer have to allow the world's thinking and values to control yours. Paul warned God's people to be wary of how damaging a worldly mindset is, and to protect themselves from adopting a godless worldview. Finally, the *sword of the Spirit* is the word of God and our greatest weapon. Unfortunately many busy professionals neglect this piece of armor, the only one designed not only for protection but also for penetrating the enemy's defense. If the bugle sounded today summoning us to fall into ranks, some of us would be hard-pressed to *find* our sword!

What spiritual battles are you fighting? What missiles are being fired in your direction? Are you linking with others for the inevitable assaults that will come?

REFLECT FOR A MOMENT

1. *Do you feel like you are experiencing spiritual warfare when you go to work? In what ways are you undergoing conflict?*

2. *List each piece of armor described in Ephesians chapter six. Evaluate how firmly each one is in place in your life. Do you have armor that is missing or inadequate for a serious conflict? If so, what do you need to do to be better prepared?*

3. *Have you experienced defeat in spiritual conflicts in which you have already been engaged? If so, what was the result? Has it wounded you? Have you become intimidated by the enemy? Have you lost respect from others? Take time with the Lord and let Him bandage, heal, and restore you so you are fully prepared for the next engagement you face.*

Spiritual Warfare

WILMER MCLEAN, A retired major from the Virginia militia, was a wholesale grocer at the outbreak of the American Civil War. McLean's home, the Yorkshire Plantation, was located in Manassas in Prince William County, Virginia. During the battle of Bull Run on July 18, 1862, Confederate General Beauregard used McLean's house for his headquarters. At one point a Union cannonball fell through the kitchen fireplace causing a great commotion. McLean had no desire to live in a battle zone and subsequently relocated his home 120 miles south to the remote hamlet of Appomattox. Three years later, on April 9, 1865, cornered by General Grant's troops, General Robert E. Lee officially surrendered his army. Ironically the end of the war took place in the parlor of McLean's new home. McLean observed, "The war began in my front yard and ended in my front parlor." Sometimes, despite our best efforts to avoid it, war finds us.

The apostle Paul warned, *"For we do not wrestle against flesh and blood, but against principalities, against powers, against the rulers of the darkness of this age, against spiritual hosts of wickedness in the heavenly places. Therefore take up the whole armor of God, that you may be able to withstand in the evil day, and having done all, to stand"* (Ephesians 6:12-13). We often think of Satan and his dominions having their headquarters in hell. But hell is not their domain. They dread that place for it is the prison God has prepared for Satan's everlasting punishment after he is finally vanquished (Revelation 20:10). It is the earth upon which Satan wages his desperate, evil battles against God's people. Scripture calls Satan *"the prince of the power of the air"* and *"the spirit who now works in the sons of disobedience"* (Ephesians 2:2). We live and work in the midst of a battlefield. And, like Wilmer McLean discovered, there is no place for us to comfortably sit out the war and avoid the tumult. Spiritual battles inevitably come.

How does spiritual warfare assault you? It happens when you are bombarded with criticism for functioning in the marketplace according to your Christian principles. It occurs during moments of temptation in the office or on business trips. It manifests itself through crises in your family or opposition from your boss or betrayal from colleagues or through illness that weakens you physically. Beware: the powers of darkness do not sit idly by while you seek to honor God in your life and professional career. Satan is a cunning and sinister general who relentlessly wages war against God's kingdom. His armory is stocked with innumerable stratagems and weapons. God's people must remain on constant alert (1 Peter 5:8).

In our day spiritual fighting has grown white hot. Satan has established strongholds in American society's most strategic positions. Various government and business leaders, educators, entertainers, and judicial officials have succumbed to Satan's deception. The media regularly exposes the fact that the forces of darkness are entrenched in corporate America. Now is not the time to seek refuge from the battle!

If there was ever a time for God's people to be on active duty, it is now. Satan is most dangerous when we adopt a cavalier attitude toward him. It is imperative that we understand two things: First, we must remember who the enemy is and who it is not. People are not the enemy, regardless of how obnoxious they may be! Second, God does not ask us to defeat Satan. Only God can do that. Rather, Christ commanded us to resist Satan and to serve God wholeheartedly as He extends His kingdom through us. Scripture assures us: God and His forces *will* be victorious!

REFLECT FOR A MOMENT

1. *Are you someone who avoids conflict? Have you been spending more time trying to avoid spiritual battles rather than being effective as a soldier of Christ?*

2. *How have you responded to opposition you have faced because you are a Christian? Have you felt sorry for yourself? Have you blamed God for your difficulties? Have you become obsessed with Satan and his activity? How do you think God wants you to respond to the spiritual conflicts that are coming your way?*

3. *Have you been aware of the spiritual battles being fought in your workplace? Are your colleagues under attack? Is your boss experiencing conflict? How might you intercede for and provide aid to fellow believers who are experiencing difficult spiritual attacks?*

Revenge!

In 1853, Cornelius Vanderbilt had become a fabulously successful businessman. The tough-as-nails, shrewd, and at times, unscrupulous tycoon had leveraged his small rowboat business on Staten Island into a shipping colossus that had made him one of the wealthiest men in America. He commissioned the construction of the *North Star,* the largest steamship in the world, as his private yacht and set sail for a victory tour of Europe. Upon his return, Vanderbilt discovered that Charles Morgan and Cornelius Garrison had betrayed him, seizing control of the Accessory Transit Company, and cutting him out of its profits. Both men were hard-nosed businessmen who now could claim to be the first men to best Cornelius Vanderbilt in business.

In response, Vanderbilt published an open letter to Messrs. Morgan and Garrison in several leading daily papers saying: "Gentlemen: You have undertaken to cheat me. I won't sue you, for the law is too slow. I'll ruin you. —Yours truly, Cornelius Vanderbilt" (Edward Renehan, Jr., *Commodore,* 199-200). The "Commodore" then launched an all-out assault on his rivals, showing no mercy until he had destroyed them. Few businesspeople have been more ruthless, or accumulated more wealth, than did Vanderbilt. However, he was also an uncouth, profane, licentious egomaniac whose family feared him. He spent his final years dying of syphilis he had contracted through his depraved lifestyle.

If you earn your living in the marketplace, it is inevitable that people will oppose, disappoint, or even betray you. The intoxicating attraction of money can drive people to ambush even their closest friends. The vital question is: how does God want you to respond? God once sent word to Eli, the judge of Israel declaring, *"Far be it from Me; for those who honor Me I will honor; and those who despise Me shall be lightly esteemed"* (1 Samuel 2:30). God promises to vindicate those who live their lives to glorify Him. For those who treat God lightly, God will not rush to their aid in their time of need.

Scripture is clear that the thirst for revenge can bring great harm to an offended party. King David's son Absalom was justifiably angry when he learned that his half brother Amnon had raped his sister Tamar. Yet rather than address the offense and go to his father the king, Absalom became obsessed with revenge. After two years of plotting, Absalom murdered Amnon and then fled into exile for three years. His relationship with his father and his brothers was irreparably damaged. He would later lead a revolt against his own father that would divide the nation in two. In a final conflict, many people lost their lives, and Absalom was callously murdered (1 Samuel 13-18). Absalom's story is one of a talented leader who squandered his life and brought great suffering upon others because of his anger toward those who had wronged him. Revenge doesn't pay.

God has promised that He will be a shield to those who walk uprightly (Proverbs 2:7). However, trusting in the Lord means that we allow Him to choose the means of our protection, as well as the timing of His justice. It doesn't mean we naively allow our competitors to continually get the better of us. It does mean that we do not become consumed with worry and anger at what others are doing. It requires us to continue to live with integrity, no matter what our enemies are doing. God is just. You can trust Him.

REFLECT FOR A MOMENT

1. *Who are some people who have harmed you during your business career? How have you dealt with them? Have you thoroughly forgiven them? Or, are you still holding a grudge for what they did? (Be honest.)*

2. *Have you allowed bitterness to creep into your heart? Perhaps it was merely anger or resentment initially, but have you allowed a previous hurt to fester in your soul until it became bitterness? If so, take time with God and ask him to root it out and to set you free. If you need to ask the forgiveness of someone whom you have wronged, do so.*

3. *Do you trust the Lord to protect you? That does not mean He will never allow you to suffer harm, but He will guide and protect and comfort you. Have you been living in fear or confidence?*

Courage

DURING THE FIRST Battle of Manassas, the untried Union and Confederate soldiers were tested for the first time. As General Thomas Jackson prepared his troops to enter the battle, Confederate soldiers were already withdrawing from the front lines. Some were wounded. Others were fleeing the conflict in fear. Still others were retreating after having been scattered by the enemy. Although disheartened to watch their comrades escaping the fierce tumult, Jackson walked his horse slowly back and forth in front of his brigade, encouraging his men. Later, John Newton Lyle, of the 4th Virginia, confessed, "I was scared. I said all the prayers I knew, even to 'Now I lay me down to sleep,' and threw in some shorter catechism and Scripture for good measure." Lyle claimed Jackson "rode about in a shower of death as calmly as a farmer about his farm when the seasons are good." Amidst the roar of battle could be heard Jackson's voice calling, "'All's well, all's well' distinct and in tones as soothing as those of a mother to a frightened child. The repose of his face was of itself reassuring" (James I. Robertson, *Stonewall Jackson,* 179). It was during this battle that Thomas Jackson was first dubbed "Stonewall Jackson" for the way he and his brigade held firm against the fierce Union assault.

Courage is one of the essential character traits of people

who make a difference in their world. It is one thing to know what you must do. It is another thing to have the courage to actually do it! It is fine to believe in the importance of living and working with integrity. It is an entirely different thing to have the courage to take an unpopular ethical stand at work. However, when we display the courage of our convictions, it inevitably inspires others to do the right thing as well.

Joshua had waited his entire adult life for the moment he would be called upon to lead his people. He had been faithful in every assignment God had given him. He had loyally served the revered Moses as his associate. Joshua was finally made the CEO of the Israelites and told to do what even his mentor Moses had been unable to accomplish—lead the Israelites into the Promised Land. And, as always, God had a word for His servant that exactly addressed what he was facing. God told Joshua: *"Have I not commanded you? Be strong and of good courage; do not be afraid, nor be dismayed, for the Lord your God is with you wherever you go"* (Joshua 1:9).

It often takes courage to do God's will. That's because His will is often difficult. In fact, it can be impossible, apart from His intervention. Yet it is often in those challenging moments that we achieve the greatest accomplishments of our life. Life's tranquil, easy times are certainly less stressful, but they are generally not our most productive. No one wants to look back on his life and wonder, "What if?" What if I only had the courage to do what I sensed God was asking me to do? What if I had not remained silent when I sensed God leading me to speak up? What if I had the courage to say "no?" Courage can save us from a lifetime of regret. The workplace can be a difficult place for Christians. Our colleagues may scorn our standards and convictions. Our boss may pressure us to compromise our ethics. We may be tempted to "play it safe" rather than take the risk of doing what God is telling us to do. There are crucial moments in our life that require courage. Those are when we must know that God goes with us.

REFLECT FOR A MOMENT

1. *What is it about living out your Christian life in the marketplace that you find most intimidating? In what area of your life do you need more courage?*

2. *How has the courage of others inspired you? In what ways would your courage motivate those around you?*

3. *Identify areas in your life that require more fortitude. Then enlist some friends to pray for you that your faith would remain strong and you would follow through with your convictions, regardless of how intimidating your circumstances may be.*

Growth in the Wilderness

JOHN CHURCHILL WAS a rising star among the British military during the eighteenth century. He was one of the prominent leaders who welcomed William and Mary to take the throne from King James II. Yet Churchill found himself in the disfavor of King William and was banished from public service for six years. More than that, his enemies viciously sought to ruin him. Even though England was at war on the continent, it refused to call on its most outstanding commander, forcing him to sit on the sidelines, fending off attacks from his political enemies. Yet his biographer, Winston Churchill would later observe, "Few features in Marlborough's long life are more remarkable than the manner in which he steadily grew in weight and influence through the whole of the six years when he was banished from favour and office... Still he grew, and at the end of this lengthy period of eclipse was felt by everyone around the summit of affairs to be one of the greatest Englishmen of the day" (Winston S. Churchill, *Marlborough*, 430-1). Churchill would go on to eventually command the British and allied forces in Europe for ten years, fighting powerful French armies, and never losing. For his storied accomplishments, he would be elevated to the Duke of Marlborough and would be widely regarded as one of the most brilliant military commanders in England's history.

There is something potent and unique about the wilderness. People grow in the wilderness in ways they cannot while occupying center stage. Isolation and even opposition can mature our character in ways that praise and accolades never will. David spent years hiding from King Saul in the Judean wilderness. It might have appeared to be a colossal waste of talent for a young man who had been anointed to become king. Yet it was not time squandered. There he began to collect his mighty men and to establish himself as a brilliant leader. Moses spent 40 years in the wilderness. It may have appeared like a promising career in the Egyptian court was being squandered in a desert. Yet it was there he learned to be the kind of shepherd God would use to guide His people. Even Jesus, at the outset of his ministry, spent 40 days in the wilderness. One might assume that after waiting until he was in his thirties before beginning His public ministry, that Jesus might have already been prepared to dramatically launch the Christian movement. Yet the Father chose to lead His Son into the wilderness immediately after His baptism (Mark 1:12-13).

To many, time in the wilderness can seem like a frustrating waste of time. We are trained to think that action and advance are signs of success. Sitting still and being overlooked for significant assignments is evidence of failure. Yet from God's perspective, His greatest work may be what He does *in* us rather than merely what He accomplishes *through* us. *Waiting* on the Lord can often be far more difficult than *serving* the Lord. That is why He must at times take us into a wilderness so we can learn to properly trust and wait upon Him. We can learn much about God's character and love for us in the wilderness that might have been difficult for us to grasp during periods of frenetic service on His behalf.

There will inevitably come times in your life where the pace slows, opposition mounts, advance grinds to a halt, and failure rears its ugly head. We may find ourselves in a parched, barren wilderness and wonder if God has forgotten us. The truth is, we may be exactly where God wants us to be. Use your wilderness experiences well!

REFLECT FOR A MOMENT

1. *Are you in a wilderness time in your life right now? If so, how do you think you have been handling it?*

2. *How difficult is it for you to wait on the Lord? Are you a person who wants to stay busy all the time? What could God teach you by making you remain still and wait for Him for answers?*

3. *Do you love God just as much when He leaves you in a wilderness as you love Him when He blesses you with activity and success? Do you view faithfulness as "success" or do you tend to only see promotions, pay raises, and accolades as "success"?*

Are We Ever Going to Get Out of This Mess?

Richard T. Case
CEO, Benchmark Associates, Inc.

THE ECONOMIC CYCLE Research Institute of NYC has correctly predicted over the last 15 years each recessionary cycle with no false alarms. Contrary to political forecasting, the Institute is currently predicting that the U.S. is about to enter another recession cycle—with unemployment hitting double digits. Further, that the U.S. business cycle is becoming shorter—with more frequent recessions the norm. Our economy is in crisis and we have little hope of a sustained recovery returning any time soon. Are we ever going to get out of this mess?

For we who are children of God, being led by God, the answer is YES! In 2 Chronicles 14, we read of Asa, the King of Judah. Asa did what was good and right in the eyes of the Lord, his God—how? Asa removed the idols that dotted the land and led his people to seek the Lord God and to obey His commands. As a result Asa's kingdom flourished. Everything seemed stable and secure. Then an enemy army of 1,000,000 came against Asa and his army of 580,000. Overwhelming! He faced an impossible situation that promised to devastate the kingdom. What was Asa's response? Give up? Resign himself to failure? Develop a sophisticated strategic plan to fight and hope for the best? Compromise and seek an alliance with an ungodly nation to avoid defeat? No. Out of his personal relationship with God, Asa cried out, stating

- Lord, it is nothing for you to help!
- So, help us.
- We rest on You.
- In Your Name (in God's authority and power), we go against this overwhelming enemy.
- You are our God!
- Do not let the overwhelming circumstances prevail against You!

Then, God answered and struck down the enemy as well as its allies. Rather than suffering a crushing defeat, Asa collected large amounts of booty. So the key questions for us are

1. Is God our God—do we have a vital personal relationship; and do we trust Him as God of all creation?

2. Have we removed the idols from our life (anything that is more important to us than God is)?

3. Are we willing to be obedient to His instructions (which implies we are hearing His instructions)?

4. Are we willing to cry out to God to seek His help, His wisdom, and His supernatural work that will lift us to victory when defeat seems probable?

We need not be afraid or resigned to the fact that, when these recessionary cycles strike our economy, our companies will inevitably suffer decline and failure. Rather, in the face of international crises, God can lead us to supernatural victory. God is not limited to current circumstances or likely economic cycles. It is nothing for Him to help us! Just ask.

REFLECT FOR A MOMENT

1. *God knows the future. How has He been preparing you for it?*

2. *Are you "resting" in God? If you are, what are you doing?*

3. *What is the most difficult challenge you are presently facing? How is God making a practical difference in your circumstance?*

Jonah and the Financial Meltdown

Jack Alexander
Vice Chairman and Partner; Rainmaker Group

HOW MANY TIMES in the last year has someone asked you

- What is going to happen in the economy?
- How long will it take for the market to recover?
- How many jobs will be lost?

Aren't we all looking for a sign—an indicator that we can rely on? Jesus said

> *An evil and adulterous generation craves for a sign; and yet no sign will be given to it but the sign of Jonah the Prophet.*

> MATTHEW 12:39 (NASB)

The obvious reference Jesus refers to is the "sign" of His resurrection to come. However, a further study of Jonah shows that God may have more to say to us through the "sign of Jonah."

Obedience—Our Response to God's Directive

The Ninevites were enemies of Israel. The idea of preaching a grace-based message of repentance was unacceptable to Jonah. God's directives violated Jonah's values and he refused to obey.

Application—in difficulty, rather than merely measuring our losses, we need to "measure" our obedience to the living God.

Grace Versus Idols

In my favorite verse, Jonah 2:8, Jonah states *"those who cling to worthless idols forfeit the grace that could be theirs"* (NIV 1984).

Difficult times reveal our idols—what do we think and worry about? The idols do not love us or provide for us. By shaking and/or destroying these idols, God is telling us to look at Him, the giver of all good and perfect gifts.

Application—Grace should be the lens through which we view life. "Forfeiting" grace carries a heavy price—we cannot give grace to others when we fail to see that everything we have is due to God's grace and mercy.

Like Jonah, God can allow us to be "swallowed" up literally through our circumstances. However, it is just as devastating for us to have the "lens of grace" removed from our lives through idolatry. Our idols cover this lens and block us from seeing with spiritual eyes.

Christ insists on being first in our life—because He is the First and the Best.

REFLECT FOR A MOMENT

1. *In what ways does your life presently compare to that of Jonah?*

2. *How do you typically respond when God asks you to do something that is difficult?*

Walking with God, in the Marketplace

GOD'S PRIMARY CALL on your life is not to have you affirm a particular doctrine or to embrace a set of religious activities, but to enter into and to enjoy a relationship with Him. Christianity is a personal, growing, intimate relationship with Jesus Christ. Jesus said, *"Come to Me, all you who labor and are heavy laden, and I will give you rest"* (Matthew 11:28). Spiritual restoration and strength come from abiding in Christ (John 15:1-8).

One of the greatest challenges for businesspeople is to maintain a close walk with Christ while they are immersed in the frenetic demands and schedule of the marketplace. With all the demands upon us, how can we carve out adequate time to spend with our Lord? How can we consciously abide in Christ throughout our workday when we are continually being bombarded with challenges, opportunities, and problems? And, how can we spend sufficient time communing with Christ when we are so busy serving Him?

We must not forget that our primary calling is not to serve Christ, but to abide in Him. If we neglect our relationship, our service will amount to nothing. It is out of our abiding relationship in Christ that our life will produce spiritual fruit that lasts (John 15:5).

How would you describe your current walk with God? Do you enjoy abiding in Christ? Are you seeing fruit resulting from your divine relationship? Would you rather serve Christ than fellowship with Him? Remember, regardless of how busy you are or how much responsibility you carry, apart from abiding in Christ, you can do *nothing*.

You Must Be Born Again!

IN MODERN SOCIETY, people's religious beliefs are viewed as "private" and expected to remain separate from their career. The result: Businesspeople claim to have God in their lives but their practices are anything but godly. Henry Ford hired a minister to oversee his factory workers' morals while Ford himself maintained a lengthy relationship with his mistress, Evangeline Cote (Steven Watts, *The Peoples' Tycoon,* 332-340). John Rockefeller was a devout Baptist. During one anxious board meeting in the 1880s, while lamenting the absence of new oil discoveries, Rockefeller stood up and pointed toward heaven, stating, "The Lord will provide" (Ron Chernow, *Titan,* 284). Yet many critics lambasted him as the most unscrupulous of the robber barons. J.P. Morgan stated he believed the Bible to be literally true and fastidiously attended church Sunday mornings and sang hymns Sunday evenings. He breakfasted with his minister every Monday morning (Ron Chernow, *The House of Morgan,* 52). Yet Morgan also bullied kings and presidents and was repeatedly guilty of infidelity. These powerful business leaders did not always allow their faith to affect how they lived or conducted business.

A devastating development in today's church is the emphasis that salvation comes simply by praying the "sinner's prayer." Many people cling to a moment, long past, when they prayed with their parents or their minister and asked Jesus to "come into their heart." For the rest of their lives, they assure themselves that they are going to heaven when they die because they prayed a prayer, walked an aisle during a revival service, or signed a commitment card at a conference. The Bible does not give such assurance. Scripture does not teach that you become a Christian when you ask Jesus to come into your heart. Jesus taught that you become a Christian when you are born again (John 3:3). When the apostle John wanted to assure people of their eternal life, he did not ask them to look back to a moment in their past when they prayed a sinner's prayer or were baptized. Rather he had people examine their present condition: Were they walking in darkness? Then they did not have fellowship with Christ (1 John 1:6). Did they hate their brother? Then they were not walking in the light (1 John 2:9). Did they love the things of the world? Then God's love was obviously not in them (1 John 2:15). Habitually sin? Evidence they did not know God (1 John 3:6). On the contrary, if they were keeping God's commandments and practicing righteousness they were indeed His children (1 John 3-5; 10). Were they overcoming the world's temptations? Then God resided within them (1 John 4:4). Did they love others as God does? That was clear evidence they knew God (1 John 4:7).

Those who have been genuinely born again *act* like they are a new creation. Jesus claimed that you identify a tree by the kind of fruit it produces (Matthew 7:15-20). A tree that claims to be an apple tree but which produces oranges is merely a deceived orange tree. A person who claims to be a Christian but produces the fruit of an unbeliever is likewise deceived. They have not been born again. Do not be tempted to overlook consistently carnal behavior by family and friends and be falsely assuaged by a childhood proclamation they made for Christ. That is doing them no favors. The present fruit of people's lives clearly reveals whether or not they are children of God. How far back would you have to look to find compelling evidence that you or your family members had truly been born again?

REFLECT FOR A MOMENT

1. *How do you KNOW you have been born again? Is there any uncertainty in your mind about this? What evidence is there from the last month that you are a child of God? How far back do you have to look in your life to find evidence you are a Christian?*

2. *Have you looked at your Christian faith more as a religion than as a relationship? Have you viewed your faith as consisting of belonging to a church, believing certain doctrines, and embracing moral lifestyles, or have you understood it to center upon relating to the Person of Jesus Christ?*

3. *What spiritual fruit have you experienced recently that demonstrates that Christ is actively working in your life? Have you been tempted to focus on serving Christ without abiding in Him? If so, what has been the result?*

Black Friday

THE BIGGEST SHOPPING day of the year! The mere thought of it sends shivers of excitement down the spine of eager bargain hunters while causing others to break out into a cold sweat. Boisterous crowds of turkey-stuffed, deal-seeking shoppers flood the malls and department stores, frantically scouting out drastic price reductions on everything from flat screen TVs to pima cotton underwear. The day after Thanksgiving, Black Friday is traditionally the day retail businesses hope to begin moving their balance sheet from the red to the black. Retailers recognize that sales during the following weeks will determine whether their companies realize a profit for that year or not.

Here's a question for you: how long do you have to go into a new year before there is a noticeable gain in your spiritual life? For example, Jesus is able to increase your faith (Mark 9:23-27). So, how has your faith in God grown this year? At what point in the year did you begin trusting God for more than you had before? Likewise, is your prayer life more robust now than it was last January? Scripture assures us that the Holy Spirit can help us to pray for deeper things than we would know to ask for on our own (Romans 8:26). Jesus said the Spirit can powerfully increase our capacity to receive deeper, more profound words from Him (John 16:12).

What month was it when you realized that God had taken your understanding of His word to a deeper level? Jesus said if we would abide in Him, His joy would fill our lives to overflowing (John 15:11). So, at what point this year did you recognize that God had expanded your joy to a dimension you had never experienced before? Is it overflowing yet? The Bible assures us that God will grant us increased wisdom if we ask Him to (James 1:5). So the question is: are you enjoying a deeper level of wisdom now than you were a year ago?

As in a business, our spiritual life could be viewed from a profit and loss perspective. Sometimes our selfish choices or our carelessness with our spiritual life causes us to take a hit spiritually. Our spiritual fervency can wane, or we compromise how we represent Jesus to others, or our power in prayer diminishes. At other times we immerse ourselves in prayer and Bible study, resulting in dramatic spiritual advancement. Our pursuit of God's will, and our obedience to do it, leads to results that can be measured like figures on a year-end sales report. Some people end the year in worse condition spiritually than when they began. Others plateau in their spiritual life, seeing no advancement the entire year. But there are those who take major leaps forward in their spiritual maturity that results in unprecedented victories in their walk with God.

Just as in the marketplace, many people find themselves playing spiritual catch-up as the Christmas season arrives. There is a surge in the attention they give to Christ, to the church and to spiritual matters in general. They have a heightened awareness of their spiritual condition as they confront the story of the Messiah's birth. They also realize that the spiritual goals they set at the year's outset have not been attained. For some, even a spiritual "Black Friday" may not be enough to recuperate the year's backsliding. What do you need to do to regain the spiritual ground you lost during this year? How will you approach the next year so you experience significant spiritual gains from its outset?

REFLECT FOR A MOMENT

1. *Is your walk with God in the same place it was last year? If so, why is that? How long has your Christian maturity been in the same place? Are you content with that or do you want to take your walk with God to a higher level?*

2. *Do you tend to try and play "catch up" with your walk with God? Do you neglect your relationship for stretches of time and then try and frantically catch up on your Bible reading, prayer, and study of God's word? If so, how has that worked for you? What might you build in to your schedule so your spiritual growth is more consistent throughout the year?*

3. *How often do you suffer from "backsliding"? Do you tend to take two steps forward in your walk with God and then take one step backward? If you do, what could you do to avoid losing ground in your spiritual life?*

Preparing to Encounter God

JEFF CLUBBS WAS home sick from his job as a Social Studies teacher when six people came to his door in Des Moines, Iowa. President Obama was coming to town the following Wednesday and wanted a home to host him. They chose the Clubbs' house. Jeff and Sandy Clubbs are ordinary people. Jeff is a teacher and Sandy is a college athletic director. They have an 11-year-old son and a 9-year-old daughter. One hundred people could attend the event in the Clubbs' backyard and the Clubbs were allowed to invite 80 of them. "My first thought was I wanted to have my kitchen redone." said Sandy. In preparation for the presidential visit, 30 additional phone lines were installed, security devices were stored in the basement, computers were set up in the upstairs office, video equipment was positioned in the kitchen, gas lines and overhead wires were mapped out, living room furniture was rearranged, metal crowd-control fences were erected, and a row of potted evergreen trees was strategically postioned. Security checks were run on the guests. The Clubbs' daughter Skyelar taped a sign outside her bedroom door: "If you're a girl or the Prez come in if not knock."

One doesn't merely pull another chair up to the kitchen table when the president stops by! How do you prepare to meet with God? When the Israelites were going to encounter

God, He instructed Moses, *"Go to the people and consecrate them today and tomorrow, and let them wash their clothes. And let them be ready for the third day the Lord will come down upon Mount Sinai in the sight of all the people"* (Exodus 19:10-11). God later commanded Joshua, *"Sanctify yourselves, for tomorrow the Lord will do wonders among you"* (Joshua 3:5).

Almighty God expects His people to prepare for their meetings with Him. Too often we simply flip open our Bibles and skim a few verses before dashing off to work, not even expecting our mechanical efforts to bring about a life-changing, profound divine encounter. We have a day set aside for worship but do we prepare for that encounter in any significant way? Weary from staying up to watch a late movie on Saturday night, we grumpily complain about the lack of parking as we arrive at church. Entering the auditorium we are bombarded with a cacophony of sounds as people excitedly rehearse yesterday's football games, describe their recent hunting trip or catch up with their friends. When the worship service begins, we rush to find our seats, search for our wallet to find something to place in the offering, whisper to our spouse about where we'll go to eat after the service, set our cell phones to vibrate, and try to find our Bible.

Too often people are walking away from their quiet time or worship service in exactly the same condition they entered it. Scripture warns, *"Do not be deceived, God is not mocked; for whatever a man sows, that he will also reap"* (Galatians 6:7). A wise person will prepare their hearts in advance for an encounter with their Creator and Lord. How much more could we experience if we focused our thoughts, confessed our sins, and prepared the soil of our hearts to receive and respond to God's word (Matthew 13:8-9)? If God matches the encounters we have with Him with the level of our preparation for them, what should we expect? Just as we would never enter a board meeting unprepared, it is an affront to almighty God to think we can commence a time of worship while completely distracted, yet experience a life-changing encounter.

REFLECT FOR A MOMENT

1. *What steps do you take to prepare for a meeting with God? Are your divine encounters random, or do you prepare for them?*

2. *How do you approach having a "Quiet Time" with God? What do you do to prepare yourself? How do you ready yourself before attending a worship service? What else might you do?*

3. *Have you ever left a church service and felt as if you got nothing out of the experience? Why do you think that is? Is it merely the fault of the pastor and worship team? Or, are there things you are doing (or not doing) that are hindering the divine encounters you could be having?*

Power Lunches

In June 2010, the Glide Foundation held its annual charity auction to undergird its $17 million dollar budget. Focusing on alleviating the suffering of the impoverished and homeless of San Francisco, the foundation heavily depends on this yearly fundraiser. Over the last several years the most profitable draw on the eBay auction block has been lunch at the Smith and Wollensky steakhouse in New York City with investment guru Warren Buffet. The 2010 winner paid $2.6 million for the privilege. Says Robert Chatwani, who directed the record-setting auction: "I tell you... some people really want to have lunch with Warren Buffet, huh?" It seems doubtful that much time will be spent discussing the weather, sports, or even the quality of the steaks.

One year the winning bid was $1.68 million and in 2008 the lunch date cost $2.1 million. Why have people been motivated to spend so much money to have a little time with Buffet? Undoubtedly bidders hope that Buffet's genius for investing and his willingness to share some of that insight over lunch will pay rich dividends. What would you talk with Buffet about if you could talk with him?

If you could spend time with anyone in the world, who would you choose? What would you discuss? Finances? Politics? Entertainment? Gossip? Theology? Trivia? What percentage of the time would you speak and how much of the time would you listen? What questions would you ask?

What if you had the opportunity to spend private time with God? What if you could ask Him your most pressing questions? What if you could listen while God shared what was on His heart? How much time would you be willing to spend with Him? What if the only time He had available was early in the morning? What if the only available time on *His* calendar happened to be at a busy time for you? What would you do?

Of course, you *do* have the opportunity to spend time with God. And, He is open to questions. He has given His people a standing offer, "*Call to Me, and I will answer you, and show you great and mighty things, which you do not know*" (Jer. 33:3). Unfortunately, we are busy people with important things to do. Sometimes we simply can't work Him in to our hectic schedule. Sadly, God could say of some of us, "*. . . and I spoke to you, rising up early, and I called to you, but you did not answer*" (Jeremiah 7:13).

Busy people don't like to waste time. John Rockefeller intoned, "A man has no right to occupy another man's time unnecessarily." It was said of J.P. Morgan, that "his imperious stare could reduce interlopers to jelly... his aura was so fearsome that crowds parted before him on the street." After saving a businessman from financial ruin, Morgan interrupted the man as he profusely thanked him saying, "No, it is a busy day. There's no time for that. Good morning." There was no mistaking when Morgan was finished talking with someone!

People typically value the time they spend in the presence of respected businesspeople. They tend to make the time count and they choose their words carefully. Every time we enter God's presence we have an unbelievable privilege. God spoke and fashioned the universe. He counseled the giants of church history. His word will one day draw history to a climactic close. The next time you enter into a conversation with almighty God, what will you discuss?

REFLECT FOR A MOMENT

1. *How do you view your time with Christ each day? Is it something you discipline yourself to do? Or is it an exciting, meaningful time you enjoy spending with your Lord and Savior?*

2. *How would you evaluate your current times spent with Christ? Are they adequate, disappointing, unfulfilling, boring, or life-changing? What adjustments could make your time spent with Christ more rewarding?*

3. *Do you find greater enjoyment spending time with friends, watching sports or news on television, going to sporting events, or spending time with Christ? (Be honest!) Why is that? Do you spend time with Christ out of guilt or because it is an enjoyable experience? Reflect on your times with God and ask Him to show you what adjustments you can make so they are more rewarding for you in the future.*

Divine Encounters

PETER HITCHENS, BROTHER of the abrasive atheist, Christopher Hitchens, had renounced his faith and was living his life as a foreign journalist on his own terms and for his own pleasure. In 1982, he and his girlfriend took a vacation, traveling throughout Europe, enjoying fine restaurants, and visiting popular tourist sites. On a visit to the Hotel-Dieu in Beaune, France, they decided to view Roger van der Weyden's fifteenth-century masterpiece, *The Last Judgment.* Hitchens was a seasoned, international journalist. He had lived in Moscow during the fall of the Soviet Union. He had survived a serious motorcycle accident, as well as mob violence in South Africa and Mogadishu. This well-educated, atheist was not easily impressed or intimidated.

Yet as he stood before Weyden's portrayal of the final judgment of humanity, Hitchens found himself deeply moved. He notes, "I had a sudden, strong sense of religion being a thing of the present day, not imprisoned under thick layers of time. A large catalogue of misdeeds, ranging from the embarrassing to the appalling, replayed themselves rapidly in my head. I had absolutely no doubt that I was among the damned, if there were any damned… I had simply no idea that an adult could be frightened, in broad daylight and after a good lunch, by such things" (Peter Hitchens, *The Rage Against God,* 101-103).

Divine encounters can occur at the least likely moment, even when you are not looking for them, or may not even believe in them. Jacob was a man no one could trust. He had brazenly lied to his father and greedily cheated his brother. His shameful conduct forced him to flee for his life into the desert. There, with nothing but a rock to lay his head upon, he experienced a life-changing dream. Suddenly heaven opened before him and he beheld angels at work carrying out their heavenly tasks right where he lay. "*Surely the Lord is in this place, and I did not know it,*" he cried (Genesis 28:16).

Jacob was not looking for a meeting with God. In fact, after his unethical behavior, he probably doubted if God wanted anything to do with him. But it was, in fact, after Jacob had hit the bottom that God had him in a place where he was prepared to listen. God had always been near Jacob. Jacob had just been too preoccupied to respond to the God who was near. God promises that, if we will seek Him with all of our heart, we will "find" Him (Jeremiah 29:12-13). This is most certainly true. But it is also a reality that God seeks after *us*. He loves us far too much to leave our spiritual lives entirely up to us. He knows that no one naturally seeks after Him (Romans 3:11). Without the Holy Spirit's drawing on our heart and His speaking to us through the circumstances of our lives, we would never find our way to God.

Divine encounters can occur during the most mundane moments of our day. We may be at work in our office, riding an elevator, talking with a colleague, reading a report, or in a meeting. Suddenly our spiritual senses detect that, just as with Jacob, God has been at work around us all the time. God fashions unique relationships with people. For one, like Peter Hitchens, God might speak through a work of art. For another, it might be through a contemporary Christian song. One could encounter God during a worship service at church, another during a walk in a park. Are you prepared for and open to a divine encounter today?

REFLECT FOR A MOMENT

1. *List the last divine encounter you experienced. Where was it? What did God do or say? How did it affect you? Do you tend to encounter God in the same circumstances and venues, or in a variety of settings?*

2. *Do you find that your Christian life is filled with ritual and religion without divine, personal encounters? If so, are you properly preparing yourself to meet with God? Are your spiritual senses alert to moments God might use to communicate with you?*

3. *Could it be that God is speaking but you are not hearing or recognizing that it is God? Consider significant or meaningful experiences you have had. Was God involved somehow? Could He have been sending a message that you did not recognize?*

God in Nature

ALBERT EINSTEIN BECAME legendary for his phenomenal cognitive powers. In 1931, Edwin Hubble took Albert and Elsa Einstein on a visit to the enormous telescope on Mount Wilson, California. The scientists explained to Elsa that, with the state-of-the-art instrument, they could determine the scope and limit of the universe. "Well, my husband does that on the back of an old envelope," she replied.

Einstein's Theory of Relativity revolutionized science. Einstein, being Jewish, claimed he was "enthralled by the luminous figure of the Nazarene." He also adamantly denied that he was an atheist. Yet he never could find his way to a personal relationship with Christ. Einstein's extensive and groundbreaking studies of the universe had convinced him that there must be a power greater than humanity, but he could never accept the personal God presented in the Christian Scriptures.

He did state, however, "I'm not an atheist. The problem involved is too vast for our limited minds. We are in the position of a little child entering a huge library filled with books in many languages. The child knows someone must have written those books. It does not know how. It does not understand the languages in which they are written. The child dimly suspects a mysterious order in the arrangement of the books but doesn't know what it is. That, it seems to me, is the attitude of even the most intelligent human being toward God. We see the universe marvelously arranged and obeying certain laws but only dimly understand these laws" (Walter Isaacson, *Einstein, 386).* To the end of his life, Einstein was working on a mathematical equation that could unlock the secrets of the universe, but he never found the Person of Christ.

The apostle Paul, a brilliant thinker of his day, declared, *"For since the creation of the world His invisible attributes are clearly seen, being understood by the things that are made, even His eternal power and Godhead, so that they are without excuse"* (Romans 1:18-20). Nature is filled with evidence that points to a Creator. He has left His fingerprints everywhere. The key is to recognize them.

The Gospel of Matthew records, *"Now after Jesus was born in Bethlehem of Judea in the days of Herod the king, behold, wise men from the East came to Jerusalem, saying, 'Where is He who has been born King of the Jews?'"* (Matthew 2:1-2). These wise men were probably astrologers. They studied the skies to understand their world. They would not have been believers, or Jewish, but Persian. They were students of nature, and particularly of the heavens. They wanted to understand their world and the secret to life. When the greatest intervention into human affairs in history occurred, they did not miss it!

For those seeking God, nature heralds His magnificence. You can see His handiwork everywhere, if you are looking. The more deeply scientists peer into space the more amazing the Creator appears. Scientific discoveries do not diminish our view of God, but cause us to pause in reverent wonder. At times we can be so busy racing to work and dashing from one meeting to the next that we fail to slow down and consider the vastness and the beauty of the world in which we live. Sometime soon, take time to look up at the night sky and carefully observe the stars. Consider the immensity of the Creator and your own smallness in comparison. Wise people study science and nature, and they eventually find Jesus.

REFLECT FOR A MOMENT

1. *In the next week, plan to go outside at night and take 15 minutes to stare into the sky. Observe the stars. Imagine the immensity of the universe. Consider the miracle of human life on planet Earth. Let God reveal to you His awesome power and His infinite love for you.*

2. *Find a good book by a Christian apologist. There are many brilliant Christian scientists who have discovered that the more they study science, the more it confirms the truths found in the Bible. Science does not disprove Scripture; it affirms it.*

3. *Do you feel the need to fully understand things before you believe them? Are you comfortable knowing that you will never completely understand God? You are limited in a physical world, while He is beyond it in a spiritual dimension. It is impossible for us to understand realities that are beyond our experience or comprehension. If you will not believe God until you know what God knows, you will forever be frustrated and lacking in faith.*

Growth, Part 1

WHILE HE IS consistently rated as one of America's greatest leaders, George Washington did not live his life from one success to the next. After he was chosen to command the revolutionary forces against the armies of England, he lost most of his early battles and at times was severely outmaneuvered. After one of his defeats, John Adams commented, "In general, our generals were outgeneraled." Yet Washington continued to grow and to learn, until he stood triumphant on the battlefield. David McCullough concluded, "He was not a brilliant strategist or tactician, not a gifted orator, not an intellectual. At several crucial moments he had shown marked indecision. He had made serious mistakes in judgment. But experience had been his great teacher from boyhood, and in this his greatest test, he learned steadily from experience. Above all, Washington never forgot what was at stake and he never gave up" (David McCullough, *1776*, 293). Life can forgive those who make mistakes but it is harsh on the unteachable.

In the final week of Jesus' life, we read, "*Then, six days before the Passover, Jesus came to Bethany, where Lazarus was who had been dead, whom He had raised from the dead. There they made Him a supper; and Martha served, but Lazarus was one of those who sat at the table with Him*" (John 12:1-2).

Jesus could not have been blamed for avoiding Bethany. His enemies were plotting to kill Him if He came back (John 11:57). Yet Jesus had returned. Why? Because He wanted to spend time with His friends. In this account, the Gospel writer highlights four people who had walked with Jesus throughout His ministry.

There was *Martha* who, as usual, was serving Jesus. She had done so earlier, only at that time she had suffered from a severe attitude problem (Luke 10:38-42). She had focused so much on serving Jesus that she had neglected to *enjoy* Him. As a result, she began to compare her service to that which was being done by others. She began to feel sorry for herself and finally accused Jesus of not caring for her. Not so this time. As Martha had spent time with Jesus, she had learned to serve selflessly and, as a result, was now glorifying God through her efforts.

Then there was *Lazarus*. In the past, Lazarus had attended meals with Jesus, but we never hear about his having a positive effect on others. But he, like Martha, had experienced a life-changing encounter with Christ. Jesus had saved his life! Now people were placing their faith in Jesus because of what He had done in Lazarus' life (John 12:11). In fact, now Jesus' enemies wanted to kill Lazarus because the divine transformation in his life was drawing many people to Jesus (John 12:10). What a difference time with Jesus had made in Martha and Lazarus's lives!

When we spend time with Jesus, we are changed. Scripture notes, *"But we all, with unveiled face, beholding as in a mirror the glory of the Lord, are being transformed into the same image from glory to glory, just as by the Spirit of the Lord"* (2 Corinthians 3:18). The longer we fellowship with

Christ, the more we take on His character and perspective. His personality is so pure and dominating that to be exposed to them, our sinful habits and attitudes are quite naturally discarded. But the key is spending time with Christ. He was willing to leave heaven and come to earth to fellowship with us. He returned to Bethany though He knew His enemies waited for Him, to enjoy His friends. What are you willing to do, to spend time with Him?

REFLECT FOR A MOMENT

1. *Consider your service for Christ. Are you serving Him in the same way, and with the identical attitude you were last year? Or, has your service for Christ matured? Is your service bringing more glory to God than it used to?*

2. *Consider your witness for Christ. Are more people being drawn to Christ because of you than were previously? What might Christ need to do in your life so you became a more effective witness for Him?*

3. *The longer you are in Christ's presence, the more like Him you become. Consider your current Christian character. What does it reflect about your time spent with Jesus? Do you need to invest more quality time with Him?*

Growth, Part 2

IN DESCRIBING THE deeper Christian life, V. Raymond Edman once wrote, "The deep dealing of God with his children varies in detail, but the general pattern seems much alike for individual cases. Into each life there arises an awareness of failure, a falling short of all that one should be in the Lord; then there is a definite meeting with the risen Savior in utter surrender of heart, which is indeed death to self. There follows an appropriation by faith of His resurrection life through the abiding presence of the Holy Spirit. As a result there is realized an overflow of life likened by the Lord Jesus to 'rivers of water' (see John 7:37-39)" (V. Raymond Edman, *They Found the Secret,* 17). Edman traces the stories of Christian leaders such as Hudson Taylor, D. L. Moody, and Andrew Murray to see how God took their ordinary Christian lives and led them deeper into a relationship than most of their contemporaries had gone. It began at a point of absolute surrender where the individuals became convinced that there was far more to be experienced of God. Realizing that, they could no longer be content remaining where they were spiritually.

As we have seen in John chapter 12, Martha and Lazarus were friends of Jesus. But, after having spent time in His presence, both moved to deeper levels in their walk with Him.

Martha's *service* became more Christ-centered. Lazarus's *witness* was magnified until many people believed in Christ because of what Christ had done in His friend's life.

Also attending the meal in Bethany was *Mary.* Mary was a person of *devotion.* In a previous encounter, she had quickly found a place at Jesus' feet and basked in His presence (Luke 10:38-42). It would seem that Mary had fully arrived in her devotion to Jesus. But as she spent time in His presence, she came to realize that there had to be greater ways still to express her love for Jesus. So she took expensive spikenard oil, and poured it on Jesus' feet (John 12:1-8). This may well have been her most valuable possession. Perhaps it had been saved for her future dowry. Yet she spent it extravagantly on Jesus, perhaps lessening her chances of finding a respectable husband one day. Further, she humiliated herself by letting her hair down and washing Jesus' feet. No dignified woman would ever let her hair down in public. Even Jewish slaves could not be made to degrade themselves by touching someone's filthy feet. She had taken her devotion to an entirely new and unprecedented level that would be celebrated for over 2,000 years.

Each of these friends of Jesus had seen his or her relationship with Jesus deepen over time. But there was one more companion who is mentioned in this account. *Judas.* He had also walked with Jesus throughout most of His earthly ministry. He had spent more time with Jesus than had Lazarus, Martha, or Mary. Yet he had remained unchanged. The Bible says that rather than being impressed by Mary's act of devotion, Judas grumbled about the extravagant waste. This was *"because he was a thief, and had the money box; and he used to take what was put in it"* (John 12:6). Judas had been a materialistic, greedy, thief when he began following Jesus and three years later, he remained the same. He had identified himself as a follower of Jesus, but he had never given his heart to his Lord. He had refused to change. His heart remained hardened and impervious to the Holy Spirit's work. The result was disastrous.

Identifying yourself as a Christian is not enough. You must remain in Christ's presence and allow Him to change you. How long have you been a follower of Jesus? Have you gone deeper? Or, have you remained the same?

REFLECT FOR A MOMENT

1. *How would you rate your devotion to Christ? Has it gone deeper? Are your worship experiences more powerful and deep than they once were? Do you enjoy Christ's presence more than you used to? Or, has it remained the same?*

2. *Consider some fresh, new ways to express your devotion to Christ. Perhaps meet with Him in a new venue. Try reading a different translation of the Bible. Use a new devotional book. Try praying out loud. Write down your prayers. Take more time to remain silent and listen. Consider fresh, new ways you might enhance your devotional life.*

3. *Have you been in some ways like Judas? Have you been a follower of Jesus but remained the same? Do you have the same sinful habits and attitudes you have always had? If so, take time to fully surrender your life to Christ. Open your heart to Him so that when you draw near to Him, you are changed.*

Standing Faithful to Our Lord in Today's World

Lynda Pitts
CEO, Legacy Marketing Group

IN RECENT MONTHS, I've found myself increasingly in awe at God's faithfulness. It is a marvelous mystery that God created us for His good pleasure so we can be in relationship with Him. He sent His Son, who knew no sin, to pay the price for our transgressions so we could experience a personal relationship with the Father, Son, and Holy Spirit. It is truly too much for my mind to comprehend and is impacting me in a deeper way every day.

Maybe it's because the world seems to be spinning more and more out of control—with the shaking of everything from the land itself to our economic structure—that I'm increasingly aware of God's faithfulness exerting an increasingly dramatic impact on our lives. We're blessed to have our Scriptures to study, with many examples of God's steadfastness to his people: Moses, Abraham, Joseph, David, Ruth, and Esther to name a few. But to *personally* experience that faithfulness is something that continues to be truly life changing.

The faithfulness of our Lord is certain: "*Know therefore that the LORD your God is God; he is the faithful God, keeping his covenant of love to a thousand generations of those who love him and keep his commandments."* (Deuteronomy 7:9 NIV).

But will *we* be found faithful by *Him*? The Lord says, *"I will raise up for myself a faithful priest who will do according to what is on my heart and mind"* (1 Samuel 2:35 NIV).

As a leader, how are you doing in your resolve to fight "the tyranny of the urgent" in order to press in and stay close enough to hear what is on His heart and mind? For me, I know that to be near Him is life itself.

Our faithfulness to the Lord has an impact on those around us, both believers and non-believers. As a believer (14 years), I have been impacted by the faithfulness of His saints, having witnessed

- Nancy, who prayed for her husband for 50 years, and who saw him accept Christ the year before she died.
- Kathy, who battled cancer for seven years, faithfully praying for her estranged husband, who returned to love and attend to her before she died. After she died, he accepted Christ, as he could no longer deny the love he saw in her and her Christian brothers and sisters.
- Two pastors, from different denominations, who 20 years ago began an interdenominational weekly prayer time to pray for one another and our city. Twenty years later, the Kingdom of God of the city worships together, prays together, and serves our city together.

I encourage you to take time to reflect on the Lord's faithfulness and how it has impacted you personally, and to realize the influence of your faithfulness on others. Let us steadfastly strive to be the Lord's faithful priest and to understand what is on His heart and mind.

Reflect for a moment

1. *Make a list of the ways God has demonstrated His faithfulness in your life over the past year. What does it reveal to you?*

2. *In what ways are you presently watching for and depending on God to express His faithfulness to you?*

3. *How does the way you are living demonstrate your confidence in God's faithfulness?*

What Follows Revival?

Jeffrey H. Coors
Chairman, Fiskeby Holdings US, LLC

THE CHILDREN OF God experienced victory and revival upon completion of rebuilding the wall around Jerusalem. In only 52 days and against fierce opposition the city wall was rebuilt. Stone by stone the remnant of Israel worked tirelessly with one hand on a hammer and the other hand on their sword. The wall was high enough to provide security from enemies and sturdy enough for entire choirs to march around on top singing praises to God.

The wall was completed in early October and the inhabitants spent the remainder of the month celebrating God's goodness. For hours on end they stood listening to the reading of God's word and hearing its explanation by the priests. They wept over it, but were told to rejoice. They celebrated with feasts. It was a national revival as the people turned their hearts back to God.

One of the most eloquent prayers in Scripture is that made by the Levite leaders extolling God's faithfulness through the generations (Nehemiah 9:5-37). They confessed their sins and pledged themselves to obey the Law of God. Their vows were recorded and they signed their names to the pledge

(Nehemiah 10). They specifically promised to "*bring the first part of every harvest to the Lord's Temple year after year*" and to bring the Levites "*a tenth of everything our land produces… We promise together not to neglect the Temple of our God.*"(vs 35-39 NLT) Their passion for the Lord was intense. This was true revival.

Nehemiah could lead the revival because of his obedient heart. He remained in Jerusalem 12 years, but eventually returned to Persia to serve King Artaxerxes. Sometime later Nehemiah returned to Jerusalem to find the people had abandoned their commitments to the Lord. The support of the Levites and the temple of God had been neglected. Work was being done on the Sabbath. These were all things they had covenanted not to do in their revival just a few years before (Nehemiah 13).

It is easier to agree to righteous living at a time of victory and revival than to persist in obedience in our daily lives. In *Experiencing God Day-by-Day,* the Blackabys point out that "Good intention without corresponding activity is disobedience" (See November 2 devotional). And "God's call is not to 'make a decision' but to obey. Deciding to obey is not equal to obeying!"

As Christian leaders in business we have had to cry out to God in desperate situations. We have seen miracles and victories at work that can only be attributed to the hand of our loving Father. We give Him glory and use these times to bring revival to our employees. We redouble our commitments to follow the Lord.

Then we slip into routine. We become distracted by everyday events and before long we can drift away from the excitement and joy we felt at the time of victory. That is when we must persist in obedience. If we do, we can join Nehemiah in proclaiming, "*O Lord, God of heaven, the great and awesome God who keeps his covenant of unfailing love with those who love him and <u>obey</u> his commands...*" (Nehemiah 1:5, NLT).

REFLECT FOR A MOMENT

1. *Have you experienced personal revival in your life? If so, how long did it last?*

2. *How faithfully have you followed through with your "good intentions"?*

3. *What are some ways you can rekindle your passion for God?*

Meaningful Time in the Scriptures Is Paramount

Steve Hughes
Management Consultant

SOLOMON NOTES IN Ecclesiastes 1:9 that, "*there is nothing new under the sun.*" An old boss seemed to borrow from this when meetings dragged noting that "everything has already been said, but not everyone has had a chance to say it." The message for today is not new but bears repeating. God repeats things to me, so I am comfortable covering old ground here.

The message is that "nothing can replace the life-changing experience of reading Scripture." A likely question from a businessperson might be "what is the schedule for this life-changing experience?"

I accepted Christ as my savior at age 11. I then wandered through junior high, high school, and college without much spiritual growth or direction. I suffered a difficult personal loss my senior year of college. Fortunately, I met a group of believers who befriended me during that time. In response to their kindness I recommitted my life to Christ. Yet, He seemed distant and silent and I didn't feel like I knew Him. I went through the motions, but was dead inside. After graduation I married a wonderful, patient woman. We were blessed with four children. Everything looked fine from the outside. I continued to go through the motions. I asked the Lord to change me but to be gentle with me. Nothing happened. A respected friend told me that any young person who could spend five minutes in the Scriptures daily could make a difference in the world. I had been afflicted with juvenile diabetes at age 14 and was acquainted with discipline. It was easy for me to check the box and read the Scriptures daily for five minutes. To be honest, I found the morning newspaper to be more interesting, so I gave it more time than the Scriptures. There was no life-changing experience in Scripture for me. In retrospect, I was impatient and unwilling to invest the time and effort required to hear from God. Instead I poured myself into work and thought mostly of business and success. When problems arose, I prayed about them, looked at Scripture and then just worked harder to resolve them myself. Then things began to change.

In my late forties our family faced issues that I could not resolve in spite of my best efforts. I sought counsel from believing friends, ministers, and others. The crowd I ran with had little experience dealing with the gnarly afflictions I was facing. I asked God to lead me and direct me through the Scriptures. I began to spend more time reading the Bible to try to learn how to address the issues. One day I came across the Psalm 119:133-134 (NASB):

> *Establish my footsteps in Your word,*
>
> *And do not let any iniquity have dominion over me.*
>
> *Redeem me from the oppression of man*
>
> *That I may keep your precepts.*

I was moved by this and wrote the verses down on a 3 x 5 card, re-reading it and turning it over and over in my mind. My thought life began to improve and I felt that I was on to something. I felt I could get rid of some of the sin in my life. So I kept working on these verses. Then, I felt the Holy Spirit telling me to study all of the lengthy Psalm 119, so I did. I was looking to Scripture to find a way to resolve tough issues, but what happened was that I came into contact with the living God. God used David's words at verses 67, 75-76 to explain my life to me—*"Before I was afflicted I went astray, But now I keep your word"* and *"I know, O Lord, that Your judgments are righteous, And that in faithfulness You have afflicted me. O may Your lovingkindness comfort me, According to Your word to Your servant"* (NASB).

Did I hear a voice? No. But it is undeniable that God was communicating with me through His Holy Spirit. It was as if I had asked God to explain the pains of my life. Without uttering an audible word He did. Isaiah tells us that He has *"worked wonders, plans formed long ago with perfect faithfulness"* (Isaiah 25:1, NASB). His plan to draw me to Him was intricate and complex and rooted in family afflictions that began to develop generations ago.

Why am I telling you this? Isn't it more of a personal testimony? Perhaps. It's my attempt to illustrate one way that God communicates with me and to add more flesh to Dr. Henry Blackaby's point that "Nothing can replace the life-changing experience of reading Scripture ." God speaks through Scripture . This is a universal message. It's for you and for me. Reading Scripture in an intentional manner is hard work, takes time, and can involve waiting, struggling, and periods of dryness. And that is OK. Waiting is a part of the process. Most executives I meet seem to be too busy to make this investment. I certainly thought I was too busy until I had no other choice. If you want to hear from God, meaningful time in the Scripture s is paramount. It bears repeating again. "Nothing can replace the life-changing experience of reading Scripture ."

REFLECT FOR A MOMENT

1. *Take time to read over a Scripture passage, slowly, and carefully, and then meditate on it.*

2. *Read through Psalm 119 (The longest chapter in the Bible!). Highlight what God says about His word.*

3. *Reflect on Bible verses that have struck you recently. Consider whether you have experienced all God intended for you through those passages.*

Leading in the Workplace

DURING AN AGE when the enemies of God flourished and the leadership of God's people was exceedingly corrupt, God declared, *"Then I will raise up for Myself a faithful priest who shall do according to what is in My heart and in My mind. I will build him a sure house, and he shall walk before My anointed forever"* (1 Samuel 2:35). Whenever times have been difficult, God's method has been to raise up people to serve Him as leaders among the people. God could have dispatched the archangels Michael or Gabriel to mobilize His people, but He has generally chosen instead to work through human instruments.

Spiritual leaders move people on to God's agenda. They take people from where they are, to where God wants them to be. Leaders may impact entire nations or they may simply lead their own children. They may influence their colleagues, or a committee at church, or a Bible study group, or a civic organization. What motivates spiritual leaders is not their own plans or desires, but God's heart and mind. When they pursue God's agenda, they have access to divine resources. When they accomplish God's will, God alone receives the glory.

What is motivating your current leadership? Is it your plans or God's? Is it His priorities or yours? Who is responsible for your success, you or God? Who is presently receiving the glory for your accomplishments, you or God? Spiritual leadership is a noble calling. Many people will benefit if you do it well.

History: Destiny or Opportunity?

DOES HISTORY MAKE great leaders or do great leaders make history? Would Napoleon have attempted to conquer the world regardless of what age he lived in or was it the social tumult following the French Revolution that drove him to wage war throughout his life?

Times of national crisis sometimes give people the singular opportunity to rise to unprecedented levels of leadership. As a young man, John Adams complained, "I shall never shine, 'til some animating occasion calls forth all my powers." Before the Civil War, William Sherman experienced failure so routinely he exclaimed, "Every castle that I build is undermined and upset at the very moment I flatter myself of its completion, but the fact is I'm getting pretty well used to it." Ulysses S. Grant's biographer noted that he "was a perfect family man. Had peace prevailed he would have lived out his days as a slightly rumpled shopkeeper in the upper Mississippi valley, indistinguishable from his friends and neighbors." History provided Abraham Lincoln the opportunity to draw upon his deep well of character to lead his nation through tumultuous times. Doris Kearns Goodwin observed, "Without the march of events that led to the Civil War, Lincoln still would have been a good man, but most likely would not have been publicly recognized as a great man. It was *history* that gave him the opportunity to manifest his greatness, providing the stage that allowed him to shape and transform our national life."

Danger, recessions, or calamities do not automatically morph mediocre leaders into great ones. But they do provide opportunities for stellar leadership. Men and women can draw upon all that God has built into their lives so they live and lead at heightened levels during urgent times. James Buchanan, Lincoln's predecessor in the White House, was imminently qualified to lead the nation but he failed miserably and is considered one of America's worst executives. History offered both men an enormous opportunity. Only one rose to the occasion.

The writer of Ecclesiastes advised, "*I have seen the God-given task with which the sons of men are to be occupied. He has made everything beautiful in its time. Also He has put eternity in their hearts*" (Ecclesiastes 3:10-11). God has placed eternity in our hearts! We innately desire to live our lives in a way that impacts the future but only God can enable us to do so. When God provides us with opportunities to impact our society, God's kingdom, and eternity, we ought to seize them. Ecclesiastes also observed, "*To everything there is a season, a time for every purpose under heaven*" (Ecclesiastes 3:1). Our nation is in a crucial season of its history. Some view these days with anxiety and despair. Others recognize unique opportunities to make significant contributions pivotal to God's kingdom and to their country. This could be a watershed era. Are you prepared to seize the divine invitations that come your way? Or, will you be cowed by the disheartening news the media routinely spews upon you? After helping craft the Declaration of Independence, John

Adams said, "When I consider the great events which are passed, and those greater which are rapidly advancing, and that I may have been instrumental of touching some springs and turning some wheels, which have had and will have such effects, I feel an awe upon my mind which is not easily described." *Carpe diem*!

REFLECT FOR A MOMENT

1. *Are you going through a difficult or a prosperous time presently? How might God use your life uniquely for His purposes during these days?*

2. *As you watch the news and see world events as well as advances in technology and science unfolding, are you intimidated by the day in which you live, or are you excited at the possibilities?*

3. *To every season there is a divine purpose. What do you sense God's purpose is for the season of life you are presently experiencing?*

Encouragers or Discouragers?

ON AUGUST 2, 216 B.C., a young lieutenant named Gisgo gaped in terror at the ominous sight of 87,000 Roman soldiers massed in the fields before him, ready to brutally destroy him and his 57,000 Carthaginian comrades. The Roman consul C. Terentius Varro, in command of the Roman legions, was determined to annihilate his troublesome enemies once and for all. Gisgo, dreading the looming tumult and convinced that death was close at hand, bemoaned the hopeless odds to his general, Hannibal. Hannibal replied, "Yes, Gisgo, you are right. But there is one thing you may not have noticed." "What is that?" queried the frightened soldier. "Simply this: that in all that great number of men opposite there isn't a single one called Gisgo" (Ben Kane, *Hannibal: Enemy of Rome*, 142). With that, the youth conceded a grin and Hannibal and the officers with him burst into laughter. When the soldiers in the ranks witnessed their general laughing with his officers, they took heart, grasped their weapons, and prepared for one of the most famous military encounters in history: Cannae. At day's end, the field was littered with over 70,000 Roman corpses compared to a mere 6,000 Carthaginian casualties. Hannibal's forces decimated one of the largest Roman armies in history and would march unimpeded toward Rome.

During a fierce battle against a French army, the Duke

of Marlborough sighted one of his cavalry officers hurriedly retreating from the fray with his men following close behind him. Commanding them to halt, Marlborough declared, "Mr. _____, you are under a mistake; the enemy lies that way: You have nothing to do but to face him and the day is your own." (Churchill, *Marlborough: His Life and Times,* 862). Winston Churchill, no stranger to courage, noted of his esteemed ancestor, "His appearance, his serenity, his piercing eye, his gestures, the tone of his voice—nay the beat of his heart—diffused a harmony upon all around him. Every word he spoke was decisive. Victory often depended upon whether he rode half a mile this way or that" (*Marlborough,* 571).

Leaders must inspire their followers, especially in times of crisis. Seasons of peace and prosperity do not call for the unique skills of leaders. But when the storm clouds gather and enemies advance, people instinctively look to their leaders in order to gain confidence and acquire direction. The need for good leadership is not exclusive to the battlefield. The marketplace also requires calm, confident, and compassionate leadership. Unfortunately, in turbulent economic times, some business leaders cloister themselves in their corner office. Others cast blame on their subordinates, or verbally abuse their staff and begin lopping off heads in a frantic effort to cut losses.

Even as Jesus' enemies were gathering in the darkness to arrest and crucify Him, Jesus assured His disciples, "*Peace I leave with you, My peace I give to you; not as the world gives do I give to you. Let not your heart be troubled, neither let it be afraid*" (John 14:27). Leaders who know Christ need not be anxious or fearful. God is in control. His purposes *will* be accomplished. If God is for you, it matters not what or who is against you (Romans 8:31). As your colleagues and staff watch you lead in times of adversity, are they witnessing your serene confidence in God?

REFLECT FOR A MOMENT

1. *Do you tend to use your words to encourage others or to rebuke and criticize people?*

2. *How good are you at encouraging others? On a scale of 1 to 10, how would you rate yourself? List three things you might start doing that would make you better at inspiring people.*

3. *Do you tend to see what is negative or do you immediately recognize the possibilities? Do you focus on opportunities or problems? Do people gain hope when they are around you, or do they become more discouraged? Pray and ask the Lord to make you the kind of person who leaves people better by having spent time with them.*

Truth AND Grace!

A CHRISTIAN CEO recently voiced his frustration after a difficult phone call with his plant manager, "It is *so* hard to show grace when an employee *really* needs a boot in the pants!" he exclaimed. A great perplexity for many Christian businesspeople is to know where grace belongs in the marketplace. Grace is an undeserved gift. It builds up, gives life, strengthens, and makes people more like Jesus, all of this while expecting nothing in return. If you lead an organization strictly by grace you might have great morale but you could also go bankrupt! Business is about smart investments and getting the best value for the dollar. Yet businesspeople are exhorted to, "*Let no corrupt word proceed out of your mouth but what is good for necessary edification, that it may impart GRACE to the hearers*" (Ephesians 4:29). How is that possible in a tough, competitive world? How can you be successful in a job that requires you to reprimand or fire people and yet still demonstrate grace? The Bible says, "*And the Word became flesh and dwelt among us, and we beheld His glory, the glory as of the only begotten of the Father, FULL OF GRACE AND TRUTH*" (John 1:14). With Jesus, grace and truth always belonged together.

Truth expresses the reality of a situation, telling it like it is…shooting straight…calling a spade a spade. At times people need someone with the courage to tell them how things really are. Leaders must dispense reality to their followers. If no one else is courageous enough to face the facts, the leader must be.

Generally people lean to one side or the other on the grace-truth continuum. We are either reluctant to hurt someone's feelings, so we withhold the truth, or we become angry and use our words as lethal weapons. Paul and Barnabas struggled with this issue. John Mark abandoned them on their first missionary journey (Acts 13:13). When it came time for Missionary Journey #2, the kindhearted Barnabas wanted to show grace and give John a second chance (Acts 15:37). Paul, however, spoke the truth: John had deserted his colleagues at a critical time, proving he was unreliable (Acts 15:38-40). They needed someone with more backbone and perseverance. Someone like Silas. Who was right? Both viewpoints had merit. Silas would indeed become a reliable colleague. However, in later years, Mark would greatly encourage the apostle as well (2 Tim. 4:11). Mark needed both grace and truth.

Sometimes the people around you require grace. They need another chance. They hope for forgiveness, without a browbeating. However, never compromise truth in order to dispense grace. Reality must still be faced. At other times, you have to deliver hard truth and act on the facts. However, as you speak the most painful truth you can still show grace. It *is* possible to fire someone gracefully! If you are speaking "truth" in anger, you probably aren't showing grace. If you have a tough word for someone, wait until you can say it without anger. Don't focus strictly on the negative, but share the positive as well. Offer hope for the future, even if your word for that day must be harsh.

Strive to give people full measures of grace and truth. People desperately need to hear the truth, and withholding it won't help them grow or mature. Likewise, everyone, including your family, needs to be uplifted by grace. Grace and truth presented together transform people. As you impart both, you can experience the indescribable joy of acting like Jesus.

REFLECT FOR A MOMENT

1. *Do you tend to focus on speaking "truth" to people? Do you feel the need to confront shortcomings and to "tell it like it is"? If so, consider if you need to balance your truth giving with more grace.*

2. *Do you tend to extend people grace, regardless of how many times they fail or disappoint you? If so, consider whether there are times you need to confront inappropriate behavior and to hold people accountable for their actions.*

3. *Have you hurt people by either being too harsh, or too lenient in how you related to them? It is difficult to always strike a balance. If you went too far one way or the other, go to that person and apologize. Seek to be reconciled. Ask God to show you how much truth and grace you should express to that person in your next encounter.*

Resiliency

WALT DISNEY IS famous for his creative genius and vision. But simply having a vision of what *could* be is not enough. There is a multitude of creative souls whose heads are brimming with fantastic ideas that will never see the light of day. Such dreaming profits people not at all.

As with most fabulously successful businesspeople, Walt Disney experienced numerous and significant failures. When he was 21, Walt's company, Laugh-O-Gram, based in Kansas City, was forced to declare bankruptcy. It was a difficult time for Disney, since he had encouraged friends and relatives to invest in his fledgling company. Then in 1928, after moving to California, Disney established Walt Disney Studios and once again began producing cartoons. However, in one of the most devastating events in his life, he was betrayed by his own employees and associates and saw his new company cannibalized. It was one of the lowest points in Disney's life. At that point he was in danger of becoming another of the thousands of aspiring writers, directors, and actors whose hopes of success in film had come crashing down on the jagged rocks of reality. But it was said that "Walt Disney seemed to never lose faith…'He was always optimistic… about his ability and about the value of his ideas and about the possibilities of cartoons in the entertainment field. Never once did I hear him express anything except determination to go ahead'" (Neal Gabler, *Walt Disney,* 72). Significantly, once Disney had recovered from his devastating setback, his next creation was Mortimer Mouse. When his wife Lillian declared she thought the name "Mortimer" was a terrible name, Disney suggested "Mickey," and the rest, as they say, is history. Successful people are not necessarily those who have avoided failure or hardship, but rather they are individuals who refused to become discouraged or to lose focus on where they were going. It has been said of Disney, "When he was enthused, as he usually was, he got others enthused too." It was Winston Churchill who claimed that "success" was going from failure to failure without loss of enthusiasm.

David had been given a vision from God that he would one day become the king of Israel. But, rather than his circumstances improving, they grew worse. King Saul became paranoid and sought to kill him. He was forced to flee from his homeland. The king gave David's wife to another man. When David fled to the city of Gath, its citizens attempted to arrest him. Forced to extremes, David had to act as if he were mad to escape with his life (1 Samuel 21:10-15). At this nadir of his life, David might easily have abandoned any thoughts that God would grant him success or that he would ever achieve his dreams. Yet this is what David wrote, "*In God I have placed my trust; I will not be afraid. What can man do to me? Vows made to You are binding upon me, O God; I will render praises to you, for You have delivered my soul from death. Have You not kept my feet from falling, that I may walk before God in the light of the living?* (Psalm 56:11-13).

Throughout every difficult challenge David faced (and there would still be many more to come), David kept his eyes on the Lord. He knew that if God had spoken, absolutely no one could ultimately thwart him from receiving what God had promised. Significantly, immediately after the Scripture relates David's low point in Gath, it describes how mighty men from all across the land began to be attracted to join him (1 Samuel 22:1-5). If David was to lead mighty men, he had to retain his confidence in the Lord! He could not lose hope. He had to stay focused on his mission, regardless of the setbacks and obstacles. Ultimately he became his nation's mightiest king, just as God had promised.

What challenges are you currently facing? Have they caused you to lose hope, or confidence? Are you being tempted to give up? Now is when your true mettle will be determined. Hold fast to what you know to be true and stay close to God. He'll do the rest.

REFLECT FOR A MOMENT

1. *Do you tend to persevere in adversity? Or, when times get tough, do you grow discouraged and give up? If so, God may keep giving you practice until you learn to keep your confidence in Him! People who quit when circumstances become difficult prove they have little confidence in God and His ability to sustain them.*

2. *It is sometimes during our most grievous trials that we are closer to God's best than we ever were before. It would be tragic to quit or lose heart only weeks or days before God's provision had arrived. If you are beginning to falter, take time to back up and get a proper perspective. Look for what is positive. Enlist godly counselors. Build a support team around you that will encourage you to hold the course until you have finished the race Christ set before you.*

Besetting Sins

WILLIAM RANDOLPH HEARST was always a controversial figure. He would eventually become one of the most powerful and influential businesspeople in America as he utilized his popular newspapers from across the country to promote his beliefs and to support his causes. As a young man, Hearst suffered the woeful neglect of his father who was a U.S. Senator. He repeatedly wrote to his father while he was a student at Harvard, seeking to gain his affirmation and interest, but to no avail. At one point he wrote, "I wrote you not long ago and inserted in my letter a mild request for an answer, but the answer never came... Will you kindly take some notice of your only son?" Notes Hearst's biographer, "All his life he had tried to prove to his father that he was worthy of his respect. If he had failed at Harvard, he had succeeded magnificently at the *Examiner,* turning a moribund, bankrupt daily into a profitable enterprise. But it had been in vain" (David Nasaw, *The Chief,* 46, 89). His father trusted him so little that, in his will, he left most of Hearst's inheritance in his mother's care.

One would think that anyone who had suffered such painful neglect as a child would naturally have been zealous to nurture and affirm his own children when he became a parent himself. But such was not the case. Paradoxically, what later frustrated Hearst most about his own sons were the very shortcomings he suffered from himself. Not one of his sons completed college, just as their father had not. Hearst would become infuriated with his offspring for their extravagant spending habits, even though he, himself, had set the example. And, even though Hearst suffered miserably from his own father's neglect, he ignored his own children just as thoroughly. Despite all he had seen that was wrong in his own father, Hearst had unknowingly become just like him. Although Hearst desperately craved parental affirmation and praise for his efforts, it seldom came. Yet Hearst was filled with criticism and ridicule for his own sons who clearly could never meet his high standards.

Isn't it amazing how we can so clearly see the sins of others but be blinded to even greater transgressions in our own life? Jeremiah 17:9 notes, *"The heart is desperately deceitful above all things, and desperately wicked; who can know it?"* One of the greatest challenges for leaders is to beware of self-deception. That is, we fool ourselves into assuming our unethical or immoral or even illegal behavior is somehow justified. Or we berate our staff and colleagues with righteous indignation, even though we would be deeply offended if someone spoke to us in the same manner. Or we condemn our associates who appear petty or proud yet excuse that same behavior in ourselves.

David could have justifiably condemned King Saul for seeking to kill one of his most reliable and trusted soldiers (1 Samuel 20:1). Yet later, when David was king, he would plot to have one of his own loyal officers murdered so he could marry his wife (2 Samuel 11; 23:39). Samuel might have criticized the lax way in which Eli raised his two wicked sons (1 Samuel 2:12-17; 22-25).

Yet Samuel's own two sons would greatly dishonor God and eventually drive the Israelites to clamor for a king to lead them (1 Samuel 8:1-5).

While it is great to study leadership principles and attend management seminars, they will do you no good if you don't evaluate your own leadership behavior accurately. It is not enough to believe that leaders ought to act with integrity. You must also thoroughly evaluate the credibility and honesty of your own actions. It is great to condemn arrogance and pride, but be careful you have not been guilty of egotism yourself. Don't assume that simply because you *believe* something, that it is thoroughly ingrained into your life. Taking what you believe and working it into your behavior can take time and focused effort. But it is worth it. Do you see the mistakes that others around you are currently making? Take a long, hard look in the mirror. You might be horrified at what you discover.

Reflect for a moment

1. *Do you have a sin that keeps finding its way into your life? If so, what is it? Why do you think you are having such difficulty with this particular transgression? Did you inherit it from your parents? Is it something unique to your character?*

2. *Do you have a "blind spot"? Are there issues in your life you often fail to detect that harm you or others? What is it? What does God want you to do about it?*

Words That Move Others

WORDS ARE POWERFUL instruments in the hands of those who know how to wield them. Edward Everett was one of the most renowned orators of his day. He once delivered a major speech that lasted over two hours. The crowd, having listened to the epic-long oration, seemed unprepared for a second discourse of similar length. Abraham Lincoln, sensing this, quickly condensed his thoughts and spoke for less than two minutes. When he was done, no one would remember Everett's speech, but history would afterward identify Lincoln's Gettysburg Address as one of the finest speeches in American history. Everett confessed to Lincoln, "I should be glad…if I flatter myself that I came as near the central idea of the occasion, in two hours, as you did in two minutes."

At times, leaders are called upon to use their words in speeches that touch large numbers. Martin Luther King Jr.'s "I Kave a Dream" speech shook his nation. Winston Churchill assumed leadership of England in its darkest hours of World War II. People were feeling demoralized and defeated. It has been said of Churchill that he "mobilized the English language and sent it into battle."

At times we must use our words to encourage our leadership team or particular individuals. The writer of Proverbs observed, "*A word fitly spoken is like apples of gold in settings of silver"* (Proverbs 25:11). It is amazing what our words can accomplish when we submit them as instruments into God's hand. Our colleague may have lost hope, but a word from us shines new light on her predicament. A friend may feel alone and forgotten, when a timely word encourages his soul.

The apostle Paul exhorted believers to avoid allowing any unwholesome word to proceed from their mouths, but instead, to speak words that edified people and gave them grace (Ephesians 4:29). What a privilege is ours to dispense grace to those around us!

But we always face a danger. Scripture also notes, *"But no man can tame the tongue. It is an unruly evil, full of deadly poison"* (James 3:8). For such a small body part, it can cause enormous damage! Business history is filled with stories of people who succumbed to using their words as a weapon. Bill Gates was notorious for firing off electronic messages telling subordinates how terrible their work was. Steve Jobs was known for the occasional angry outburst. Getting "Steved" became a part of tech jargon meaning something that was unceremoniously terminated, whether it was people's jobs, or their projects. Jack Welch would yell so loudly at people in his office when he was upset that his voice could be heard throughout his executive office complex. These leaders were highly successful, but could succumb to the temptation to abuse people with their words.

Some people are naturally gifted at using words. They come easily. But for others, words are a challenge. If you are a leader, you must cultivate your use of language until it becomes an effective tool in your leadership arsenal. Winston Churchill used to practice giving speeches for hours, ensuring they exerted their greatest impact when he delivered them.

Churchill's friend, F. E. Smith once noted, "Winston has spent the best years of his life writing impromptu speeches." Your words can be a powerful instrument. Are you using them well?

REFLECT FOR A MOMENT

1. *Are you comfortable with using words? Are you at ease when speaking in public? Are you effective at encouraging others? If you are, you can probably become still better, with practice and attention to detail. If you struggle in this area, don't give up. Get help. Find a coach. Read books. Take a class. The use of words is too important for you to not be at your best when using them.*

2. *Do you regularly work on developing your arsenal of words? Reading books and learning new words are crucial. The larger your vocabulary, the greater the supply of words at your disposal. Speaking may not come easily to you, but you can improve if you make the effort.*

3. *The greatest hindrance to public speaking is shyness. Yet shyness is primarily self-centeredness. It is being so consumed with worry about what others think of us, that we fail to share words that could encourage people. Ask God to help you take your eyes off of yourself and your feelings of inadequacy, and put your focus on God's assignment for you and the people you will encourage through the words you share with them.*

Using or Blessing?

IN 336 B. C. KING Phillip of Macedon was murdered by his bodyguard. His 20-year-old son, Alexander, was proclaimed king in his place. Alexander was an extremely ambitious young man. Historians speculate that he may have had his father murdered, since his father Phillip had remarried and any future child would usurp Alexander as the rightful heir. Alexander began a series of campaigns to conquer the known world. He defeated the Persian Empire, which had been the largest kingdom of that day. He also conquered Israel, Egypt, and Syria along with Asia Minor. He then set out with the enormously aggressive aim to subdue India.

Alexander was a brilliant military commander who never lost a battle. He employed military tactics that are considered classics in modern studies of warfare. Yet after some harrowing battles in which Alexander was wounded, his troops finally rebelled and refused to advance any further. Fearing the prospect of facing other large armies and exhausted by years of campaigning, Alexander's army mutinied at the Hyphasis River, refusing to march further east. This river thus marks the easternmost extent of Alexander's conquests. The Greek historian, Plutarch notes,

> As for the Macedonians, however, their struggle with Porus blunted their courage and

stayed their further advance into India. For having had all they could do to repulse an enemy who mustered only twenty thousand infantry and two thousand horse, they violently opposed Alexander when he insisted on crossing the river Ganges also, the width of which, as they learned, was thirty-two furlongs, its depth a hundred fathoms, while its banks on the further side were covered with multitudes of men-at-arms and horsemen and elephants. For they were told that the kings of the Ganderites and Praesii were awaiting them with eighty thousand horsemen, two hundred thousand footmen, eight thousand chariots, and six thousand war elephants.

On Alexander's return, he came to Babylon where he contracted an illness from which he died at the age of 32. Some historians speculate he was poisoned by one of his generals. As Alexander lay dying, his soldiers filed slowly past him to see him one last time. Alexander could only wave to them in silence.

As Joshua, another mighty war hero, approached the end of his illustrious leadership, he reminded his people, "*Behold, this day I am going the way of all the earth. And you know in all your hearts and in all your souls that not one thing has failed of all the good things which the Lord your God spoke concerning you. All have come to pass for you; not one word of them has failed*" (Joshua 23:14).

Alexander led his people to the extreme of human endurance in order to gain his own personal glory and fame. He used his people rather than blessing them. Joshua also won great military conquests. But he did so for God's honor. When Joshua's task was done, he readily laid down his position and blessed his people. Joshua led people to experience God's best. Alexander led people to increase his fame. Joshua blessed people. Alexander used them.

How do you view the people you work with? Are they a means to an end? Are you using them to achieve your goals? Do people around you exist to make you look better? Or, are you striving to ensure that the people around you experience every good thing that God has promised?

REFLECT FOR A MOMENT

1. *Are you an ambitious person? If you are, what are you ambitious to achieve? Does your ambition ever tempt you to manipulate people so you can achieve your goals?*

2. *Do the people you work with truly know you care about them? (Do you care for them?) What is the evidence that you are concerned about the people you work with?*

3. *Have you ever sought to ask God what His "best" is for those you work with? How focused are you in helping others receive all God has for them?*

Team

Brent Garrison, Ph.D.
Director of CEO Relations, CEO Forum

*From that day on, half of my men did the work,
while the other half were equipped with spears,
shields, bows, and armor*

NEHEMIAH 4:16 (NLT)

WE ARE FAMILIAR with the storyline of the book of
Nehemiah and its powerful leadership lessons. Nehemiah
demonstrates great wisdom in assigning team-specific
duties to the men so the construction on Jerusalem's walls
could continue, while protecting them against the threats of
Sanballat.

It's easy to see the value of teamwork when watching
athletics, for if a teammate misses a block it is on video for
everyone to see and critique. However, talent isn't enough to
win a championship, for we know teams that win with less
raw ability than losing teams possess. So what allows teams
with less individual skill to win? It occurs when people work
well together, as a team. In fact, a player with superior talent
may prevent people from gelling together into a team. The
same thing can happen in the marketplace.

Why is it sometimes difficult for a group of talented people to work together effectively as a team? It makes perfect sense when we look at the problem through the lens of Scripture. The Bible declares we are all sinners. When we put a group of "sinners" into leadership positions (add the dynamics of quotas and money), there will be conflict. People can (and will) be selfish, jealous, petty, and stubborn, for that is their nature (Ephesians 2:1-22). It is therefore understandable that there will be challenges when people work together. Even redeemed people manifest inappropriate characteristics as they struggle with the flesh and the spirit.

While working with people can be challenging, doing so is definitely worth the effort. That is because, being made in the image of God, people have intrinsic value. As followers of Christ, we should look at each colleague and employee as having profound worth, and pray that each person would come to Christ through faith. People in the marketplace need leaders who will authentically care for them and demonstrate Christlike leadership rather than treating them as if they are merely a means to an end.

You might be thinking, "He doesn't know my team!" OK, so the team you have is challenging. Remember, they are sinners and will therefore manifest selfish behavior, but they are invaluable in God's eyes. He sent His Son to die for them and they need you to care for them and believe in them in the same manner. You might be the first person who has demonstrated concern for them, and that just might change their life. You may have to make the tough decision to release the contrarian for the sake of the team, but do so with a heart that cares.

Creating an effective team is one of your most important

tasks for a business leader. It will often be difficult to develop a team that gels, but realizing that teamwork is challenging because of our nature might give you that understanding spirit to pray for and care for that difficult team member.

Lead well this week (Romans 12:8).

REFLECT FOR A MOMENT

1. *Are you presently leading a team? If you are, rate its current effectiveness on a scale of 1-10.*

2. *If you are presently working on a team, are there people with whom you are struggling to work with? If so, why is that? What might you do to help your colleagues?*

3. *How do you see "sin" affecting your team dynamics? What might God do to address that problem?*

Are you Leading Like Jesus?

Marjorie Dorr
Retired Chief Strategy Officer, Wellpoint;
Retired CEO, Anthem BCBS Northeast

ARE YOU SEEKING to serve or be served? Matthew 20:25-28 says, *"Jesus called them together and said, 'You know that the rulers of the Gentiles lord it over them, and their high officials exercise authority over them. **Not so with you**. Instead, whoever wants to become great among you must be your servant, and whoever want to be first must be your slave—just as the Son of Man did not come to be served, but to serve, and to give His life as a ransom for many.'"* (NIV)

These verses highlight Jesus' admonition to not lead as others do but to focus our attention on a more excellent way. There are many leadership programs and techniques in the market today for business leaders to follow. However, for those who claim to follow Christ, Jesus gave us a mandate to be servant leaders. Leading like Jesus is an expression of obedience to the Lord whom we love.

Learning to lead like Jesus is, at its essence, learning to love like Jesus. Millions of dollars are spent to train people in leadership skills—changing people from the outside—which has proven to be largely ineffective. However, Jesus, asks us to lead from the inside—to change our heart from self-serving leaders to servant leaders. We must alter our heart to first love God and worship Him—not money, not power, not appreciation, not success. For this to happen, our hearts must be attached to the vine (John 15:5). One way for us to maintain that connection is to spend time in solitude, meditating on God (Psalm 1:2). So how did Jesus model this?

He consistently withdrew from the demands of His schedule to pray. Mark 1:35 says, *"Very early in the morning, while it was still dark, Jesus got up, left the house and went off to a solitary place, where he prayed."* Luke 11:1 reminds us that *"One day Jesus was praying in a certain place."* And Mark 6:31 shows the importance of solitude as Jesus calls the disciples to, *"Come with me by yourselves to a quiet place and get some rest"*(NIV) Jesus understood the demands of being a leader—the constant pressures of people 24/7—the conflicts, the exhaustion. Jesus knew that leaders need to replenish their spiritual energy or else they will be crushed under the pressure. If Jesus took the time in solitude for rest and replenishment with the heavenly Father—why don't we? Sin leaves no room for God in our heart. When we edge God out through busyness and neglect we often become prideful and think we can lead on our own (EGO). Or we lead by fear refusing to trust God and walk by faith.

Jesus did not neglect intimacy with His father. Where or what most fosters an atmosphere or attitude of solitude for you? Are you willing to invest more time in solitude in order to lead like Jesus?

REFLECT FOR A MOMENT

1. *Would you say that you are currently "leading like Jesus"? Why or why not?*

2. *What is one thing you could change about your leadership that would enable you to lead more like Jesus would? What is preventing you from making that change?*

Relationships that Honor God

FEW THINGS IN our world have been tarnished by sin as much as have relationships. As soon as evil entered into humanity, alienation, deception, and murder began occurring. Sin causes us to be selfish. It makes us look at people in terms of what they can do for us, rather than what we can do for them. It causes us to justify our harmful behavior toward others and to nurse every grievance others commit against us. Sin leads us to treat people in the exact opposite manner in a manner than God intends.

The apostle Paul described the way we should treat others, *"And be kind to one another, tenderhearted, forgiving one another, even as God in Christ, forgave you"* (Ephesians 4:32). We are to be kind and thoughtful toward those around us. We ought to be quick to forgive faults committed against us. We should relate to others in ways that make people better because they are associated with us.

It is easier to be kind to some people than to others. But God expects us to act in a Christlike way to each person you relate to. What does loving your spouse as Christ would look like? How would Christ love your child or colleague or boss? Christ set a high standard for loving others. He laid down His life for them. He expects nothing less from us (Ephesians 5:25).

Heroes to Your Children

CLARK KENT WAS famously mild mannered and inauspicious at work, but he would transform into a superhero when off duty. Unfortunately, the opposite is true for many business leaders today. At work they accomplish seemingly superhuman feats, overcome every challenge, build winning teams, solve every problem. But when they return home at day's end, they morph into Clark Kent—tired, distracted, and disinterested in building a team or addressing problems.

Cornelius Vanderbilt leveraged his railroad and shipping interests to become one of the world's wealthiest people. Yet he was extremely embarrassed by his son Corneel. Vanderbilt viewed his offspring as lazy and irresponsible. He grew so estranged from him that Vanderbilt refused to see Corneel even when he was on his deathbed. After he was largely ignored in his father's will, Corneel spent his final night gambling away his remaining assets and then shot himself to death in a New York City hotel room he could not afford to pay for. Vanderbilt had been slightly less scathing of his other son, William, whom he denigrated as a "blatherskite."

Winston Churchill, one of the twentieth century's greatest leaders, experienced regular frustration with his son Randolph. After his son had a benign tumor surgically removed, Churchill mused, "What a pity to remove the one part of Randolph that is not malignant."

Henry Ford loved his son Edsel, yet in a horribly misguided effort to toughen him up, Ford constantly humiliated his son, trying to arouse his anger. Ford pitted his henchman Harry Bennett against Edsel and routinely took Bennett's side. Eventually Edsel's fragile health collapsed under the constant pressure. Charles Sorenson, one of Ford's chief lieutenants, observed that Ford's mistreatment of his only son was the greatest mistake of his life.

Andrew Mellon was a fabulously successful businessman but he constantly struggled to relate to his son Paul. Near the end of Mellon's life, after having given millions' of dollars worth of paintings to the National Gallery of Art, he wanted to dispose of two paintings which he felt were of inferior quality. When his son asked for them, Mellon offered to sell them to him for $50,000. According to Paul, his father did not "seem to care about how I really feel about anything."

John Rockefeller was a brilliant businessman but he struggled to relate to his daughter Edith once she became an adult. For the final 20 years of her life, Edith could not bring herself to visit her father.

J.P. Morgan liked his son Jack but worried he "lacked fire and grit." Living with such a domineering father, Jack suffered numerous insecurities. His biographer observed, "Another son might have rebelled. Jack sulked and pined, waiting for approval."

Are businesspeople truly successful if they develop fabulously profitable companies but fail to lead their children to love and obey God? God promises, *'As for Me,' says the Lord, 'this is My covenant with them, My Spirit who is upon you, and*

My words which I have put into your mouth, shall not depart from your mouth, nor from the mouth of your descendants, nor from the mouth of your descendants' descendants', says the Lord" (Isaiah 59:21). Are your children impressed by your business success or by your walk with God? What is it about you they are most likely to emulate?

REFLECT FOR A MOMENT

1. *Where do you receive your most accolades and sense of accomplishment? At work or at home? Where are you shown most respect, at work or at home?*

2. *Many people confess that they give their best efforts at work where they are striving for bonuses and promotions, and then give leftovers to their family when they arrive home at the end of the day. Have you done this? If so, why?*

3. *Working people often become so focused on their responsibilities and pressures at work that they fail to view their families the way God does. Take a moment to pray for each person in your family. Ask the Lord to show you how you can specifically bless them this month.*

Mighty Men

JOHN ROCKEFELLER'S BUSINESS acumen is legendary. He raised Standard Oil to such heights that he ultimately surpassed the business luminaries of his day such as Astor, Vanderbilt, Carnegie, and Morgan. What is less widely known, however, is that though Rockefeller's name was synonymous with his company, he never owned more than 30% of it. He always encouraged his colleagues to purchase stock in the company, giving his lieutenants a vested interest in its success and making it necessary for him to cooperate with others when leading the business. In the process, men such as Henry Flagler, John Archbold, and Henry Rogers became enormously wealthy along with their boss. Rockefeller always claimed the primary reason for his success was the confidence he placed in people and the loyalty toward him and the company it generated in return.

Outstanding business leaders surround themselves with extraordinary people. J.P. Morgan was known for enlisting the best business talent of his day, including Harry Davison, Tom Lamont, Dwight Morrow, and Russell Leffingwell. In 1901 George Perkins, an up-and-coming executive for the New York Life Insurance Company, came calling on Morgan to request a donation of $125,000 for a charitable cause. Favorably impressed by Perkins, Morgan gave $25,000, but declared he would donate the entire amount requested in exchange for a favor. Perkins asked what that might be, to which Morgan replied, "Take that desk over there." Morgan always demonstrated a keen eye for talent as he built his famous bank. Henry Ford had executives such as James Couzens and Charles Sorensen to help him build his auto empire. Under Jack Welch, General Electric teemed with executive talent who were regularly being recruited to serve as CEOs of other companies. GE used to publish a book annually that listed its top managers, with pictures and bios. It stopped doing so when it discovered that executive headhunters were using it as a directory for new clients.

King David took the defeated, war-torn, divided nation of Israel and fashioned it into a Middle Eastern empire. One of the keys to his phenomenal success was the "Mighty Men" he gathered around himself (2 Samuel 23:8-39; 1 Chronicles 11:10-47), including Adino the Eznite who had killed 800 men. Jashobeam and Abishai each killed 300 men at one time. Benaiah was renowned for his strength and bravery. Scripture indicates these valiant warriors, *"strengthened themselves with him in his kingdom"* (1 Chronicles 11:10). As they loyally served and fought for David, they also *"strengthened themselves."* David became a powerful king with these warriors at his side, and they gained renown while in his service.

The question is: how do you attract outstanding men and women to work with you? Mighty men are not attracted to mediocre leaders. In today's business world, talented employees are crucial for business success. But where will the most gifted employees choose to direct their allegiance? Money alone doesn't motivate such people. They will work for those they respect and who maximize their full potential. Are your people becoming great under your leadership? Do you bring out the best in those around you? Have you developed your own cadre of outstanding associates? Are other companies constantly trying to hire them away from you? What does the caliber of the people around you reveal about the quality of your leadership?

REFLECT FOR A MOMENT

1. *Evaluate the caliber of the people who are working with you. What does the quality of the people on your team suggest about your leadership?*

2. *Do you feel threatened by colleagues who are more skilled or knowledgeable than you are? Or are you comfortable finding the most outstanding talent to work with you? What is it you look for in selecting team members?*

3. *Why would anyone want to work with you? What advantage is it to people to work with you as opposed to working with others? Do people enjoy working with you?*

Laughter

SOME PEOPLE ARE a lot of fun to be around! Laughter follows them wherever they go. Such leaders make it fun to come to work. Richard Nixon was not one of those leaders. He always felt uncomfortable around people. He used to schedule White House staff parties on dates he knew he would be out of town. Nixon's cynical view of others influenced the attitudes of his associates as well. Ronald Reagan, on the other hand, had a knack for making people laugh. After his death, a White House aide recalled that he always knew when the president had returned from a trip by the sound of the laughter pealing down the hallway. When Reagan was shot by would-be assassin John Hinckley Jr., a bullet lodged dangerously near the president's heart. When Reagan first talked with his wife Nancy, he joked, "Honey, I forgot to duck!" Such humor endeared the president to his friends and even to some of his foes.

Daniel Goleman in his work on emotional intelligence demonstrates that people pick up their emotions from the people who are around them. Those with the strongest personalities or greatest authority tend to exert the most influence on the emotions of other people. When leaders wring their hands with worry, the staff is understandably nervous as well! When leaders remain calm or are filled with joy, their emotions become contagious. It is up to leaders to interact with those they lead closely and often so their positive outlook rubs off.

One evening, after a hard day's work, Jesus and His disciples departed from the crowds and sailed across the Sea of Galilee in some small boats. Jesus was so weary that he lay his head on a pillow and fell fast asleep. Suddenly a violent windstorm swept across the sea and it appeared that the boats were in imminent danger of sinking. Jesus continued to sleep. The disciples, in a panic, woke Jesus and asked if He cared that they were all about to perish. In response, Jesus said, "Peace, be still," and calm prevailed. Jesus had such a profound sense of heavenly peace in His life that it prevailed upon those around Him.

Just as gloom and despair can quickly contaminate the ranks, so confidence and optimism are also contagious. After difficult fighting at the Battle of Shiloh, during the Civil War, an officer asked General Grant if he wanted to prepare the men to withdraw at daylight. Grant replied, "Not at all sir...we're whipping them now!" Grant's forces ultimately gained the victory. After years of having Union forces led by negative or worrisome generals, the northern forces finally had a leader who, though perhaps not a brilliant commander, was a confident and optimistic one. The change in attitude altered the war.

Max De Pree, Chairman of Herman Miller, suggests, "Joy is an essential ingredient of leadership. Leaders are obligated to provide it." There may be times when we are struggling with our attitude. We may not feel very joyful ourselves! Yet we have a stewardship of influence. Our attitudes will affect those around us. People will either have a miserable time working around us, or they will be encouraged. It depends on how we act. If everyone you worked with took on your attitude, what would your workplace be like? Before you walk into work tomorrow, take a moment to examine your attitude. Ask God to make any necessary corrections in you before you impact others any further.

REFLECT FOR A MOMENT

1. *Are you a fun person to be around? What is the evidence? Do people like to work with you? What is the evidence?*

2. *Do you laugh often? When was the last time you laughed with gusto? Are you known for your joy? What is your prevailing mood at work? Do you think that is what God wants it to be?*

3. *Do you struggle with your attitude at work? Do people or situations irritate you easily? If they do, take some time with the Lord and ask Him to fill you with His joy. You cannot have the joy of the Lord filling your life and not be someone who is fun to work with!*

Forgiveness

THE GILDED AGE occurred in America between the end of
the Civil War and the beginning of World War I. It featured
spectacular fortunes being made by what became known
derogatorily as the "Robber Barons." Men such as Vanderbilt,
Rockefeller, Morgan, and Gould reached unprecedented
heights. Two men, Andrew Carnegie and Henry C. Frick, met
in 1881 during Frick's honeymoon. Frick owned H. C. Frick
& Company, which transformed coal into coke, which was
necessary for steel production. Carnegie, with one of America's
largest steel producing companies, needed a steady supply of
coke for his factories. Together they formed a partnership
that made both men fabulously wealthy. Each man stood at
five feet two inches tall, but both were tough as nails and had
egos that far exceeded their physical stature. Frick became
chairman of Carnegie Steel Co. but the meddlesome Carnegie
could not help but interfere in Frick's work. They eventually
suffered a major falling out in which Carnegie forced Frick
from the company after they had filed lawsuits against each
other. Frick built a large mansion on Fifth Ave and 70th Street
to dwarf Carnegie's. The two estranged friends, though they
moved in the same circles and lived on the same street, never
reconciled. Years later Carnegie sent word to Frick that he
wanted to meet with him. Frick responded by saying, "Tell

Mr. Carnegie I'll see him in hell, where we both are going." While both men became enormously wealthy and successful, their friendship was permanently fractured.

Perhaps nothing damages relationships more than pride. Pride causes us to focus on ourselves. It makes us see things from our own, limited, perspective. And perhaps, most importantly, pride prevents us from humbling ourselves, confessing our wrongdoing, and saying we're sorry. Countless relationships have been permanently severed because pride refused to allow the aggrieved persons to be reconciled.

Some of the most troubling words Jesus ever spoke, were, *"Love your enemies, bless those who curse you, do good to those who hate you, and pray for those who spitefully use you and persecute you"* (Matthew 5:44). Jesus also claimed that the manner in which we treated those who harmed us would be the exact measure by which God would treat us for our sins against Him (Matthew 18:35). Scripture declares that not only are we to forgive others, but as God's children, we are to be ministers of reconciliation (2 Corinthians 5:18). We ought to leave a trail of reconciliation behind us wherever we go and not a series of former friends.

At the close of the Civil War, there was widespread popular opinion in the Northern states that Robert E. Lee ought to be hung for his role in the deaths of thousands of Union soldiers. General Grant threatened to immediately resign in protest if Lee, who had surrendered honorably, was harmed. Grant and Lee had fought fiercely against one another. Yet Grant set their differences aside.

Christ went to incredible lengths to achieve reconciliation between God and us. He owed us nothing. It cost Him everything. And now, that same Christ is seeking to live out

His life in us. He continues to have a heart for reconciliation. He is unwilling that we have any severed relationships in our lives. He knows how to restore broken relationships. His power is ultimately sufficient to overcome any obstacle. Do you have a relationship that Christ wants to mend?

REFLECT FOR A MOMENT

1. *Do you currently have any broken relationships? If you do, who are they? How do you think Christ feels about them? What do you think He wants you to do about them? When will you do that?*

2. *Christ has given you a ministry of reconciliation. Are you someone who causes strife between others, or are you a person who mends fences and reconciles estranged people? Ask the Lord to give you the wisdom to be a reconciler.*

3. *Have your actions offended someone? Is anyone presently upset with you? Take a moment right now to jot down some specific things you might do to be reconciled. Put dates beside them indicating when you plan on taking those important actions.*

Two Are Better Than One

IN 1948, BILLY GRAHAM was still fashioning his internationally renowned ministry. During a two-week series of meetings in Modesto, California, Billy gathered his team together. Men such as Grady Wilson, George Beverly Shea, and Cliff Barrows had been drawn together with Billy to form what would become the Billy Graham Evangelistic Association. Simultaneously, they were becoming good friends. Billy was concerned about the number of evangelists who were crossing moral and ethical lines and bringing disgrace to Christ's name. That day, the group of associates drew up what they would later refer to as the Modesto Manifesto, in which they committed themselves to certain principles that would protect them from committing the same ethical and moral mistakes others were making. They pledged to stay above reproach concerning money. They identified ways they could protect themselves from sexual sin. They committed themselves to working with local churches, rather than criticizing them. Finally, they pledged themselves to be absolutely honest in all of their publicity. As a result, though no Christian ministry received greater exposure or opportunities than they would, each man remained true to his commitment and the group of colleagues remained friends through over six decades of collaboration.

When Billy Graham was 78, he reflected on the team of friends he had worked with for six decades. He called Grady Wilson his "God-given balance wheel," because he helped add humor and laughter to the team. Of Cliff Barrows, Graham described his "humility and willingness to be a servant" as well as his spirit of reconciliation, that helped the team to work peaceably together. Of George Beverly Shea, Graham observed, "I don't believe I've ever heard him utter an unkind or critical word about anyone" (Billy Graham, *Just As I Am,* 781-786). Good friends, and trusted colleagues, this extraordinary group set an example of godly teamwork.

Scripture advises: "*Two are better than one, because they have a good reward for their labor. For if they fall, one will lift up his companion. But woe to him who is alone when he falls, for he has no one to help him up*" (Ecclesiastes 4:9-10). The marketplace is filled with pressures, temptations, and disappointments. It is foolish to assume that you can face them without godly friends to walk alongside you. Some people believe it is unwise to develop friendships at work. Yet while one must always relate to others with integrity, we spend too many hours each week at our jobs to not have friends among our colleagues.

The writer of Proverbs warns that: "*A man who isolates himself seeks his own desire; he rages against all wise judgment*" (Proverbs 18:1). A sign that someone is in danger of moral or ethical failure is that they isolate themselves from others. People who shun accountability are playing with fire.

Friends come in various personality types, temperaments, and senses of humor. If variety is the spice of life, having a diversity of friends adds much to the quality of your existence. Proverbs advises, "*A man who has friends must himself be friendly, but there is a friend who sticks closer than a brother"* (Proverbs 18:24). For you to enjoy godly friends yourself, you must be willing to love people as if they were your own brother or sister. As the Lord places friends alongside your life, they will strengthen, protect, and cheer you on so you accomplish far more than you ever would have, had you lived your life in isolation.

REFLECT FOR A MOMENT

1. *List the friends who are closest to you. Take a moment to evaluate them. What do you think of their number? Their variety? Their proximity? The length of your friendships?*

2. *Are you someone that others seek out to be their friend? What kind of friend are you? Rate yourself as a friend on a scale of 1-10. What might you do to become a better friend to others?*

3. *Do you have a tendency to be a private person? Do you have difficulty sharing your life with others? Do you prefer to be alone? It is dangerous for anyone to live their life in isolation. If you sense you need more friends in your life, especially at work, ask the Lord to show you how to be a better friend to people than you have been previously.*

Relationships at Work That Remain above Reproach

BILL CLINTON SERVED as president of the United States between January 20, 1993, and January 20, 2001. Clinton was the first Democratic president to win back-to-back elections since Franklin Roosevelt had done so in the 1930s. Clinton was generally popular and left the White House with an impressive 65% approval rating. This was due in part to the economic prosperity the nation enjoyed during his tenure, evidenced by Congress passing a balanced budget in several years during Clinton's presidency. But there was also a dark side to Clinton. During 1995-1996, the nation became familiar with the name of Monica Lewinsky, a White House intern who became sexually involved with the president. Rumors began to swirl of other women with whom the president had acted inappropriately as well. It appeared that, despite his intelligence and political talents, Clinton had an adulterous attraction to women.

In November 2009, the media disclosed that the revered golfing legend Tiger Woods had been committing adultery. Despite being married, with two children, and regularly promoting himself as a wholesome family man, this revelation exposed the dark side of Woods. Over the next several weeks, Wood's life unraveled before the watching eyes of millions of people around the world. Numerous other women began stepping forward to admit that they, too, had committed adultery with Woods. Woods' wife eventually divorced him, and his golf game plummeted.

In 2001, Yale University Press published a scholarly book with the provocative title, *Why Smart People Can Be So Stupid.* The book explored how brilliant individuals could rise to the top of their field and beat out thousands of competitors, but then self-destruct by making wildly reckless and foolish decisions with their lives.

Scripture is filled with wise counsel on how we can work closely with people of the opposite sex without succumbing to temptation. Notice what it says: *"I have made a covenant with my eyes; why then would I look upon a young woman?"* (Job 31:1) Job understood that temptation would always be available, but he wisely chose to prevent sexual sin from entering his heart by not looking in a lustful way at women. The Psalmist invited God to regularly search his heart to ensure no deception or lust or greed had entered therein (Psalm 139:23-24). We can be sure that the Holy Spirit will be quick to find our secret sins, if we will invite Him to search us. Lustful actions result from lustful looking. That is why the psalmist prayed, *"Turn away my eyes from looking at worthless things, and revive me in your way"* (Psalm 119:37). That is the power of media. It is impossible to watch hours of television and movies that glorify adultery and fornication without it affecting you. The antidote for sinful actions is godly thinking. David claimed, *"I have set the Lord always before me; because He is at my right hand I shall not be moved"* (Psalm 16:8).

As you go to work, you will encounter extremely diverse

people. Some are promiscuously looking for their next victim. Some are unhappy with their marriage and they can make your life unhappy too. What begins as a simple flirtation, or office teasing, can quickly deteriorate into something far more sinister. No one can protect your heart for you. Guard yours well. There is much at stake if you don't.

REFLECT FOR A MOMENT

1. *What actions do you regularly take to guard yourself from compromising situations with people of the opposite sex? Do you think you have adequate safeguards in place to protect you from sexual sin? If you don't, what additional protection could you put in place, soon?*

2. *Are you inadvertently allowing sinful thoughts to fill your mind through the television, movies, music, and books you allow in your life? Your thinking will affect your actions. What further steps might you take to keep your thoughts pure?*

3. *Do you make a regular habit of inviting the Holy Spirit to search your heart and mind for anything that is unclean? Take some time this week to invite the Holy Spirit to do so. Spend time in God's word and let the Spirit help you identify areas of weakness or danger in your life.*

Bringing Others with You

ON AUGUST 8, 1914, Captain Earnest Shackleton began his quest to be the first person to travel across the continent of Antarctica. Over 5,000 men had applied to join his crew. Shackleton had previously been knighted by King Edward VII for his attempt to be the first person to reach the South Pole. He had made it to within 112 miles before being forced to return to his ship. This time, however, he was determined to succeed. Unfortunately, on January 19, 1915, Shackleton's ship, the *Endurance,* became entrapped in ice and was carried along with the ice flow. The crew remained imprisoned aboard ship until October when the vessel began taking on water and had to be abandoned. For several months the crew camped on an ice floe. When it began to break up, they set out in three small lifeboats 346 miles to Elephant Island. The weather on this desolate island was formidable and well outside shipping routes from which help might come. Finally Shackleton decided to sail for a whaling station located over 800 miles away. Taking four companions with him, they sailed for fifteen days on open seas, braving hurricane force winds that could capsize them in an instant. Landing on South Georgia Island, Shackleton then hiked 32 miles across a mountain range to get to a whaling station. He quickly made arrangements to rescue his crew, eventually bringing every man back to safety. Shackleton's exploits and efforts to save his crew became legendary.

When Jesus came to earth, His heavenly Father gave Him 12 disciples. For the next three years, Jesus walked with those men. He traveled with them, ate meals with them, taught and cared for them. Near the end of Jesus' life, He prayed to his Father and gave an account of His relationship with those twelve friends. He declared, *"While I was with them in the world, I kept them in Your name. Those whom You gave Me I have kept; and none of them is lost except the son of perdition that the Scripture might be fulfilled"* (John 17:12).

Jesus saw His relationships as a divine stewardship. He knew that the world would seek to destroy his friends and rob them of God's best (John 17:14-16). In response, Jesus sought to bring God's word to bear on their lives and to walk with them in such a manner that they remained true to their faith. As a result, Jesus came to the end of his life and claimed that none, but the traitor Judas, had fallen away. And, for the remainder of their lives, none of the 11 would abandon their relationship to Christ.

Have you ever considered the reason God placed the friends He did in your life? God has a purpose for everything He does. What did He wish to infuse into your friends' lives when He placed you into a relationship with them? What was it God intended to do in your life by giving you the friends He did? At times we can treat our friendships selfishly, relating to people solely on the basis of what they do for us. Yet it may be that, for people to experience everything God intends for them, *we* must play a role. Perhaps God intends for you to encourage a friend during a trying time in his life. Maybe you are to intercede when your friend faces temptation.

Perhaps God desires for you to inspire your friend to strive for God's best in her life. How tragic for you to have friends who are discouraged and failing while you do nothing to come to their aid. If you were to give an account to God for the stewardship of your friendships, what would you say? Have you walked with each friend until they experienced God's purpose for their life?

REFLECT FOR A MOMENT

1. *Take an inventory of your closest friends. How are they doing? Are they struggling or prospering? How are their marriages and children doing? How is their walk with God? What might God do through your life to be a further encouragement to them?*

2. *Have you had friends who fell by the wayside? Have they experienced divorce or bankruptcy or broken relationships? Have they dropped out of church? Could it be that God placed you in their life for such a time as this? What might God want you to do to help them in their difficult time?*

3. *Do you receive more from your friends than you give? Do you view your friendships based on what others do for you? If so, take time with the Lord to let Him show you how to invest in your friends' lives. God can lead you to live your life in such a way that the people around you become better for having been your friend.*

Making an Impact for Christ in the Marketplace

Tom Starnes
Chairman and CEO, Inflexis

IT'S RELATIVELY EASY for me to share my faith at work these days. I run a small, privately held company where the executives are believers. But that was not the case earlier in my career when I worked for a few Fortune 500 and even Fortune 50 companies. There was never any discussion of faith at work—either around the conference table or the water cooler. If there were believers in these firms, I didn't know them and I didn't know how to live my faith in the workplace. It took years of study, practice and a supportive boss who loved Jesus, for me to learn ways to do this.

A good friend of mine, Dave Ramos, after graduating from Harvard Business School, ran global marketing for Nortel. Earlier in his career he had been in the top 1% of salespeople at IBM. He studied ways to make an impact in large public companies without "crossing the line" of evangelism and now runs his own consulting business called The Dashboard Group. He has developed an approach of integrating his faith in the marketplace that most of us can use. It's good for business, and for the Kingdom. Below I have extracted seven major points from a course Dave designed called, *Jesus: The Ultimate People Developer* and have added my own perspective to each point. The core concept is to develop people in the same manner in which Jesus worked with Peter.

1. Jesus affirmed Peter. He affirmed him not for his accomplishments, which would be substantial, but for his potential. And, He did it publicly. Tell people you believe in their abilities.

2. Jesus blessed Peter...abundantly. We all have ways we can do this. There's the typical salary, bonus, and stock but there are also less expensive, more personal options such as buying a book for someone and writing a note of encouragement in the cover jacket.

3. Jesus asked Peter to do things Peter didn't think were possible. You've probably heard the saying, "If you want to walk on water, you've got to get out of the boat." Ask employees to push beyond their normal aspirations. I should add that in studies done by Harvard Business School, only one common success factor of senior managers has been identified...consistently high expectations of the organization.

4. Jesus disciplined Peter. He did this in love. If you correct an employee and they know you did it because you care about them, not only will they appreciate your concern, others will take notice. People are drawn to honesty, sincerity, and kindness. If you can demonstrate these qualities, many others will want to work for and with you.

5. Jesus empowered Peter. In fact, Jesus told Peter He would give him the keys to the power of heaven. It's frustrating

to have responsibility without authority. Give your managers authority and they will do their best to prove they have earned your trust.

6. Jesus favored Peter. This one is a little tricky but it's a biblical concept. Peter was one of "the few" and was given extra time with Jesus. Not all your employees will go the extra mile. Find the ones who will and put your "extra mile" into their development.

7. Jesus prayed for Peter. He prayed before selecting him as a disciple and that Peter's strength would not fail. You can pray for your employees. And, if you're doing the first six, you're probably going to have opportunities to pray *with* a few people.

I doubt you'll find any secular business book to disagree with these concepts. In fact, there's a good deal of research supporting these actions to develop high performance executives. As Bill Hybels, Senior Pastor at Willow Creek Community Church, says, "No matter what your business card says, we are all in the people business."

REFLECT FOR A MOMENT

1. *Are you more of a "task"-oriented person or a "people"-oriented person? How has that affected your relationships at work?*

2. *What are three things you do that make people at work better?*

3. *What is one habit or behavior you practice that has had a harmful effect on your colleagues? How might you address that?*

Is Prayer a Part of Our Business?

Paul Spence
CEO, The STI Group

GEORGE MÜLLER (1805-1898) was a Prussian-born English evangelist and philanthropist He was a man of faith and prayer who established orphanages in Bristol, England. Müller prayed about everything and expected each prayer to be answered. Many times, he receivedunsolicited food donations only hours before they were needed to feed the children, further strengthening his faith in God. For example, on one well-documented occasion, they gave thanks for breakfast when all the children were sitting at the table, even though there was nothing to eat in the house. As they finished praying, a local baker knocked on the door with sufficientfresh bread to feed everyone. He frequently and periodically led his staff to pray for specific and documented prayer request. Müller prayed in millions of dollars (in today›s currency) for the orphans and never asked anyone directly for money. In his lifetime he cared for 10,024 orphans and he never took a salary in the last 68 years of his ministry, but trusted God to put in people›s hearts to send him what he needed. He never took out a loan or went into debt. And neither he nor the orphans were ever hungry.

Shortly after reading *The Autobiography of George Müller*, I was asked to speak to a group of college students about the subject of living out my faith in the workplace. As I prayed and sought God's face on what He would have me speak to the students, I began to reflect upon the significant events in my business career. In each of these significant events, without exception, a period of serious prayer with other committed believers preceded each of these events. These events included times of major expansions within the business, times of difficulty where there seem to be no solution, and in some cases possible bankruptcy – needs that only God could provide. Psalms 91:15 states, "He shall call upon Me, and I will answer him; I *will be* with him in trouble; I will deliver him and honor him."

At the beginning of 2010, our business, like most American businesses, was facing a faltering economy and an uncertain future. Following the example of Müller, a group of business leaders within our company agreed to meet with me every Monday morning for six months to fervently pray for our business. We also decided that we would make a specific documented list of needs, continue to pray, and watch to see how God would answer our prayers. It was amazing how faithful God answered every specific prayer request in ways that we couldn't even imagine!

The scriptures are replete with promises and instructions to believers to come to God in prayer:

- Psalms 32:8, *"I will instruct you and teach you in the way you should go; I will guide you with My eye."*

- Jeremiah 33:3, *"Call to Me, and I will answer you, and show you great and mighty things, which you do not know."*

As business leaders, it is expected for us to cast the vision of our organizations, lead out in times of uncertainty, and to make wise decisions for those that follow us. As leaders who are committed to Jesus Christ we have been given the most powerful privilege to call upon the God of the universe to guide us. But I wonder if we are all guilty of ignoring what could transform us as leaders as well as invoke the blessings of God upon our businesses? As business leaders, are we leading out in prayer within the business or is prayer an afterthought only to implore God to bless our humanly devised plans? Let's continually encourage one another to make prayer a cornerstone of all we do in the marketplace.

Applying Wisdom to Our Decisions

OUR LIVES ARE the product of the decisions we make. We can't always control our circumstances or what others do, but we have complete autonomy over our own decisions. Poor decisions lead to an impoverished life. Wise choices result in joy and contentment. The writer of Proverbs wrote, "*The fear of the Lord is the beginning of knowledge, but fools despise wisdom and instruction*" (Proverbs 1:7). Wisdom begins by taking God and His word extremely seriously! Wisdom is also something that accumulates. The apostle James offered, "*If any of you lacks wisdom, let him ask of God, who gives to all liberally and without reproach, and it will be given to him* (James 1:5).

Thriving in the marketplace requires sagacity. Temptations come by the bushel. People will attempt to deceive you. Problems can escalate with growing complexity. There are times when it may appear that there is no "correct" answer. Yet a decision must be made. In times like these, wisdom is indispensable.

Could the decisions you have recently made be characterized as "wise"? Has the fruit of your decisions been palatable? Are you growing in wisdom? God has provided bountiful wisdom to you as you live out your life. Are you making full use of it?

This One Thing I Do

STEVE JOBS RETURNED to lead Apple in 1997 after a string of disappointing quarterly results led to CEO Gil Amelio's resignation. Upon his return, Jobs found that Apple had widely diversified its product lines. He concluded, "Apple is in serious financial straits and we can't afford to do anything extra...We've got to focus and do things we can be good at." Under his direction, the company reduced its offerings to just four computers: two desktops and two laptops, providing two for personal consumption and a pair for professional users. This narrowed focus would ultimately contribute to Apple's remarkable turnaround.

For over 20 years, Starbucks had been a model of success and innovation. Yet in 2008, Howard Schultz returned as CEO after he grew concerned that the company he had founded was losing its way. Despite its phenomenal growth, he sensed it had strayed from fundamentals. Stores now brimmed with DVDs, CDs, and various coffee-drinking accessories, but the actual coffee-drinking experience had deteriorated. In 2007, *Consumer Reports* rated the quality of Starbucks coffee behind that of McDonalds. Something had to change, so Schultz took extreme measures. He closed 600 stores, eliminating 12,000 positions. He also removed numerous items that had crept onto store shelves, and returned the company to its primary business: coffee. In February 2008, all 7,100 Starbucks stores closed at 5:30 p.m. so the baristas could be retaught how to make a perfect shot of coffee. As the company regained its focus, it also returned to profitability.

Successful leaders have always understood the power of focus. Andrew Carnegie's business philosophy was simple, "Put all your eggs in one basket and then watch that basket." It was said that General Dwight Eisenhower's great strength lay in his attention to detail, "complemented by his intuitive knowledge of which detail to pay attention to."

Business leaders today, more than ever, must be diligent to maintain priorities as they lead. Do they open new stores? Enter new markets? Diversify their products? Enlarge their leadership team? Executives must constantly be intentional about how they allocate their valuable time: Work? Family? Health? God? Church?

Jesus offered straightforward counsel for businesspeople, *"But seek first the kingdom of God and His righteousness, and all these things shall be added to you"* (Matthew 6:33). Jesus understood that our life's focus determines our success. It is impossible to have a dozen priorities. To have many priorities is to have none. We make personal progress when we focus our life, over time, in the same direction. Talented business leaders will always be inundated with new opportunities and a myriad of challenges. Clients, colleagues, and causes will clamor for their attention and investment. The key is to stay riveted onto our specific calling and purpose. To grow and thrive in our walk with God is not to allot to Him leftover minutes seized from the scrap-heap of more pressing responsibilities. Other than Jesus, who has impacted the world for the better more than the apostle Paul? Paul was a busy, talented, driven leader, but his desire to know and serve God was his life's supreme goal. He determined, *"One thing I do...I press toward the goal for the prize of the upward call of God in Christ Jesus"* (Philippians 3:13-14). How long is the current list of your life's priorities?

REFLECT FOR A MOMENT

1. *Are you a focused person? Do you keep your eyes on the goal and refuse to become distracted? Or, have you lost your clear focus on your mission and goals? What would you need to do to regain your focus?*

2. *Jesus commanded us to seek first His kingdom. Are you doing that? Or, have you made Christ's kingdom a secondary priority? If you have, take time with the Lord and let Him help you make the kingdom of God the most important priority in your life. Let Him show you what needs to be reordered, or even removed, from your life so you can regain your proper focus.*

3. *Have you allowed urgent issues to crowd out crucial ones? Do you let the loudest voice drown out the most important concern? Have you become a slave of technology rather than using it to serve you? Jot down those things that continually distract you from getting the most important tasks accomplished. Make a plan to address those distractions. Plan to live your life intentionally and wisely.*

Wisdom

HISTORY CHRONICLES THE accomplishments of people who displayed courage. George Washington was famous for fearlessly charging into the fray of battle and yet miraculously never being wounded. He once commented, "I heard the bullets whistle, and, believe me, there is something charming in the sound." Winston Churchill, no stranger to danger himself, fought in the Second Boer War as well as World War One. He once confessed, "There is nothing more exhilarating than to be shot at without result."

The marketplace, like most fields of human endeavor, requires courage if one is to succeed. For those people of great courage, enormous possibilities may await. One of the toughest businessmen of his era was Henry Clay Frick. Standing only five feet two inches" tall, he was afraid of no man. Having partnered with another fiery five feet two inches tycoon in Andrew Carnegie, Frick was giving oversight to Carnegie Steel Company's most modern steel plant at Homestead, PA, in 1892. Frick had informed the Amalgamated Association of Iron and Steel Workers Union that its skilled workers would be required to take a 15% reduction in pay. A strike ensued. Determined to break the unions once and for all, Frick ordered in hundreds of Pinkerton detectives to protect the plant. Upon their arrival on July 6, shooting occurred that led to 13 deaths and hundreds of injuries. The militia had to be summoned to bring order to the strife-ridden mill. On July 23, while Frick was in a meeting in his office, Alexander Berkman, an anarchist, burst into Frick's office and shot him twice in the neck and then began stabbing him with a knife. When the doctor arrived, Frick refused anesthesia while the bullets were being dislodged so he could better help the doctor locate them. Frick spent ten days in bed, during which time his newborn son died from the complications of his premature birth. His son's funeral was August 4 and on August 5, Frick was back at work. Frick's courage and toughness, not surprisingly, became legendary. He would go on to become an immensely wealthy man and develop an art collection that can still be viewed at his former Fifth Avenue home in Manhattan.

Courage is a character trait that is widely esteemed. Fear, is loathed. That is what makes the following statement so troubling, *"The fear of the Lord is the beginning of wisdom"* (Psalm 111:10). For many, the very thought of being afraid of anything is anathema. Yet in our modern, liberalized culture, it appears particularly appalling to speak of "fearing" God. Yet Scripture repeatedly instructs us to do that very thing (Deuteronomy 4:10; 6:2; 28:58; Psalm 19:9; 34:9; 86:11; Matthew 10:28).

Our problem is that fear is always viewed as a negative, harmful experience. Yet it can also be lifesaving. Those who have no fear neglect to take precautions that could save their life. Those without fear may not fully recognize that they are mortal. Fearlessness is not the same as courage. We can demonstrate courage while we feel great fear. That's what makes it courage.

But when we come before God and see Him as He truly is, it ought to cause us to fear for our finiteness as creatures and for our accountability to our eternal Creator for our sins. Fear of God humbles us and compels us to listen and obey. It reveals that we understand how far distant we are in nature from our Creator. And, in our fear, as we listen, and obey, we will inevitably gain wisdom, which only derives from having a proper, and reverent view of almighty God. Do you fear God enough to gain His wisdom?

REFLECT FOR A MOMENT

1. *Do you fear God? If so, what is the evidence? How does your fear of God affect how you live? How does it determine how you relate to God? How has it impacted the way you became wise?*

2. *Do you struggle with the concept of fearing God? You may have been taught you should love God, but not fear Him. You may have assumed that fear was something people did in the Old Testament, but not today. If so, prayerfully study the Scripture passages that instruct you to fear the Lord. Let the Bible shape your beliefs and actions, not popular opinions.*

3. *Do you have a teachable spirit? Are you humble enough to learn from your mistakes as well as from Scripture? If you have not humbled yourself enough to fear God, you may not be humble enough to learn from Him either. Prayerfully ask the Lord to increase your humble, teachable spirit.*

Seeking Counsel

DESPITE THE NUMEROUS challenges the United States has faced throughout its history, its single greatest crisis undoubtedly was the Civil War. More soldiers were killed in that war than in any other conflict. The foundations of the republic were fiercely shaken during the national strife. Such a turbulent period called for outstanding leadership. It is no wonder that in asking historians to rate the performance of U.S. presidents, Abraham Lincoln is perennially ranked at the top. He overcame his nation's most devastating crisis.

Doris Kearns Goodwin, in her Pulitzer-Prize winning book, *Team of Rivals,* analyzed Lincoln's presidency and noted that his brilliance lay in his ability to enlist and utilize the outstanding leaders of his day for the nation's cause. While Lincoln ultimately made the final decision, he enlisted the best thinking available to him. Lincoln explained, "We needed the strongest men of the party in the cabinet...I looked the party over and concluded that these were the very strongest men. Then I had no right to deprive the country of their services"(319). Several of the men in his cabinet had run against him for the presidential nomination and thought they were better suited to lead than was Lincoln. At least one of the men had openly mocked Lincoln before he had become president. Nevertheless, Lincoln conscripted his previous opponents and critics and wielded them into an unbeatable team.

General Eisenhower operated by the principle, "Make no mistakes in a hurry." He understood that, as a leader, his mistakes would cost others much more than it would cost himself. He could not afford to be careless or unprepared with others' lives.

The writer of Proverbs sagely observed, *"Where there is no counsel, the people fall; but in the multitude of counselors there is safety"* (Proverbs 11:14). One of the means God uses to speak to us is by providing counselors who can offer us wise advice. There are, of course, several prerequisites if we are to benefit from counselors. First, we must enlist godly advisers. Such people rarely offer their services unsolicited. Second, we must be prepared to hear things we find unpleasant. John Gardner noted, "Pity the leader who is caught between unloving critics and uncritical lovers." Third, we must cultivate the ability to recognize good advice. King Rehoboam had not one, but two sets of counselors (1 Kings 12:1-20). Unfortunately for him, and his kingdom, Rehoboam could not distinguish between good and bad advice. Being unable to recognize godly advice places us in the same position as those who have none. Finally, we must accept and follow wise counsel. The most brilliant insights will avail us nothing if we do not act on them. Even King Solomon, who was himself a brilliant leader, failed to follow his own counsel, and he and his descendants suffered grievously as a result (1 Kings 11).

Wise leaders conscientiously and fervently enlist godly counselors to walk with them. Such leaders invite their advisors to be brutally honest. They would rather know the truth about their situation than be merely affirmed by their fawning associates. Godly leaders also walk closely with the Lord so they are in the best position to recognize when God speaks through one of their colleagues. We live in a complex and rapidly changing world. The stakes are high and the penalty for fools even higher. It behooves us to seek wisdom, wherever it may be found.

REFLECT FOR A MOMENT

1. *How would you rate the caliber of your advisors? Have you gathered top-notch people around you who can offer you outstanding counsel? If you have not, take action now to gather advisors who can help you in areas in which you need advice.*

2. *Can you receive unwelcome counsel? Do you accept advice well? If you become defensive or argumentative, people will not tell you what you need to hear. Ask trusted friends their candid opinions of how teachable and receptive you are to other's advice. Their answers might surprise you!*

3. *Are you walking closely enough with the Lord that you would recognize His voice if He spoke through one of your friends? Be sure you are walking closely enough with the Lord that you recognize a word from the Lord when you receive one!*

Prepared

His very birth was unfortunate. It came on "Mausoleum Day," the day solemnly remembered each year when his great-grandfather, Albert, died of typhoid. Yet on December 14, 1895, Prince Albert Frederick Arthur George of York was born. At his birth, expectations for his future appeared modest. His great-grandmother, Victoria, still sat upon the throne in her sixty-year reign. His grandfather Edward continued to wait into his fifties for his turn to assume the throne. Edward's oldest son, Edward, had died prematurely, thus putting his younger brother George in line for the throne. George had two sons. The eldest was Edward, who would one day become king. The second son, like many second sons throughout Europe, would grow up in the shadow of his older sibling destined to one day be the heir to the family fortune. To make matters worse, Albert (or Bertie, as he was called), suffered from an almost debilitating stammer. While his brother Edward was a charming and eloquent public speaker, Bertie struggled painfully to pronounce certain words and dreaded having to make public speeches. His father had little patience for his son's stammer, and would impatiently yell, "Get it out," to only humiliate him further. Bertie also had the misfortune of being left-handed, which at that time, was considered abnormal. He was therefore forced to learn to write with his right hand. He was also knock-kneed and, as a remedy, forced to wear painful braces on his legs for several hours each day.

On October 31, 1925, Bertie gave a speech to a large gathering in which he stammered painfully throughout. He was humiliated. The following year, he began meeting with an Australian speech therapist named Lionel Hogue. His father would later observe, "Bertie has more guts than the rest of them put together!" When, in 1936, Edward VIII abdicated the throne to marry Wallis Simpson, Bertie was thrust onto center stage to become King George VI. Unbeknownst to the world at that time, World War II was rapidly approaching and the king would be called upon to make heroic efforts on behalf of his nation, including making a number of crucial speeches to uplift his people's morale. Bertie had no idea, as he worked to overcome his natural weaknesses, that one day he would be given a history-making role to play.

The apostle Paul declared that Christ is *"able to do exceedingly abundantly beyond anything we could ask or think, according to the power that works within us"* (Ephesians 3:20). Paul knew full well the impossibility of a former murderer and blasphemer being used mightily by God, yet Christ had accomplished that very thing. The world desperately needed Paul to become more than anyone thought possible. It took much work and study on Paul's part, but it wholly depended upon God's grace and power to accomplish the feat.

Our world desperately needs people who believe that with God, *all* things are possible. Too many assume they are limited by their weaknesses, or circumstances, or previous mistakes. Yet opportunities may come that invite us to accomplish something significant. Those moments may catch us by surprise. But when they knock at the door, we must be prepared. Have we worked hard to better ourselves? Have we sought to overcome our weaknesses? When our moment comes to undertake an important task, will we be ready?

REFLECT FOR A MOMENT

1. *What are your greatest areas of personal weakness? What have you done to overcome them? How hard are you trying to improve yourself in those areas? If called upon to work in those areas of your life, would you be prepared?*

2. *What are your expectations for your life? Do you assume God will use your life for His purposes? Or, do you believe you are too "ordinary" to accomplish anything important? When we claim we are too "ordinary," we are saying more about our belief in God than about our own limitations.*

3. *Have you allowed other people's expectations and evaluations to determine what you expect for your life? People's opinions should not set limits on your life. Take time with God and let almighty, infinite God share with you what is in His mind for your life. With God, ALL things are possible! Live like it!*

A Holy Temple

JOHN ROCKEFELLER WAS a devout Baptist who religiously abstained from alcohol and tobacco. At the age of 78, he finally dispersed his spectacular wealth to his heirs and to charities, retaining a paltry 20 million to finance his final years. This appeared almost meager in light of the fact the retired tycoon would live another 20 years to be 98. Likewise, Henry Ford, a contemporary of Rockefeller's, would reach the age of 83. Yet great wealth and business success were not always accompanied by strong health.

J. P. Morgan, though he lived to be 75, was a chain smoker. When his health began to deteriorate, his doctor prescribed that he decrease the cigars he smoked to only 20 per day! Cornelius Vanderbilt lived to be 83, but he lived his life in excess and died from complications of syphilis he had contracted through his wanton lifestyle. Walt Disney lived to be 65. He was a chain-smoker whose constant, hacking, cough became his trademark. His staff knew when he was walking down the hallway by the sound of his cough. His daughter once asked him not to attend her performance at a school play for fear his constant coughing would cause her to forget her lines.

For others, the stress of business is what ultimately killed them. William Vanderbilt, the heir to Cornelius, inherited almost 100 million dollars in 1877. His father had regularly referred to him as a "blockhead" and a "blatherskite," and as a result, William desperately sought to be a good steward of the enormous wealth that had been passed on to him. His assets doubled in less than nine years to 200 million dollars. Yet in his early 60s, he confessed, "The care of $200,000,000 is too great a load for my brain or back to bear…It is enough to kill a man." At age 64, while in the middle of a meeting, he collapsed to the floor and died from an apoplectic stroke.

Scripture exhorts, "*Or do you not know that your body is the temple of the Holy Spirit who is in you, whom you have from God, and you are not your own? For you were bought at a price; therefore glorify God in your body and in your spirit, which are God's*" (1 Corinthians 6:19-20). We are meant to live our entire lives in a manner that glorifies God. We do that not only by our moral lifestyle and our church involvement. We can also honor God by our business ethics and the way we treat our families. We further glorify God by the way we care for our physical bodies.

At times businesspeople live paradoxical lives. They care deeply for the health of their company but they shamefully abuse their own physical well-being. They keep their companies lean, but they allow themselves to gain many unnecessary pounds. They eliminate wasteful practices in their business but refuse to relinquish bad habits in their personal lives. Yet one could wonder how someone who kills himself with overeating, alcohol, or tobacco could be entrusted with the health of a company.

The challenge for many businesspeople is that their schedule and work demands require much time. Business travel can be wearisome. Business lunches can challenge the best-intentioned of eating regimes. We must remember that our bodies are a divine gift. We are stewards of them. How we treat our bodies reflects on our Creator. How does your body currently reflect on God?

REFLECT FOR A MOMENT

1. *How would you rate your current health? Are you overweight? Do you properly exercise? Do you eat and drink healthily? Do you maintain unhealthy habits? How do you think your physical health and lifestyle are currently reflecting on your Creator?*

2. *What are your greatest challenges to living healthily? How does your work life make it difficult to take proper care of your body? Take some time to list ways you can take better care of yourself. Then enlist a small group of friends, tell them your goals, and ask them to hold you accountable for achieving them.*

3. *Have you considered your physical health to be a spiritual issue? Scripture calls your body the temple of God. If you cannot control your physical body, how can you expect to control your emotions, or thoughts, or actions? If you cannot be entrusted to care for your own body, why should someone entrust you to care for their business?*

Changing Our Habits

PETER ARNELL IS the founder of Arnell and a leading branding and design expert who has worked with such companies as, Samsung, Chanel, Reebok, Mars, Pepsi, Home Depot, and Fendi. Paradoxically, as he was helping companies rebrand their image, his own personal appearance and health was completely out of control. His weight ballooned to over 400 pounds. He eventually decided that if he was to ever enjoy his grandchildren, he had to drastically change some of the destructive habits that were destroying his life.

Arnell suggests that, "True change springs from an idea whose time has come" (Peter Arnell, *Shift,* 18). Arnell chose an unusual method for altering his life. He claims, "I started looking to oranges to transform my life." He would eat up to 50 of them *a day.* As he began to adjust his eating habits, he started to lose weight. He eventually shed 256 pounds and settled on his ideal weight of 150 pounds. Arnell found an unusual means of rebranding himself into the person he knew he could, and ought to be.

For followers of Christ, we have a source of help that is far more powerful than even the tastiest orange. It is the power of God. Paul stated, *"For the kingdom of God is not in word but in power"* (1 Corinthians 4:20). Christianity is not meant to merely be a religion of words, but a lifestyle characterized by divine power. There is no bad habit or sinful practice or human limitation that is beyond the God's power to set us free. The writer of Hebrews urged believers to "*lay aside every weight and the sin which so easily ensnares us*" (Hebrews 12:1). The problem for many people is that they have developed harmful habits and routines that continually trip them up and robs them of God's best. We may have acted the same way for so long that we feel as if we cannot break those habits, regardless of how important it is for us to do so.

John Jacob Astor, the founder of the Astor fortune, claimed, "The man who makes it the habit of his life to go to bed at nine o'clock usually gets rich…It's all a matter of good habits and good habits in America make any man rich." Peter Drucker intoned that routine "makes unskilled people without judgment capable of doing what it took near genius to do before." The key is to eliminate unhealthy routines by God's power, and then to cultivate healthy practices, also by God's power!

The Gospel of Luke notes that Jesus often withdrew into the wilderness to pray (Luke 5:16). Apparently he also regularly went to the Garden of Gethsemane to commune with His Father, as Judas knew right where to find him on the night of his betrayal. It was a routine Jesus developed in His life that guided and strengthened Him throughout His ministry.

There are two areas of life on which businesspeople must focus. The first is to eliminate habits that hold them back from God's best for their lives and business. The second is to develop healthy routines that strengthen them physically, emotionally, and spiritually. As Drucker says, when you have healthy routines, you are able to accomplish as much or more than can undisciplined people of genius. So what healthy habit will you, by God's power, implement into your life in the coming days? What is preventing you from beginning today?

REFLECT FOR A MOMENT

1. *Do you need to "rebrand" yourself? Do you like who you are and how you look right now? If not, why don't you do something about it, now? Ask God what it is He would like to see in your life. Then, by His power, strive to become that person. Settle for nothing less.*

2. *Do you have healthy or unhealthy routines in your life? What are the defaults in your life? (Those behaviors you naturally resort to when you are tired or going through the motions.) What positive routines do you need to build into your life so you become a healthier person?*

3. *Is your life and your body a testimony to the power of God? The Gospel is not about words, but about power. Are you talking about the power of God while your actions and your health declare that God's power is ineffectual for you? Trust in God's strength to help you have victory in EVERY area of your life.*

Thinking Differently

LEADERS THINK DIFFERENTLY than followers do. They have to. While followers can be content focusing on the trees, leaders must see the forest. While staff may concentrate on today, executives must concern themselves with tomorrow. It was said of George Washington that one of his greatest strengths was the ability to see things as they were and not as he wished them to be. Howard Gardner, in his book, *Leading Minds,* suggests that, while leaders often exert *direct* influence, such as by issuing orders, enacting legislation, or spending money, leaders also exert *indirect* leadership through their thinking process.

However, business leaders today face a dilemma. Nicholas Carr points this out in his book, *The Shallows: What the Internet Is Doing to Our Brains.* He notes that our brain is constantly adapting to our experiences. He argues that by using computers and particularly the Internet, our brains are being re-wired to think like the Internet. He argues, "Sometimes our tools do what we tell them. Other times we adapt ourselves to our tool's requirements" (47). Studies have shown that the human mind can retain at most seven elements at the same time if it is to properly store new information into its long-term memory. Yet today, people are being continually notified of messages and changes in stock value as well as text messages, incoming e-mail, and social media notifications. With such a bombardment of media messages, our minds cannot properly assimilate the data. Carr suggests that "frequent interruptions scatter out thoughts, weaken our memory, and make us tense and anxious" (132). He suggests that regular use of the Internet has made people unable to read more than a computer screen's worth of text at a time and to read at a superficial level. We skim more than we read. He also argues that what we are doing when we multitask is "learning to be skillful at a superficial level" (141). He posits that intensive multitaskers are "suckers for irrelevancy" (142). Carr also argues that "the brighter the software the dimmer the user" (216). He suggests the Internet is altering the depth of our emotions (221) and today's search engines serve as "amplifiers of popularity" (217). He suggests that tools such as Google simply draw us to the most popular sites rather than the most thoughtful or even helpful ones. In other words, today's Internet tools are gradually doing more and more of our thinking for us. Perhaps, even more significantly, it is changing the *way* we think and *what* we think about.

What is Scripture's response to this issue? It urges us, *"And do not be conformed to this world, but be transformed by the renewing of your mind, that you may prove what is that good and acceptable and perfect will of God"* (Romans 12:2). Scripture exhorts us to resist the world's efforts to influence, shape, and guide our thinking. Without even realizing it, we can allow modern media to change the way we view things. Accustomed to watching the news on television while seeing updated weather reports on the side of the screen and headlines scrolling at the bottom, we find it nearly impossible to sit in front of our Bibles and to read more than a chapter. We must rely on the Holy Spirit's help to guard our minds from the world's intrusions. The Spirit will alert us when biblical values and perspectives are being challenged. But we must immerse ourselves in God's word so our minds are filled with it, rather than today's headlines and related commentary. Are you thinking biblically? Or, is someone, or some thing, thinking for you?

REFLECT FOR A MOMENT

1. *Do you like to multitask? While you may be able to accomplish many things, are you doing them well? Can you focus? Can you think deeply on a matter? If you can, what is the evidence?*

2. *Do you spend more time on the Internet than reading books? Do you read more fiction or nonfiction? List the last three serious books you read. Were they required for your job or because you wanted to become informed of important issues? What are two important books you know you need to read in the next couple of months? Make plans to obtain them and read them.*

3. *Are you a deep thinker? Do you consider issues others miss? Do you discover solutions to difficult problems? If your brain is like a muscle, how much vigorous exercise have you given it lately?*

Margin

In 1992, Dr. Richard Swenson wrote a much-discussed book entitled *Margin: Restoring Emotional, Physical, Financial, and Time Reserves to Overloaded Lives.* In it he argued that, quite simply, people have limits. They can only handle so much stress, so many expenses, and so many commitments before they reach a saturation point. His formula was: Power-Load = Margin (*Margin,* 92). He claimed that modern society was encouraging people to live their lives right to the limit of their capacity, with nothing held in reserve. As soon as they received an unexpected bill, or crisis, or emotionally draining relationship, or disappointment, people had no reserve with which to respond in a healthy and productive manner. As a result, people were burning out and feeling overwhelmed with life. Swenson called marginless living "the disease of the 1990s." But clearly things have grown worse since his book was first published.

Businesspeople are particularly susceptible to marginless living. With economic downturns and belt tightening, companies are doing more with less. Employees often shoulder far more responsibility than they used to. In times of high unemployment, no one wants to decline work that an unemployed person would gladly embrace. Business professionals also face pressures because they are often talented individuals who are sought after as volunteers by numerous organizations. Their church needs their time. Their children's Little League team wants them to help out. Their children need help with schoolwork and being shuttled to their multitudinous lessons. When we add the need to stay current in our field as well as to spend devotional time with God, we can soon feel as if we have far too many responsibilities than we can handle. Without realizing what is happening to us, we gradually become more and more frustrated and less and less joyful.

The truth is that our Creator knows full well that we have limits. That is why He set a pattern for people when He rested on the seventh day of His creative activity. Scripture indicates, *"And on the seventh day God ended His work which He had done, and He rested on the seventh day from all His work which He had done"* (Genesis 2:2). Clearly God did not need to rest. But He set a pattern of scheduling restoration into our lives. The Sabbath is God's response to our need for margin. To make things perfectly clear, God codified this pattern in the Ten Commandments. Out of the ten most important divine laws given to humanity, one of them forbids people from working seven days a week (Exodus 20:8-11).

When Christ came to earth, He did not do away with the Law, but rather He fulfilled it. He looked upon those who were weary and stressed, and announced: *"Come unto Me, all you who are weary and heavy laden, and I will give you rest"* (Matthew 11:28). Christ never gives us more than we can handle. He won't overextend us. He never allows us to face a crisis for which His grace is not sufficient to carry us through. But we must lean on Him. We must walk with Him closely enough that we experience His strength as well as His peace.

Like a branch abiding in the vine, as we abide in Christ, He infuses us with the strength and wisdom to handle every situation.

How would you describe your life? Peaceful? Content? Rested?

REFLECT FOR A MOMENT

1. *Do you have adequate margin in your life? If you were surprised with an unexpected bill, or crisis, could you handle it, healthily? If you don't have margin in your life, what are some steps to build it in?*

2. *Do you feel overwhelmed with your responsibilities and pressures at work and home? Do you need to care for your soul and emotional health? Do you need to accept Jesus' invitation to come to Him for rest? Are you abiding in the Vine and drawing upon Christ's strength and peace?*

3. *Do you regularly take time to rest? Do you have a Sabbath in your schedule? Do you go hard all the time or do you have regular times of rest built in to your schedule? If you don't, why don't you sit down with your calendar this week, and begin to schedule some in?*

Overreaching

HENRY FORD WAS brilliant in many ways. Between 1900 and 1908 there were 501 car companies established. Yet Ford would best them all with the introduction of the Model T in 1908. Ford had a genius for car construction and transformed mass production with the development of the assembly line. He also revolutionized industry by introducing the $5 workday. Buoyed by his rising fame and enormous wealth, the entrepreneur began to espouse his views on other social and political matters. At the outbreak of World War I, Ford adamantly opposed American involvement, claiming he wanted to spare American lives from European battlefields. Thinking that, as a successful businessman, he could talk reason to the European belligerents, Ford enlisted a cruise liner dubbed the "Peace Ship" and set sail for Europe in 1915 along with a motley collection of anti-war activists. The entire endeavor became one of the most embarrassing events in Ford's storied life.

Ford would often promote his views against smoking and drinking, as well as popularizing traditional dances such as the Two Step and the Waltz. He also promulgated a virulent anti-Semitism. One contemporary critic accused Ford of being among wealthy businesspeople who "assume that because they have made a great success and shown exceptional ability in one field of action, therefore their opinions are of equal weight in all others" (Steven Watts, *The Peoples' Tycoon,* 225). Ford ran for the U.S. senate and barely lost. On June 25, 1916, the *Chicago Tribune* carried a scathing article against Henry Ford, calling him an "ignorant idealist" for espousing ideas it considered harmful to America while being ignorant of the facts. Ford defended himself by suing for libel. Ford ultimately found himself on the witness stand in court, trying to prove he was not ignorant. In that he failed. He was repeatedly asked basic questions about American history to which he consistently gave the wrong answer. At one point Ford defensively argued, "I could find a man in five minutes who could tell me all about it." It became painfully clear that, while Ford knew much about constructing automobiles, his knowledge about many other basic areas of life was appallingly meager. Over time, as Ford grew older, he became worse at offering his opinions on matters he clearly had not thought deeply about. His biographer notes, "He increasingly appeared as, at best, a slogan-spouting, irrelevant old man chained to the past, and, at worst, a dangerous reactionary" (*The People's Tycoon,* 430).

Scripture offers much wise counsel with regard to our speech. Proverbs 22:29 claims, "*Do you see a man who excels in his work? He will stand before kings; he will not stand before unknown men.*" Certainly skill in our profession will provide us a platform for greater influence. The great temptation will be for us to speak on matters for which we have little knowledge or upon which we have given scant serious thought. Scripture sagely advises, "*Whoever guards his mouth and tongue keeps his soul from trouble*" (Proverbs 21:23). The key is to watch over our mouth to ensure that we do not say more than we know! Success and leadership positions will provide us a platform for influence. But we must always be cognizant of what we know, and what we do not know. We are most influential when we speak on that which we truly understand, and we defer to others, and seek their counsel, on matters for which we are uninformed. What are you known for? Do people take your words seriously? What do you really know?

REFLECT FOR A MOMENT

1. *Are you an expert in certain fields? If so, what are they? What are some fields you do not know very well? How often do you voice your opinions on matters on which you are generally uninformed?*

2. *How effective are you at guarding your mouth? Do you avoid expressing opinions that you have not carefully thought through? Are you respectful of others' viewpoints?*

3. *We cannot learn anything new while we are speaking. In conversations do you do the majority of the talking or the listening?*

Redeeming the Time

GEORGE C. MARSHALL emerged from World War II as one of its most respected and celebrated military leaders. As the top U.S. Army commander, his task after the Japanese attack on Pearl Harbor was to rapidly build the U.S. military to a strength that could defeat its enemies. Marshall placed orders to purchase 60,000 planes, 45,000 tanks, and 8,000,000 tons of merchant shipping in 1942. He planned for 125,000 planes, 75,000 tanks, and 10,000,000 tons of shipping in 1943. The U.S. would ultimately spend 160 billion dollars on its military during World War II and build its military forces to over eight million people.

One day Marshall was busily writing at his desk when Brigadier General Leslie R. Groves, the military director of the atomic bomb project, entered his office. Groves respectfully waited until Marshall was finished. Marshall then scanned the request for 100 million dollars to be approved, and signed it. As Groves was about to leave, Marshall said, "It may interest you to know what I was doing. I was writing the check for $3.25 for grass seed for my lawn" (Ed Cray, *General of the Army,* 315). While Marshall was famous for his normally wise use of time, he recognized the incongruity of delaying a 100-million-dollar project to develop the world's most powerful weapon while he invested three dollars on grass. While we may never have to make 100-million-dollar decisions, we all will face important and unimportant matters.

The apostle Paul urged believers, "*See then that you walk circumspectly, not as fools but as wise, redeeming the time, because the days are evil*" (Ephesians 5:15-16). The most precious resource we own is our time. Without it, nothing else we possess matters. Yet, as Marshall realized, we must decide each day and each hour how we will invest our time. Those who have changed their world have had no more time available to them than those who wasted their lives.

In the workplace, time is money. Valuable employees manage to get the most out of their day. Nevertheless, there are innumerable time wasters always lurking in the shadows seeking to squander our most precious resource. Studies show an enormous amount of time being spent by today's employees logged in to social media or surfing the net while on company time. Text messaging and e-mails bombard us while we try to complete projects or to study important documents.

People will thoughtlessly waste our time, if we let them. Small talk in the hallway about sporting events or the latest movie can whittle away precious minutes. Urgent but secondary issues can distract us from that which is essential. A thousand little things clamoring to be done can prevent us from accomplishing the one major project that had to be finished. At the end of a hectic and exhausting day we may realize, to our chagrin, that while we seemed busy all day, we never managed to complete our most pressing tasks.

Jesus was one of the busiest people of His day. People were constantly clamoring for His attention. Critics watched Him.

The needy followed Him. Yet Jesus never seemed to be in a hurry. He never raced to His next appointment. Yet at the end of the day, Jesus had accomplished every assignment His Father gave Him. No one distracted Him. He redeemed His time. How like Jesus are you, with your time?

REFLECT FOR A MOMENT

1. *How good are you at using your time? Are you behind in your work? Do you seem to have more to do than you have time to complete? If so, review your schedule. Prayerfully ask the Lord to show you if you are using your time effectively.*

2. *Are you a victim of time wasters? What are the biggest wasters of your time? Honestly reflect on what wastes the most time. Do you squander time on the Internet? Do you spend too much time watching television or movies? Do you love to visit with colleagues? How might you address these issues so they do not continue to dissipate your precious time?*

3. *Do you make it a practice to tackle your most important jobs first? Or, do you let numerous smaller tasks eat away your day so you never have time to complete your most important ones? How might you reorder your schedule so your critical work is always completed in a timely manner?*

Planning Versus Preparing

Mark Nelson
President, Chevron International Pte Ltd., International Products

As BUSINESS LEADERS, we often find ourselves facilitating a planning effort…creating a plan for corporate funding, for resource optimization, for investors, and even planning for specific scenarios. In most cases, planning leads to clarity of execution, aligned people, and delivering on commitments. We each have consequence history that would tell us effective planning can create value.

James 4:13-16 says, *"Now listen, you who say, 'today or tomorrow we will go to this or that city, spend a year there, carry on business and make money.' Why, you do not even know what will happen tomorrow. What is your life? You are a mist that appears for a little while and then vanishes. Instead you ought to say, 'If it is the Lord's will, we will live and do this or that'"* (NIV). What is the message here? Are we not to plan? Did Joseph plan his journey as a child to eventually be a powerful leader in Egypt? Did Moses plan to tend sheep for 40 years? Did Saul plan to join the followers of Christ he so frequently persecuted?

James' admonition is critical to business leaders in that we are required to plan for our organizations, but we might need a different vantage point for our personal lives. When people focus on achieving their personal goals, they negate the opportunities God can provide. James' advice seems to be that if we want to establish a goal, we should come to God for verification. I personally have, at times, accomplished objectives and still felt a bit empty. Conversely, I have interacted with folks who may have experienced a considerable setback (missed an objective) but were experiencing fulfillment. Upon reflection, I was planning and these fulfilled individuals were preparing...preparing to serve God in whatever His master plan held for them.

Can you imagine Moses tending sheep suggesting to his wife that he would part the Red Sea and lead the Israelites from Egypt? Or Joseph, while being traded into slavery, contemplating that he would one day be accountable for financials of the entire Egyptian Empire? Many business leaders I know have confessed that if you had told them a few years ago that they would be where they are today they would not have believed you.

Let's make sure we are allowing God to prepare us for His plan.

REFLECT FOR A MOMENT

1. *How do you normally make your plans? What role does God have in your planning? What role ought He to have?*

2. *If God wanted to add something into your schedule, how could He do it? God knows the future. We do not. How could He guide you into the future? What process do you have to incorporate God's guidance into your planning?*

Choose This Day
Joshua 24:15

David Ratcliffe
President, CEO, Southern Company

As I MATURE in my life and faith, I am increasingly compelled by the notion of choices. Joshua 24:15 is Joshua's challenge to the Israelites to choose whom they would serve. Like them, we must choose also. Obviously our first and most important decision is what we will do with the person of Jesus Christ. There is no more critical choice to be made in our lives. The challenge of "choice" is mine, not my wife's, my mom's, my dad's, or anyone else. It is I, and I alone, who must choose. And, there is no middle ground since not to choose is to choose!

Beyond that most important decision, the real challenges begin. They involve the specific choices we make concerning how we will live our life. Our instructions are clear: we are to choose the mind of Christ (Philippians 2:5) and the lifestyle that Christ instructed. As Paul said, *"wretched man that I am, the things I want (and know) to do I don't do"* (Romans 7:15-24). I find great solace in the fact that one of our greatest Christian role models also struggled with always choosing the correct response!

I have tried to improve on the habit that Stephen Covey refers to as "proactivity" (*7 Habits of Highly Effective People*). He notes that we can choose how we respond to life's issues and to the people we encounter. In fact, only we can choose. It is not just a right or an opportunity; but for followers of Christ, it is a responsibility and provides accountability. For we are called to be "in this world but not of this world." We are to be different and if we are to be successful then we must become better at the discipline and process of making choices. We must choose to be Christlike in those times when the world deals us cruel and unfair circumstances or offers angry remarks or opposition. That means our response cannot be to retaliate. We must leave justice in God's hands. He is fully capable of handling our problems (and our opponents!).

As we develop the discipline of choosing to become more Christlike, we mature in our walk with Him. Our reward is that we are freed from the world's expectation for us. We also develop the ability to rise above even our most difficult circumstances. It really is liberating to choose how we will respond. I am nowhere near where I want to be. Like Paul said, I am a wretched man. Yet I find that the more Christlike my choices become, the more joy I embrace. I know that will be your experience too!

REFLECT FOR A MOMENT

1. *How effective are you at making wise choices? How often do you have to rescind an earlier decision? Are you living with many regrets from your previous choices?*

2. *Have you developed a process for making decisions? Or, are you haphazard each time you have a choice to make? How much of your decision making is based on your feelings? How much of your decision making is determined by seeking the Lord's guidance?*

3. *What choices could you make this month that would lead you to become more like Christ? List three decisions that could strengthen your walk with God. Now make specific plans to carry them out!*

This Is the Time to Pray and Seek God's Will

Richard Case
CEO, Benchmark Associates, Inc.

IN 1787, AFTER months of work, the delegates to the Constitutional Convention from the 13 original states had reached an impasse about central government versus state rule. Larger states were pushing for representation according to population and smaller states for equal representation. They were ready to give up and disband. It was then that Benjamin Franklin proposed a day of going to the local churches and seeking God's wisdom. After this day of prayer in hearing from God, they returned to the Convention and came to the remarkable solution we have today—the U.S. Constitution.

In the challenging days in which we live, we are all facing such uncertainty that we wonder if there are any real solutions ahead. God is calling us again to humble ourselves, seek Him, hear His voice, and expect His solutions to become clear to us. When we lack wisdom (when we are unclear concerning His will or His solutions to our circumstances), He invites us to ask Him. He promises to reveal His wisdom—but (and it is a big condition)—we must ask, believing He will tell us. We must determine that when we ask, He will answer with His generous wisdom (see James 1:5-8).

David teaches us how this works in 1 Samuel 23. Being pursued by King Saul, David was focused on his adverse circumstances when he became aware of a city, Keilah, near his camp that was about to be ransacked by the Philistines. He asked God if he should go and save Keilah. God said, "Yes, go." David's men said, "This is not a good idea, we are having enough problems of our own—it is too dangerous." David could have said, "You're right," or "You have to go because God said so," but instead he went with his men, back to God and sought confirmation. God again said (He does not mind clarifying again, particularly when we are seeking unity with those around us), "Yes, go"—and "I will deliver the Philistines into your hands." David and his men heard God speak, immediately obeyed, and went and saved Keilah.

Saul recognized the perfect opportunity to kill David since Keilah had only one way out of the city. David heard that Saul was again coming after him (he had good market researchers working for him), so he asked God, "Will the men of Keilah deliver me into the hands of Saul? Is Saul coming after me?" He thought that since he had just saved Keilah, certainly its citizens would protect him, but David understood the value of not being presumptive about anything without the wisdom of God. God answered that Saul was coming after him and that the men of Keilah would indeed betray him to Saul. He left Keilah and, as a result, his life was spared. Ultimately God fulfilled His promise of making David king of Israel and bringing the Messiah through his lineage.

Instead of moving toward resignation or fatalism over these days, instead of trying to figure all this out on your own—go to God and ask Him for wisdom—He promises to give it and will lead you through the morass you are facing into His plans for you—plans for good, not evil, plans of hope and a future (Jeremiah 29:11). Believe Him.

REFLECT FOR A MOMENT

1. *How does prayer factor in to your decisions? Do you pray over every major decision your make? What about minor ones? How do you decide when you need God's guidance?*

2. *Do you recognize when God is seeking to guide you? When was the last time you sought specific guidance from God about a matter and He provided it to you? Do you think this is meant to be normative for the Christian?*

3. *What types of issues do you think God wants to be involved with in your life? Does He care about your business decisions? Does God simply concern Himself with "spiritual" issues? Why don't you seek God's guidance on some mundane issues in your life this week? Invite God to become actively involved in the ordinary living out of your life. See what God can do!*

Leaving a Legacy

OUR LIVES CAN influence people we never see. At times this is because of the *breadth* of our influence. Our actions can affect people working in other departments or offices at our company. Our decisions may influence people working in other cities or even various nations. In the global market in which we function, a decision made in Connecticut can exert an immediate impact on Cameroon. But our lives also exert a *length* of influence. That is, long after we have acted, people can still experience the consequence.

God cautioned those who would ignore His commands. He warned, *"For I, the Lord your God, am a jealous God, visiting the iniquity of the fathers upon the children to the third and fourth generations of those who hate Me, but showing mercy to thousands, to those who love Me and keep My commandments"* (Deuteronomy 5:9-10). Our lives can affect others for generations to come.

Those who recklessly defy God and disobey His commands are inadvertently bringing grief to their descendants. A broken marriage, an addiction, or a weak character quality in our life can inflict devastation to the generations that follow us. Long after we are gone, our descendants can be feeling the pain of our foolish choices. Conversely, when we choose to love God and heed His word, we transmit a blessing to descendants we may never meet. How will the coming generations remember you?

Leaving a Spiritual Legacy

THROUGHOUT HISTORY GREAT leaders have often found it difficult to pass on their success to their offspring. The Duke of Wellington, Napoleon's conqueror, was always formal with his own children and withheld signs of affection. His oldest son, Douro, was so intimidated by him that he once mused, "Think what it will be like when the Duke of Wellington is announced and only I come in" (Richard Holmes,*Wellington: The Iron Duke,* 262). Many children of famous tycoons never demonstrated a fraction of their parents' business aptitude. William Randolph Hearst loved his children but was often absent from them. His son Bill observed, "In not spending more time with his wife and children, my father made the biggest mistake of his life. It left an emptiness in all of us" (David Nasaw, *The Chief,* 356). Perhaps that is why none of Hearst's children completed college and each suffered turbulent, failure-riddled business careers. When Hearst's oldest son George underperformed at one of his father's companies, Hearst fired him, concluding, "He is apparently too lazy to occupy a position by himself and do any work" (David Nasaw, *The Chief,* 358).

While it is certainly not a sin for your children to choose a different career path than yours, it *is* tragic when they choose not to embrace your faith in God. The Bible reveals that many successful leaders failed to lead their children spiritually. God used Abraham, Isaac, Jacob, and Joseph to launch the Israelite nation. God knew the power of successive generations building upon each other's walk with God. Moses was a dynamic leader but when he chose his successor, his own son Gershom (Exodus 2:22) was not up to the task so he appointed Joshua. Joshua's honorable pledge is legendary, *"But as for me and my house, we will serve the Lord"* (Joshua 24:15). While Scripture is silent about Joshua's children, after Joshua's death, *"another generation arose after them who did not know the Lord nor the work which He had done for Israel. Then the children of Israel did evil in the sight of the Lord..."* (Judges 2:10-11). Eli was a national leader but his sons Hophni and Phinehas were corrupt and did not know God (Judg. 2:12). Samuel was a revered statesman but his two sons Joel and Abijah disgraced their priestly office (Judges 8:3). King Hezekiah was one of the most righteous leaders in Judah's history, but he reared Manasseh, who was arguably his nation's wickedest monarch (2 Kings 21:1-2, 9). How could such godly leaders fail so miserably to teach the next generation to follow God?

D.L. Moody was the best-known evangelist of his day. Yet his sixteen-year-old son Will renounced his faith. Moody wrote him a heart-wrenching letter, "I sometimes think it is my fault, if I had lived more consistent you would not be so disgusted with what is so near my heart...if I have ever said or done any thing unbecoming a Christian father I want you to forgive me and I would rather die than stand in your way" (*Moody,* 238).

How tragic to walk closely with God ourselves but not to help our children develop their own solid faith in Him. Our enthusiasm about following God does not guarantee that our children will share our zeal or understand our spiritual pilgrimage. We must be as intentional about helping our children develop their faith in God as we are in assisting them with their education and embarking on careers. Moody relentlessly pursued his prodigal son until he embraced his faith once more. Are your children following and even surpassing your walk with God?

REFLECT FOR A MOMENT

1. *Are you a first generation Christian? If so, what kind of spiritual heritage do you believe God wants to pass down to the generations from your life? If you have a godly heritage, who were some of your ancestors who passed their faith down to you?*

2. *How are you living your life so it exerts a positive impact on your descendants? How much time do you spend explaining your faith and your decisions to your children and grandchildren? What are you doing to specifically pass on your spiritual legacy?*

3. *Think about ways you can pass on a Christian heritage to your descendants. Give your Bible to your children as a keepsake. Save your spiritual journals to be read by future generations. Make a recording of your testimony or spiritual journey. Record prayers you have prayed for those who follow you. Highlight the spiritual markers of your life that can encourage the generations that follow.*

Serving Your Own Generation

IN 1889 ANDREW Carnegie penned an essay that ignited vociferous debate among America's business leaders. He charged, "The man who dies thus rich dies disgraced." In 1901, Carnegie sold his steel company for $480 million, retaining for himself $225,639,000. It instantly made him one of the world's wealthiest people. He spent the remainder of his life giving away his fortune to better the world. Largely impressed by Carnegie's actions, John Rockefeller established the Rockefeller Foundation in 1913 and soon donated 183 million to it. He and his son would ultimately contribute over 1.5 billion dollars to charity.

The March 2011 edition of *Forbes* announced there were 1,210 billionaires in the world, scattered among 54 countries with a total estimated worth of $4.5 trillion. While the United States still boasts the most billionaires (413), in 2011 Moscow housed more billionaires than any other city (79). Mexico was home to the globe's wealthiest person: Carlos Slim at $74 billion.

Business leaders have often used their resources for the betterment of humanity. Many have invested in education or medical care. Some, like Najib Mikati, take on the thankless job of trying to rebuild their nation (Lebanon). In 2011, Bill Gates was the world's second wealthiest person ($56 billion).

He would have been the wealthiest had he not already given away $30 billion. Warren Buffet was the third wealthiest ($50 billion). This duo travelled around the world urging fellow billionaires to donate half their wealth to charity. If America's billionaires responded, $600 billion would be raised to address the world's greatest issues. As of the end of 2010, 40 had accepted the challenge. Many business leaders, having enjoyed financial success, now feel compelled to invest their energies and resources into helping others. As they move further into their careers, they want to contribute to society while they still have the opportunity.

David rose from an inconsequential shepherd boy to his nation's greatest leader. He enjoyed power and prestige but he also sought to leave a legacy. Scripture summarizes his life by saying, "*For David, after he had served his own generation by the will of God, fell asleep, was buried with his fathers, and saw corruption*" (Acts 13:36). God intends for us to "serve" our generation in whatever time God grants us. What a tragedy to spend our entire lives feverishly accumulating promotions and possessions but doing nothing to enhance the lives of others. Unbelievers give vast amounts of time and money to charitable causes out of their sense of decency and good will. *How much more* ought those who profess Christ as their Lord to live in a manner that builds God's kingdom and changes their world? *Now* is the time to live our lives in a manner that impacts our world. Yesterday is past and tomorrow may be too late.

In a 2005 commencement address at Stanford, Steve Jobs mused to those beginning their business careers, "Remembering that I'll be dead soon is the most important tool I've ever encountered to help me make the big choices in life. Because almost everything—all external expectations, all pride, all fear of embarrassment or failure—these things just fall away in the face of death, leaving only what is truly important." Each of us has a limited time to serve our Lord. Each of us has a unique calling to fulfill. The clock is ticking. How have you been investing your life? What adjustments ought you to make?

> *"So teach us to number our days, that we may present to You a heart of wisdom."*
>
> PSALM 90:12 (NASB)

REFLECT FOR A MOMENT

1. *What are some ways you are investing in the future? How are you investing your finances? How much is going to your heirs and how much to the Lord's work? How generously do you share what you have with ministries that affect eternity?*

2. *Are you living your life as if you and your possessions will last forever? Or, are you living your life with a keen awareness that your time on earth is limited? How are you living with a sense of urgency? What are you presently investing in that will outlast you by many years or generations?*

3. *What does serving the Lord's purposes in your generation look like? How has God uniquely equipped and blessed you in order to bless your generation? How has God's call on your life given you a sense of purpose as you live and work?*

Building for Eternity

NORTH CAROLINA'S MOUNTAINS attract thousands of tourists annually. In summer, people come from across America to escape the sweltering heat. The lush, green mountains provide breathtaking views. In the region around Asheville stand two impressive structures, both designed to accommodate numerous visitors.

One is The Biltmore Estate. In 1889 George Vanderbilt poured the inheritances he received from his grandfather Commodore Vanderbilt, the wealthiest businessman of his era, and his father William into the construction of America's largest private residence. It took six years to build and entailed the construction of a private railway spur to bring construction materials to the 146,000-acre estate. Perched on a magnificent site with a panoramic view of 50 mountain peaks rising above 5,000 feet, the house boasted 255 rooms including a bowling alley, indoor pool, exercise room, a 20,000 volume library, and a cavernous banquet hall. In December 1895, George opened his luxurious residence to his wealthy relatives. Although his siblings owned lavish mansions on Fifth Avenue, they were duly impressed with the monument George had built to showcase the Vanderbilt millions. Vanderbilt commissioned extensive experiments in forestry and horticulture. On March 6, 1914, a heart attack caused George Vanderbilt's untimely death at the age of 52. He had occupied his dream home for less than 19 years. His wife was soon forced to parcel off much of the surrounding lands to meet the enormous maintenance expenses. Today, the Biltmore is a popular tourist attraction that brings thousands of visitors each year to gawk at the enormous wealth enjoyed by America's elite.

Not far from the Biltmore in the small community of Montreat sits another home, that of Billy and Ruth Graham. They built the modest house on a mountainside as a place to provide much needed privacy and where they could raise their children. Nearby sits The Cove. It was established by the Billy Graham Evangelistic Association with the goal of encouraging Christians and ministry leaders through solid Bible teaching. The Cove is designed to accommodate up to 500 guests at a time. Lining its halls are pictures and memorabilia from the numerous crusades Billy Graham undertook worldwide. A Christian radio station on the property broadcasts Christian music and programming. The Vanderbilt estate and The Cove sit miles, yet worlds apart. One is a public display of opulence. The other is a base from which to extend God's kingdom.

Jesus told the parable of a successful businessman who had a knack for turning a profit. This man built larger coffers and increased his investments without any thought of using his wealth to help others. There seemed no end to his potential for accumulating riches. But alas, the end was closer than he imagined. Like George Vanderbilt, he died unexpectedly and his heirs received what he spent a lifetime accumulating. Jesus concluded, *"So is he who lays up treasure for himself, and is not rich toward God"* (Luke 12:21).

Billy Graham collected riches in heaven. He never built a palatial mansion nor did he accumulate enormous wealth. People will not tour his former home to view his priceless possessions but will celebrate a life that invested heavily in the kingdom of God. Graham and the thousands who responded to his preaching will be enjoying the dividends of his investment for eternity.

REFLECT FOR A MOMENT

1. *You more than likely work hard. What has your labor primarily been for? How long will your accomplishments last? How long will they be remembered? Will your labor be viewed by others positively or negatively?*

2. *If your life were to abruptly end this week, would your house be in order? Would you be ready to pass on what you have to the next generation? What do you need to do so you are prepared to hand over all you have to the next generation?*

3. *How much time do you invest in the development and encouragement of the next generation? Do you invest in mentoring the younger generation? Are you training people to some day replace you? How are you living your life with an eye to the future?*

Measuring Your Legacy

IN THE EPIC days leading up to the revolutionary war, John and Abigail Adams conducted a fascinating correspondence concerning the state of America. Abigail observed, "We have too many high sounding words and too few actions that correspond to them." Her husband, John, serving at the epicenter of his nation's greatest political leaders, concluded, "We have not men fit for the times." Both John and Abigail would be called upon to make enormous personal sacrifices for their nation. John would serve as the first vice president under George Washington and then succeed Washington as America's second president. His son, John Quincy Adams would later become the sixth president of the United States. Not only did this couple discuss the shortcomings of their nation, they rose up to make a lasting difference.

Many people are so busy dealing with day-to-day concerns that they give only fleeting attention to matters of the future. Even fewer consider how their daily lives have eternal ramifications. Yet God created us for eternity and it is only from that vantage point that our lives gain their true meaning and perspective. Many of us want to make a contribution to humanity that will outlast us, to leave a legacy. For some people, the only meaning for their lives is found in their efforts to live as comfortably as possible during the brief decades they traverse the planet. Consequently it is not surprising when they grow discouraged and disillusioned immersing themselves in mundane tasks having no lasting value.

Horace Mann intoned, "Be ashamed to die until you have won some victory for humanity." Successful businesspeople have the material means to leave a legacy. John Rockefeller, Andrew Carnegie, Henry Ford, and Bill Gates all established enormous foundations for the betterment of mankind. Andrew Mellon claimed, "Every man wants to connect his life with something eternal." As a result, he created the National Gallery of Art in Washington D.C.

Milton and Catherine Hershey were unable to have children, so in an effort to leave a legacy, Hershey built an entire town in Pennsylvania as a modern utopia. Having no heir to his fortune, the industrialist willed his millions to a foundation that supported a boys' orphanage. By 2005 the foundation was sponsoring over 1,100 boys. The value of the endowment from Hershey's gift reached eight billion dollars making it greater than that of Harvard or Yale Universities. While there have been critics who charged that the town and boys' school are not fulfilling all of the tycoon's intentions, the town of Hershey, Pennsylvania, and the boys' school continues to function and thrive. Nevertheless, despite the enormous funds supporting the school, even it will not last for eternity.

The apostle Paul cautioned, "*Each one's work will become clear, for the day will declare it, because it will be revealed by fire, and the fire will test each one's work, of what sort it is. If anyone's work which he has built on it endures, he will receive a reward*" (1 Corinthians 3:13-14). How long will your life's investment endure? Until you leave your company? Until your heirs spend their inheritance? What are you investing in today that will outlast your grandchildren?

What are you giving your life to that will last for an eternity?

REFLECT FOR A MOMENT

1. *Of all the work you have done, what of your labors or investments will last the longest? What of your accomplishments will be most appreciated by the next generation? Why?*

2. *How are you preparing your heirs to handle what you give them one day?*

3. *What is the one great contribution to society and to the Church that your life has, or will, make?*

Investments

You think *you* have problems! How would you have liked to be Warren Buffet? An economic downturn in 2008 caused the value of his personal assets to drop by 25 *billion* dollars! As of April 2009, they had been reduced to only 38 billion. To make matters worse, his financial free-fall reduced him to second place among the world's wealthiest people behind his good friend, Bill Gates at 40 billion. Fortunately for Gates, he only lost 18 billion so he was able to overcome Buffet and regain the top spot. The year 2008 was difficult for billionaires. Their number dropped from 1,125 to 793 worldwide (*Forbes,* 3 March 2009).

Buffet spent most of his life making money. When he was ten he read the book, *One Thousand Ways to Make $1,000.* It offered a seemingly sure-proof path to wealth. Buffet made it his goal to become a millionaire by age 35 (Alice Schroeder, *The Snowball,* 64-65). His story is legendary. He launched numerous companies while he was still a young boy. Yet even as he reaped financial success he was always reluctant to part with his money. He arranged a deal with a local newsstand to buy week-old magazines at a reduced price. Buffet gambled on horse races. When he was 16, he lost his first bet of the day and then continued betting, desperately trying to recoup his losses. By day's end he had parted with $175, a considerable sum at that time. All the way home Buffet painfully calculated how many papers he would have to deliver on his paper route to recoup his devastating losses (*The Snowball*, 109).

Buffet hated losing money. Fortunately for him, over the years he earned much more than he lost. Not everyone recovers from financial losses. Adolph Merckle with assets valued at 9.2 billion dollars was the fifth wealthiest person in Germany. Yet when his company entered turbulent financial waters in 2008, he vainly attempted to stave off financial ruin. Losing all hope, he made his way to a nearby train station and stepped into the path of a speeding locomotive (*Forbes,* 3 March 2009, 76). For some, the loss of wealth is irrecoverable. Others view it merely as a road bump. It depends on the role money plays in your life.

Christ left heaven's throne room to serve God's kingdom purposes. Though a King, He did not spend His time pursuing wealth. He knew His earthly sojourn was brief. He invested in eternity. Jesus sagely advised, *"Do not lay up for yourselves treasures on earth, where moth and rust destroy and where thieves break in and steal; but lay up for yourselves treasures in heaven, where neither moth nor rust destroys and thieves do not break in and steal. For where your treasure is, there your heart will also be"* (Matthew 6:19-21). The problem with money is that it can become all-consuming: the obsession with earning it; the fear of losing it; the pride of accumulating it; the stress of preserving it; the pressure to distribute it. Jesus knew money could gain a stranglehold on the most pious. He recognized the rich young ruler was controlled by his money. So Jesus sought to pry him loose of its suffocating grip (Luke 18:22-23). Christ will work to establish His priority in your life. He knows accumulating money is dissatisfying. Buffet ultimately chose to give away the bulk of his fortune. Does your money possess you? It is easy to tell. Observe how easily you give it away and how much you suffer when it is lost.

REFLECT FOR A MOMENT

1. *How important is money to you? How easily can you give it away? How painful is it when you lose it? Does money play too important a role in your life?*

2. *What is your plan to invest your wealth in eternity? How have you been intentional about ensuring that the most money possible is invested in the Lord's kingdom work? How many different ministries and Christian efforts do you currently support? How could you increase the level of support you are giving?*

3. *Do you receive more joy out of earning or giving your money? Are you a "cheerful giver"? Take time to pray and ask God to place His heart for giving generously over yours. Don't quit praying until you are as generous a giver as God is!*

Small Beginnings

"It was the worst retail store I had ever seen. Sam had brought a couple of trucks of watermelons in and stacked them on the sidewalk. He had a donkey ride out in the parking lot. It was about 115 degrees, and the watermelons began to pop, and the donkey began to do what donkeys do, and it all mixed together and ran all over the parking lot. And when you went inside the store, the mess just continued, having been tracked in all over the floor. He was a nice fellow, but I wrote him off. It was just terrible." Thus was described the launching of Sam Walton's third Wal-Mart store in Harrison, Arkansas. Not a spectacular beginning!

One of the qualities that made Sam Walton ultimately so successful was his eternal optimism. Regardless of how poorly something began, he always assumed it would get better. In Sam's early years he took a management position at J.C. Penney. When the regional manager stopped by and examined Sam's store, he declared, "I'd fire you if you weren't such a good salesman. Maybe you're not cut out for retail" (*Sam Walton,* 23). Sam didn't give up, however. When he later began opening stores across the country, his daughter Alice tearfully confided to a friend, "I don't know what we're going to do. My daddy owes so much money, and he won't quit opening stores." Ultimately, of course, Sam's early, small, relatively unimpressive efforts grew into the largest retail chain and employer in the world. Many of the greatest accomplishments in human history have begun inauspiciously.

God declared, *"For thus says the High and Lofty One who inhabits eternity, whose name is Holy: I dwell in the high and holy place, with him who has a contrite and humble spirit, to revive the spirit of the humble, and to revive the heart of the contrite ones"* (Isaiah 57:15). God is high and lifted up. But on earth, He delights in those who are humble. Even when God sent His Son to earth, He did not start Him out in a palace, but in a stable. Jesus claimed that His kingdom was like a mustard seed (Matthew 13:31-32). It begins as something seemingly small and insignificant, but it gradually grows into something large and widespread. Jesus did not begin His earthly ministry with great fanfare. In fact, He told His first disciples that He had nowhere to lay His head. Yet they followed and, eventually developed a movement that covered the globe.

The world loves to celebrate size and numbers. The bigger it is the better. The faster the growth is, the more impressive. Yet this mindset is dangerously seductive. When we begin something with plentiful resources, we do not feel totally dependent upon God. When we have many people heralding our spectacular launch, we may not feel we need God's guidance. When we launch ventures with much fanfare, we attract people who are looking for quick and easy success. While strong beginnings are certainly not sinful, they tend to foster carnal attitudes and self-sufficient behaviors.

The problem can be that we do not have the patience to wait until that which is small has had time to develop and gain strength. In 1905, Alex Y. Malcolmson had a falling out with Henry Ford. In a pique of anger, he sold his shares for $175,000. Malcolmson would later declare bankruptcy, while his relinquished shares would have been worth hundreds of millions of dollars only ten years later. Don't despise small beginnings!

REFLECT FOR A MOMENT

1. *Are you easily seduced by size? Do you assume that bigger is better? Perhaps you need to take time to study the Scriptures and to beware of that which the world is impressed with!*

2. *Are you discouraged by smallness? If you are a part of a humble beginning, don't lose heart! Some of history's greatest ventures began small and without fanfare. What is one "small" thing you are a part of right now? If you do not belong to anything that is small, perhaps you need to find something that you can help grow.*

3. *Have you lost patience with smallness? Could it be that you are in danger of walking away before a project or effort reaches its potential? If God has called you to something small and seemingly insignificant, be certain you do not abandon it if God has not released you from it.*

Being Remembered

WILLIAM VANDERBILT WAS a warmhearted, kind man, who inherited 100 million dollars from his father in 1877, making him one of the wealthiest men of his day. In less than nine years, he grew his wealth to $194 million. Yet perhaps what he is best known for were two infamous quotes in the *Chicago Daily News*. In an interview on 9 October 1882, he declared, "The railroads are not run for the benefit of the 'dear public' —that cry is all nonsense—they are built by men who invest their money and expect to get a fair percentage on the same." In 1883, when asked about a popular fast mail train that was being discontinued, he retorted, "The public be _____! I don't take any stock in this silly nonsense about working for anybody but our own." While technically he was correct, his honest comments were public relations disasters and came to symbolize the calloused attitudes of the "robber barons" of the Gilded Age.

John Jacob Astor was famous in his day as one of the wealthiest men in America. But perhaps he is best known for being the wealthiest person on the *Titanic* during its maiden voyage. When the ship struck an iceberg, the captain informed his most illustrious guest before he sounded the general alarm, so Astor could be saved on a lifeboat. Astor declined, however. Instead he ensured that his pregnant wife

Madeleine was safely aboard a lifeboat. Astor's body was eventually recovered with $2,500 in cash in his pockets.

Randy Pausch was a popular computer science professor at Carnegie-Mellon University. On August 15, 2007, Pausch learned that his pancreatic cancer had metastasized and that he was almost certainly going to die. He was asked to deliver a final lecture at his university on September 18, 2007. His title was, "Really Achieving Your Childhood Dreams." On that day, the lecture hall was filled. Though everyone knew he was dying, his lecture was on living. He subsequently put his thoughts into a book entitled *The Last Lecture,* that became a bestseller. Pausch died on July 27, 2008, leaving behind his wife and three young children. But through his book and Web site, he continues to be remembered, and to exert an ongoing positive influence on people worldwide.

Scripture concludes, "*A good name is to be chosen rather than great riches*" (Proverbs 22:1). Biblically, our "name" represents the reputation of our character. It is what we are known for. We generally develop our reputation through our words and primarily through our actions. Yet not all words and actions are of equal value. We might speak kind words 100 times to our child, but in a moment of frustration, spew out a few angry insults that are remembered long after our kind words are forgotten. We might do 100 different effective projects for our company, but what we may be remembered for is the unethical behavior that led to our eventual dismissal. Often it is not how we began, but how we ended, that carries the most weight with people. Certain words and actions have a way of being indelibly imprinted into people's minds, regardless of what else we say and do.

The question for each of us is: how will we be remembered?

One careless word can undo 1,000 thoughtful utterances. One selfish action can erase the good of 1,000 noble actions. Every day we are investing in our name. We cannot control what people think about us; but we can control our words and actions.

REFLECT FOR A MOMENT

1. *What kind of "name" have you been developing with others? If your actions and words have been contributing to your name, or reputation, are you pleased with the name you have built? If not, how do you wish it was different?*

2. *Sometimes one thoughtless, negative word or action can negate hundreds of positive ones. Have you been careless with your words or actions? Do people know you more for something negative or something positive? You cannot erase past words or actions. However, you can live your life today in such a way that you begin to restore your name into a positive one, once more.*

3. *What positive actions are you doing today that will be fondly remembered long after you are gone? What could you do to enhance the positive reputation of your name for years to come?*

Scattering

JOHN JACOB ASTOR was one of the first notable multimillionaires in American history. Astor was born in Germany in 1763 into a butcher's family. He immigrated to America in 1784 and eventually made his fortune in the fur trade. He developed a shipping business and then began investing heavily in real estate in the New York City area. Even as a multimillionaire, Astor was notoriously cheap. He once declared that a friend's hotel would never succeed, evidenced by the fact he placed too large of lumps of sugar in the sugar bowl. He would become upset if his children took more butter than they could use on their bread. Astor's fortune eventually grew to $25 million, which made him the wealthiest man in America. Yet he was always reluctant to part with his money. A minister once called on Astor and proclaimed that, "You are indeed fortunate to have such a great fortune…It increases your ability to do good." To which Astor replied, "Oh, the disposition to do good does not always increase with the means" (Lucy Kavaler, *The Astors*, 35). At his death in 1848, Astor made his only large benefaction, giving $400,000 to the Astor Library, which would become the New York City Library. Most of his wealth went directly to his son William, who would be tasked with carrying on the family legacy. William would live to be 83 and would eventually double his wealth to $50 million. Yet, in light of the fact he was for many years the richest man in America, his donations to charity were negligible. His intent was to pass on as much of his wealth as possible to his heirs, as his father had done.

Warren Buffet, in contrast, would come to dwarf the Astor millions. Yet he believed that inheritances were simply "unearned wealth," of which he did not approve. He made his children do chores to earn their allowance and often turned down their requests for money. His children grew up knowing their father would not give them money except for their education. On June 26, 2006, Buffet donated 85% of his Berkshire Hathaway stock to the Bill and Melinda Gates Foundation. At that time, his donation was valued at 37 billion dollars. He would not leave a foundation or institution with his name on it in perpetuity. He would disperse his enormous wealth in a manner he felt would do the most good to others.

The world tends to encourage people to hoard what they have. Yet Jesus told a story about a successful businessman who had accumulated more wealth than he could possibly use. His solution was, "*I will do this, I will pull down my barns and build greater, and there I will store all my crops and my goods.*" Jesus commented, "'*Fool! This night your soul will be required of you; then whose will those things be which you have provided?' So is he who lays up treasure for himself, and is not rich toward God*" (Luke 12:18; 20-21). Jesus made it clear that hoarding our possessions rather than investing in His kingdom is shortsighted and foolish. The writer of Proverbs noted, "*There is one who scatters, yet increases more; and there is one who withholds more than is right, but it leads to poverty*" (Proverbs 11:24). Being a wise steward of our resources means we care for our own needs as well as for our family. But our heart ought to be predisposed to give. Our assets *will* be disposed of one day. Either we will have the privilege and joy of doing so, or someone else will.

REFLECT FOR A MOMENT

1. *How much effort have you made to build your retirement funds? How much wealth do you anticipate passing on to your heirs? How much wealth do you plan to invest in God's work while you still have control of it?*

2. *What is your view on passing on inheritances? Do you agree with Buffet that it is not right to do so? Buffet has tried to invest his money in a way that it exerts the most impact. How are you doing that?*

3. *Do you receive more delight from gathering or from scattering? Do you enjoy seeing your wealth pile up or being dispersed the most widely?*

God's Blessing

WHEN THE ANGELS announced the coming of the Messiah, they declared, *"Do not be afraid, for behold, I bring you good tidings of great joy which will be to all people"* (Luke 2:10). The Christian message brings great joy! It is the most encouraging, amazing, and life-changing news mankind has ever received. Those who believe it, embrace it, and obey it, will experience abundant life. Jesus promised that if we would abide in Him, His joy would fill our lives to overflowing (John 15:11). How can you identify people who are experiencing the truth of the Gospel? They have joy!

The greatest human condition is to be the recipient of God's blessing. No earthly pleasure can compare with the satisfaction that comes when God is pleased with you and chooses to bless you. This can be experienced in business and financial success, but it involves much more. The joy of the Lord can be experienced in both prosperity as well as bankruptcy. The sense of God's pleasure upon your life brings peace and contentment regardless of your circumstances. Notably, the joy of the Lord is such that *no one* can remove it from you (John 16:22).

The world loudly proclaims that, to be happy, we must possess the best house, car, clothes, spouse, and job available. The media urges us to be perpetually striving for more and better. Yet it is but a hopeless pursuit of a mirage. Those who recognize the source of true joy and contentment will wholeheartedly embrace Christ. They will find their pleasure in Him. They will bask in God's presence and infinite goodness.

From where do you draw your joy? Have you found true pleasure in Christ? Have you had the profound delight that comes from being blessed by God?

Abundantly

THE BUSINESS WORLD categorizes its processes into pairs (profit/loss; revenue/expense; asset/liability), with the ultimate goal of the positives outweighing the negatives. Life is sort of like that—some relationships and activities add to its quality while others diminish it. Jesus warned about *thieves* whose purpose it is to *"steal and to kill and to destroy"* (John 10:10). There are numerous behaviors, attitudes, people, and activities that rob us of the life God created us to enjoy. Conversely, Jesus assured His disciples that He had come so *"that they may have life, and that they may have it more abundantly"* (John 10:10). Whoever or whatever dominates your life will determine whether you experience a diminished or an abundant life.

Mark Twain candidly confessed, "I am opposed to millionaires, but it would be dangerous to offer me the position." In truth, much of Twain's heartache resulted from his constant, but futile attempts to accumulate wealth. Cornelius Vanderbilt admitted, "I have been insane on the subject of money-making all my life." Such an obsession led him to become America's wealthiest tycoon, but it also resulted in heartache and suicide among his children. By 1883, his son William had doubled his inheritance in six years from 95 million dollars to 200 million. But by his early sixties, William was weary and disheartened.

He noted, "The care of $200,000,000 is too great a load for my brain or back to bear...It is enough to kill a man. I have no son whom I am willing to afflict with the terrible burden. There is no pleasure to be got of it as an offset—no good of any kind. I have no real gratification or enjoyments of any sort more than my neighbor on the next block who is worth only half a million." In a similar fashion, John Jacob Astor, commenting on his inherited fortune complained, "Money brings me nothing but a certain dull anxiety."

The biographer of Andrew Mellon, one of the wealthiest men in the 1930s, noted that he "rarely smiled and hardly ever laughed." His marriage ended in a painful divorce. Henry Ford II, grandson of Henry Ford, was married three times. Says his biographer, "Henry was married to the Ford Motor Company, and marriage to him was always a form of polygamy." A time will inevitably come at the end of our life when our net worth or the profitability of our company appears meaningless. In light of this fact, we ought to invest our life in those things that bring us, and others, abundant life. We were created to enjoy life, *every day*.

The psalmist declared, "*In Your presence is fullness of joy*" (Psalm 16:11). Spending time in God's presence brings inexplicable joy! In addition, those who "*delight in the law of the Lord*" will prosper in all they do (Psalm 1:2-3). Godly children provide abundant satisfaction (Proverbs 15:20; 23:24), while he who begets a fool "*has no joy*" (Proverbs 17:21). In addition, God intends for us to find complete marital contentment and pleasure from our spouse (Proverbs 5:15-20). God is extremely clear on how to experience *abundant* life.

The world incessantly clamors to enhance our life. However, its methods rob us, rather than bless us (Proverbs

14:12). Evaluate your current activities and commitments. Are they leading to the *abundant* life God intends? Or, are they robbing you, and others? Life is too brief and precious to squander! Live each day with joy. As Jonathan Swift advised, "May you live all the days of your life."

REFLECT FOR A MOMENT

1. *Are you presently experiencing an ABUNDANT life? Why or why not?*

2. *Have you been seduced by the world to seek happiness from it? Have you assumed money or possessions could bring you joy? Have you discovered it cannot? Have you inadvertently modeled for your children the love of money?*

3. *Have you come to experience the joy of the Lord? Do you enjoy God? Have you learned to enjoy the simple pleasures in life that bring much joy? What is it that has been giving you the most pleasure in your life, lately?*

Waiting

BETWEEN 1995 AND 2000, numerous technology companies were launched in the hope of capitalizing on the booming popularity of the Internet. Investors poured millions of dollars into companies with few tangible assets. Companies that added an "e-" before their name, or a ".com" to the end, instantly attracted investors. The companies often operated at an initial loss, hoping to eventually gain significant market share in their particular field and ultimately to realize enormous profits. Many of the founders of these companies became instantly wealthy. The soaring stock seduced numerous investors to jump on the bandwagon while stock prices continued to soar. During the 2000 Super Bowl, 17 technology companies paid two million dollars each to purchase 30-second advertisements. March 10, 2000, marked the peak of the dot-com bubble.

In 1999, Warren Buffet, famed investor, gave a speech to an exclusive group of business leaders in Sun Valley about investing. While the business community was clearly enamored with the rising technology industry, Buffet had fastidiously refused to invest in its stocks. This seemed odd, since Buffet had a penchant for finding profitable investments, and he was a good friend of Bill Gates. Buffet insisted on investing in value and not in the popular stock of the day.

Even when his Berkshire Hathaway stock prices languished, he refused to compromise his convictions and jump on the dot-com bandwagon. He explained, "In the short run, the market is a voting machine. In the long run, it's a weighing machine" (Alice Schroeder, *The Snowball,* 16).

During 2000-2002, the dot-com bubble burst and over five trillion dollars in company value was lost. Refusing to be rushed or hurried into unwise investments, Buffet experienced astronomical success in the following years.

Scripture exhorts us *"Wait on the Lord; be of good courage, and He shall strengthen your heart. Wait, I say, on the Lord!"* (Psalm 27:14). God knows how to bring the maximum joy and abundance to our lives. But we must trust Him. His ways are not our ways. His timing is not ours. We can become impatient, wanting to experience financial success or to obtain a management position *now.* When a shortcut to success and happiness presents itself, we can be sorely tempted to jump on the bandwagon. But Scripture also encourages us to wait *patiently* on the Lord (Psalm 37:7). That can be the hard part!

Why does God make us wait for things? If He loves us, why doesn't He immediately shower us with everything that makes us happy? It is because God cares more about our *relationship* with Him than our *gifts* from Him. Waiting reminds us of who is ultimately in control of our life. It causes us to turn our attention (and our prayers) toward Him. It tangibly demonstrates His lordship over our lives.

We can be tempted to forgo waiting on the Lord and to simply take matters into our own hands. Those who have done so know what the result can be. We only have one life to invest. There will be innumerable dot-com schemes to throw your life into, but beware. If you are impatient, you may recklessly forfeit your future and miss what God intended to give you, if only you had waited. Scripture promises, "*Those who wait on the Lord shall renew their strength; they shall mount up with wings like eagles. They shall run and not be weary, they shall walk and not faint*" (Isaiah 40:31). Wait on the Lord. It's worth it!

REFLECT FOR A MOMENT

1. *Are you presently waiting for something? How are you handling it? Do you have difficulty waiting? If so, why is that? What might it cost you if you grow impatient?*

2. *If God is making you wait for something, how have you been spending the time? Have you grown frustrated? Or, have you been focusing more on Christ? Have you concentrated more on the gift or the Giver?*

3. *Why might God ask you to wait? What might God build in to your character and walk with Him that He can accomplish better by making you wait, than if He had immediately given you what you wanted? Are you willing to wait as long as it takes until you receive what God has for you? What is the alternative?*

Embracing Your Birthright

EDWARD ALBERT CHRISTIAN George Andrew Patrick David was born on June 23, 1894, with great fanfare. His great- grandmother, the formidable Queen Victoria, rejoiced at his birth. David, as he was known by his family, grew up to be popularly described as "Prince Charming." Winston Churchill took it upon himself to train him as a public speaker, and with considerable success. The young Prince of Wales made successful trips to North America, Australia, South Africa, and India. He drew large, enthusiastic crowds wherever he went. Yet David was unhappy. He constantly complained that he had no private life of his own. His father, King George V, had warned his son, "Don't think you can act like other people…You must always remember who you are." Yet King George worried about his son. When his son was 40, the king declared, "After I am dead the boy will ruin himself within twelve months" (Phillip Ziegler, *King Edward VIII*, 174).

Then David met Mrs. Wallis Simpson. She was an American who had divorced her first husband and was married to Earnest Simpson. David fell in love with her and began a torrid affair. She eventually divorced her second husband to marry David, who became King Edward VIII. But Edward was warned that the people would not accept their king marrying a woman who had two living husbands. Edward claimed that only she could make him happy. His mother warned him that she would never accept Mrs. Simpson as his wife, and the prime minister cautioned that marrying her would cost him his throne. Nevertheless, after having been King of England for less than a year, Edward VIII abdicated on December 10, 1937, so he could marry Wallis Simpson. Edward thereafter was known as the Duke of Windsor. He held various minor posts during World War Two, but after the war, he never fulfilled another official government role. Edward grew extremely bitter at his lot, and often suffered from boredom. He remained married to Wallis for 36 years until his death in 1972. Edward was the son of the king, yet he forfeited his inheritance to indulge in the sins of his flesh.

The apostle Paul claimed, *"The Spirit Himself bears witness with our spirit that we are children of God, and if children, then heirs—heirs of God and joint heirs with Christ, if indeed we suffer with Him, that we may also be glorified together"* (Romans 8:16-17). Paul was describing the unbelievable truth that we have the incomparable privilege as creatures of dust, to be adopted into God's royal family. Believers are made heirs of God, and joint heirs with Christ. We enjoy free access into God's presence. The storehouses of heaven are at our disposal. God's armies are mobilized for our defense. It is truly mindboggling.

Yet incredibly, there are those who forfeit their heavenly birthright. They are adopted as sons and daughters, yet they live as aliens. They prefer the cheap trinkets and gaudy earthly pleasures over the joys of heaven. They become consumed with their lust and greed and surrender the treasures that were theirs. Whereas they may have once been of service to their King, they are no longer. Lives that showed such promise now live with regrets. How are you living? As a child of the King? Are you delighting in your heavenly inheritance? Live like the royalty you are!

REFLECT FOR A MOMENT

1. *Are you living like a child of the King? Do you live with the constant awareness that all the resources of heaven are at your disposal? What confidence does being a child of the King give you?*

2. *Have you been tempted to forfeit your spiritual birthright? Have you been willing to harm your relationship with the King in order to dabble in the pleasures of sin? Why do you think Christians are so willing to forfeit something of value for pleasures that are temporal and ultimately dissatisfying?*

3. *Have you found yourself wanting to have the "best" of both worlds? Do you want all the privileges of being a child of God while still being free to dabble in the worldly sins that appeal to you? How successful have you been at doing both?*

Balance?

ONE OF THE most elusive goals for people is balance. We are often urged to carve out proper amounts of time for work, family, recreation, God, friends, rest, and hobbies. Since time continues to be our most precious commodity, properly balancing each responsibility forces us to continually fight a losing battle to find sufficient time for every priority. Something inevitably suffers neglect. Nevertheless, although the proponents of balanced living continue to fervently preach their message, the reality is that history has largely been made by imbalanced people. Think of the people who have exerted the greatest influence on human affairs. How many of them lived what you would call "balanced" lives? They were passionate. They were focused. But balanced, they were not. In order to be unusually effective in one area of their life, people tend to neglect other, important responsibilities.

Many a famous Christian leaders have experienced dramatic success in one area of their life while simultaneously neglecting other important aspects of their lives, such as their family. William Carey, a shoe cobbler from England was so passionate about impacting India for Christ that he volunteered to go as Britain's first missionary, even though it literally drove his wife insane. George Whitefield, the incomparable preacher of the 1700s, married Mrs. James, a widow. At the close of the wedding ceremony, Whitefield delivered a sermon and then preached twice daily throughout the following week. He then left for a month-long preaching tour, returning on Christmas Eve, and then departed on the 26th. When A.W. Tozer, the inspirational preacher and author, died, his widow remarried Leonard Odam. When she was later asked how her second marriage was going, in light of having been first married to such a well-known man of God, she replied, "I have never been happier in my life. Aiden loved Jesus Christ, but Leonard Odam loves me."

Jesus was an extremely busy person. He was constantly surrounded by crowds of people. Further, He had the ability to alleviate people's illnesses and to meet their needs. The pressure to do all He could would seemingly have been intense. But you never see Jesus in a hurry. You never witness Him feeling overwhelmed at all of His tasks. At one point Jesus was traveling through the bustling streets of Jericho. He spied Zacchaeus, the chief tax collector, sitting in a tree (Luke 19:1-10). Jesus instantly knew that His Father's priority for that moment was to spend time with the notorious sinner. At other times God's will was to move on to other villages (Mark 1:37). Periodically Jesus retreated from the crowds to spend time with His disciples (Matthew 16:5, 13). In other moments Jesus took time to teach the multitudes (Mark 6:34). The key for Jesus was not in properly allocating sufficient time on His calendar for each of His priorities. The key was to understand His Father's will (John 5:19-20). As a result, Jesus ultimately completed everything His Father assigned to Him (John 17:4).

God knows what your priorities should be for each day. Today it might be a project at work. Tomorrow it might be your daughter. God can accurately guide you each day to ensure you accomplish what you must for that day. If you follow His lead, you will live a life that may not always appear balanced at the moment, but will be complete, and full over time.

REFLECT FOR A MOMENT

1. *Have you attempted to live a "balanced life"? How effective has that been?*

2. *Have you suffered at times from imbalance? Have you focused so exclusively on certain activities that other priorities such as your family, were unnecessarily neglected?*

3. *Take time to seek God's will each day. He can guide you each day to know what is most important at that particular time. You must seek Him regularly though, because each day, your priority might change. Your life may seem imbalanced on any given day, but over time, God can guide you to attend to every important responsibility in your life.*

Living the Life That Is Really Life—Clear Focus

George Clark
Jr. Managing Director, Freestone Partners, LLC

Looking for that blessed hope, and the glorious appearing of the great God and our Savior Jesus Christ.

TITUS 2:13 (KJV)

AS BELIEVERS WE have the true hope! That hope is eternal life with our Lord. However, as humans, and as leaders, many of us live with divided hope. There is much in the world that clamors for our attention. We know our true hope is in heaven, but our eyes are focused on the temporal hope of the world.

> *"No man can serve two masters. Either he will hate the one and love the other, or he will be devoted to the one and despise the other. You cannot serve both God and money."*
>
> MATTHEW 6:24

As my career developed, I struggled with many things such as my health or raising my children from newborns into teenagers. Along with these challenges came the continual temptation to place my trust in what was temporal or worldly. As a leader, the priority of things like meeting the objectives of our different constituents or making budget creeps into my focus. But daily, as I spend time with the Lord, He gently reminds me that I am to work with all my heart and with excellence in everything that I do. I am not to place my hope in anything other than Him. Many leaders today extol erratic values. We begin to place a priority on power, prosperity, or riches. Consequently, we should not be surprised when those who follow us are inconsistent in their values in life and work.

It is difficult to trust in the Lord with all that you are with less than a single-minded focus on Him. It is a moment-by-moment decision to choose Jesus over the distraction in front of us.

Earlier this month, I had the opportunity to choose between trusting God or being upset that I did not get my way. Having struggled with upper back problems for over a year, I decided to try a minimally invasive treatment that had a high chance of success. It did not work. I have seen several doctors and tried most anything they thought would help. After prayer and reflection, I stopped to praise God. Why? Because I know that this is His perfect will. I am asking Him to open my eyes to His teaching and to strengthen me to do His will. While I am uncertain if and when God will allow my back to recover, I walk each day in confidence that the pain is here for my good and His glory.

It is my choice: Where is my focus? Do I trust Him? How about you?

In what or whom do you trust? Your business success? Your family? Your Lord and Savior? Look at your calendar and credit card statement from last month. These should verify your answer. What would your coworkers or family say?

Let's focus on Jesus and lift each other up daily. It's not just the best way to live; it is the only way.

REFLECT FOR A MOMENT

1. *Do you tend to trust more in your own skills and experience, or in Christ? How can you make sure you keep your trust and focus squarely on Christ?*

2. *Can you praise God even when you do not get what you want? Can you rejoice in Christ even when He allows you to suffer pain? How can you do that?*

3. *People are watching you and how you live your life. What do they see? If they were to model your behavior, what would they do?*

Wow! Take It In!

James Barnett
President, DaySpring Cards

DURING MY YEARS as a young boy (the youngest of seven children), our family took only two major vacations. The first was to the west coast when I was four years old. Eight of the nine of us piled into the car (with no air conditioning!) to travel from Arkansas to California. The other big trip was when I was 11. This time six of our family members went to the east coast pulling a trailer for lodging through the Great Smokey Mountains, to Washington DC and on to New York City. Then it was on to Boston and back across to Niagara Falls. It was awesome!

Because we traveled so little during these years (cost and a big family!), I remember vividly the impact those trips had on me. I was deeply impressed by the sites, monuments, and activities we were able to experience—encountering so many magnificent places and things for the first time. God's beauty and some of man's creations were wowed me big time!

Many years later when my wife and I had our own three children, we decided that each summer we would take a trip for two weeks to see our great country and God's beautiful creation. So along with my sister and brother-in-law and their two kids (nine of us in all), we decided a great goal would be to cover all of the national parks and major sites of the US over a 10-15 year period! We would rent a 12-or 15-passenger van and off we would go…usually 4,000 miles in two weeks… cheap hotels and lots of hiking and sightseeing. We were moving…and taking it in.

After seeing so many beautiful and wonderful sites for days and days and listening to me say again and again, "Wow, take it in," the kids became less and less impressed and excited. In fact, they grew a little bored! Our "wow factor" had worn out. We had shown them so many magnificent things they weren't interested anymore.

We often do the same thing in our spiritual life. As new believers we are impressed with God. Over time, the excitement wanes and we grow less and less enthralled. Then we hit tough times, hardships, disappointments, etc. and we lose the "wow" of God. While we have some "mountaintop" experiences along the way, we discover that much of life is lived in the valley or on the mountainside. Yet, because we lose perspective and "life" beats down on us, we fail to be impressed even when God does something awesome in our lives once again.

We also see this happen repeatedly in Scripture. Jesus performed miracle after miracle, and, while people were impressed for a time, they wandered back to "the mountainside of life" and failed to really take it in.

As we mature in our journey with Christ, I want to encourage you (as I encourage myself) to not lose heart in our day-to-day activity. While most of life is lived out "on the mountainside," God is always at work. Look for where He is working and join Him. Mark the times He reveals Himself to you, His beauty, His power, His answers to prayers. Remember and record the spiritual markers of life when God illuminates Himself to you…and He becomes a little more real to you.

When you get discouraged, take time to recount the specific times in the past He has shown Himself to you and you said, "Wow! Take it in!" Check out Matthew 8:23-27 when Jesus calms the storm. It closes with verse 27: "*The men were amazed and asked, 'What kind of man is this? Even the winds and the waves obey him!'*"(NIV) Never lose your amazement for God!

Reflect for a moment

1. *Have you lost your amazement at the goodness of God? From the time you first became a Christian, have you lost your amazement and wonder at who God is? If you have, what happened? How might you regain it?*

2. *Have certain spiritual habits become rituals instead of moments for worship? Attending worship services and having quiet times can become boring rituals rather than exciting encounters with Christ. If that has happened to you, how might you restore the excitement and freshness of your times with God? Could you change your routine? Could you do some things differently? Think of some practices that will enhance and invigorate your time with God.*

Navigating Today's Bitterness and Anger

Clarence Otis
Chairman and CEO, Darden Restaurants, Inc.

WE LIVE IN a time of increasing division and contention. It is a time when, more and more, we see people disparaging (and even demonizing) those of different circumstances and points of view—whether the similarities and differences in perspective have to do with personal temperament, cultural and social background, vocational and professional training, or some combination of these. People seem more deeply wedded to their own opinions about today's social, political, and moral issues and more angrily hostile toward those who hold a different viewpoint, even on complicated matters that are far from black and white.

In his letter to the Church at Corinth, Paul addressed a group of believers who were struggling with petty disagreements and offenses. These too were based, to a large degree, on differences in personality and background, and echo the disunity we have today. Paul challenged the Corinthians to refrain from placing too much stock in their own opinions or in the views of people generally, saying, "*Where is the wise? Where is the scribe? Where is the disputer of this age? Has not God made foolish the wisdom of this world?*" (1

Corinthians 1:20).

Paul disavowed his own opinions as well, glorifying instead the wisdom of God, telling the Corinthians, "*My speech and my preaching were not with persuasive words of human wisdom, but in demonstration of the Spirit and of power, that your faith should not be in the wisdom of men but in the power of God,*" (1 Corinthians 2:4-5). He admonished those in the church at Corinth who had aligned themselves with this apostle or that, telling them, "*For when one says 'I am of Paul,' and another, 'I am of Apollos,' are you not carnal? Who then is Paul, and who is Apollos, but ministers through whom you believed, as the Lord gave to each one. I planted, Apollos watered, but God gave the increase. So then neither he who plants is anything, nor is he who waters, but God who gives the increase*" (1 Corinthians 3:4-7).

Paul pointed out that each Christian is, in fact, unique, with different gifts. He explained that these disparate gifts were intended to work together for God's purpose: "*For to one is given the word of wisdom through the Spirit, to another the word of knowledge through the same Spirit, to another faith by the same Spirit, to another gifts of healing by the same Spirit, to another the working of miracles, to another prophecy, to another discerning of spirits, to another different kinds of tongues, to another the interpretation of tongues. But one and the same Spirit works all these things, distributing each one individually as He wills. For as the body is one and has many members, but all the members of that one body, being many, are one body, so also is Christ. For by one Spirit we were all baptized into one body*" (1 Corinthians 12:8-13).

Paul gloried in the fact that God created people uniquely. Each person has unique gifts, strengths, insights, perspectives, and concerns. When God brings people together, it is so He can allow people to work together for His purpose. If God delights in diversity, why do we make our differences a source of such discord? Why do we hold fast to our own opinions and remain unwilling to subject them to constructive criticism and, perhaps, improvement by others—even when those others are fellow Christians? Is it because we have too much love for ourselves and not enough for others? Does Paul capture us and the self-righteous, close-mindedness we can exhibit when he says, "*Though I speak with the tongues of men and of angels, but have not love, I have become sounding brass or a clanging cymbal*" (1 Corinthians 13:1).

There's no doubt that important matters are at issue today. Is that sufficient reason, though, for us to retreat into our own viewpoint and reject those with different perspectives that may reflect their unique positioning in the Body of Christ? Is such rejection not a sign of too much self-love and too little love for thy neighbor? Through Paul, God teaches that we stand a better chance of discerning His will when we love others and respect and take their perspectives and concerns seriously. If we're alienated from one another because of our differences, don't we fail to take advantage of the diversity with which God has blessed us? And with such failure, aren't we further from, not closer to, discerning God's will? As believers, we must take care to avoid the social, political, and moral anger percolating around us. We must remember "*Love suffers long and is kind; love does not envy; love does not parade itself, it is not puffed up*" (1 Corinthians 13:4).

REFLECT FOR A MOMENT

1. *Are you more concerned with people or with being right? Are you willing to be gracious with people to maintain unity, rather than offending someone in your effort to win an argument?*

2. *Are you an argumentative person? If so, why do you feel the need to always win a debate or get the best of others? Is it difficult for you to build up others, even if it means yielding ground to them in a discussion?*

3. *Do you always distinguish clearly between matters that cannot be compromised and issues that are merely matters of personal opinion? Some issues should be died for. Many matters can be compromised for the sake of harmony. Have you been good at distinguishing between the two?*

Responsibility

David Fagin
CEO (Ret) Golden Star Mining

UPON ENTERING THE Holy Land which had been promised to Moses, in Joshua 1:6, Joshua instructed the people: "*Be strong, courageous, be careful to obey Moses law, not turning to the right or to the left that you may be successful wherever you go.*" How it must grieve Jesus' heart that leaders so often fall short of these simple instructions. News stories have recently reported many leaders that have committed great sins, including church leaders, politicians, businessmen, and sports stars, many of whom claim to follow Jesus. Society has become so numbed by such failures, that it is no longer embarrassed or shocked. However, rather than dwelling on these shortcomings, Christian business leaders should redouble their efforts to demonstrate self-control to protect the reputations of both Jesus and themselves from such weakness in character.

In Joshua 1:8, we are told to meditate on God's word day and night and to obey everything written in it so we will be prosperous and successful ambassadors for Christ. In order to do this, we must walk closely with Jesus daily, absorbing his love, compassion, and strength, and using the same tools that He used to ward off the world's temptations. Jesus faced the same ones (and more) than we have. Unlike Jesus, we are not perfect and we will fail, some of us often. But because of our love for Him, our faith in the Gospel, and His sacrifice for us, we know we will be forgiven. Those around us can be forgiven too, if they will only repent and follow Him.

In Romans 13:12, we are told to put on the "armor of light" and to behave decently. The apostle Paul provided further instruction to protect us in Ephesians 6:10-17. Paul describes the "full armor of God" in word pictures and encourages us (1) to live in truth, (2) to strive for righteousness, (3) to remain vigilant to maintain peace, (4) to remain faithful to ward off the evil one, (5) to seek salvation in every thought, (6) to listen to the Spirit through the Word, and (7) to remain in prayer at all times while praying that every person and situation will be conformed to the will of God.

As business leaders, we have a unique opportunity to influence the lives of many people. We must choose whether to impact them for good, or for ill. This includes our employees, shareholders, regulators, advisors, suppliers, customers, and competitors. Because of our leadership status, we may also influence those unrelated to our work because of our leadership status such as our family, friends, neighbors, those we meet in industrial or professional associations, and others. How do they view our behavior? What do they think of our character? If they know we claim to be Christian, and yet see attitudes of arrogance, pride, thoughtlessness, and selfishness…they will know us only as hypocrites.

By these passages and many others, it is clear that leaders have a much greater responsibility to God than most of those around us. Luke 12:48 says, *"From everyone who has been given much, much will be demanded"*(NIV). Because it was His plan, God granted and enabled us to attain the positions we hold or have held. We should be grateful for His mercy and generosity and share God's full blessings with those in our lives. If we don't, we may unwittingly drive others away from His kingdom.

REFLECT FOR A MOMENT

1. *How do you feel about having "responsibility"? Do you see that word as negative or positive? Do you tend to embrace responsibility or to resent it? Why?*

2. *The more God gives us, the more He expects. As you have been given positions of leadership, how have you experienced this truth? Why do you think God does this? Why have so many leaders proven to be irresponsible? What can you do to continue being trustworthy as God increases your responsibility?*

3. *God told Joshua to meditate on His word day and night so he could obey everything God commanded. How is that possible for you to do? What would meditating day and night look like in your life? Why is it important that you do so?*

Welcome Home

Terry Noetzel
Deloitte Consulting LLP

RECALL, IF YOU would, a recent business trip. Perhaps it was extended…and had its share of challenges. What was it like to be away from home? What was it like to return home, to gather round the dinner table and share that first meal back with your family?

Recently, God has had me camped out in the parable of the Prodigal Son (Luke 15:11-32). Certainly, all three characters have much to teach us, but God has focused my attention on the Prodigal.

Notice the Prodigal's departure: he said to his father *"give me my share of the estate"(NIV)*; then the Prodigal gathered all that he had and set off for a distant country. It's remarkable that a son would demand his inheritance. In reality, he was saying, "Father, I wish you were dead! Since I can't wait for you to die, just give me all that I have coming after your death, as well as what you need to live on, so I can get out of here." This is a radical rejection of the Father. Of course, I would never do that.

Or would I? The Father calls me to walk at His side, to allow Him to provide for me in every area of my life, to live in intimate relationship with Him. Yet there are times, ways, and habits where my actions and thoughts in effect say "I'll just figure it out myself" or "I really want this particular outcome, so I'll make it happen."

Subtle? Perhaps. But isn't this living as if I don't have a home and must go off to the distant country and make one for myself? Isn't it nonetheless a rejection of the Father, a denial that my true home can only be found in Him?

While in the distant country the Prodigal squandered his inheritance on fleeting, temporal, worldly pleasures. God allowed famine in the distant country, but there is no shortfall at home. Eventually, the son came to his senses and began rehearsing the speech he was going to make. Note, however, that the son did not even consider the possibility of complete forgiveness. He set his sights on survival and planned his negotiating strategy for a business relationship with the Father. As a hired hand, he'd be entitled to compensation for services. Yes, he'd survive, but he wouldn't live in the fullness of who he really was, the true son of the Father. The wayward son did recognize that living at home, even as a hired hand, was far better than the impoverished lifestyle he was experiencing in the distant country. So he began his journey toward home.

Even while far off, the Father caught sight of him and *ran* to meet him. Amazing! The son attempted to blurt out his lines, but the Father ignored his words. He was already forgiven! The Father was overjoyed that His son had returned. Rather than a business relationship, the Father restored him to full sonship with the family ring and a royal robe. Then the celebration began! The Father whose love never wavered, celebrated the return of the one who had heartlessly rejected him.

It's clear, isn't it? God has so much more in store for you than you can imagine. His love is so complete and unconditional, that He will not only let you walk away, but He will run to you as soon as you turn and take the first steps toward Him. With a Father like that, why would you ever want to leave home?[1]

REFLECT FOR A MOMENT

1. *What is your favorite aspect of the parable of the Prodigal Son? Why is it? Who do you identify with in that parable? Why?*

2. *When have you been like the younger son? How have you rejected your heavenly Father's love for you? Why have you done so?*

3. *How has the love of the Father encouraged you? When have you experienced His warm welcome when you returned to Him? Are you presently walking at a distance from Christ? Do you need to return into a full, intimate walk with God once more? If so, what is preventing you from returning to Him now?*

---

1 Inspiration for this devotional should credited to the writings of Henri Nouwen in *The Return of the Prodigal Son: A Story of Homecoming.*

Final Challenge

IT HAS BEEN my enormous privilege to work with men and women who spend their workdays in the marketplace. They are remarkable people. Somewhere in their life, God got a hold of them. Nothing has been the same since. Their families have felt the impact. Their colleagues have been encouraged. Their churches have been revived. In short: their lives are making a profound difference in their world.

These people had understood they were gifted in business, but they had not known why God had equipped them in that particular way. Once they understood God's call to a personal relationship with Him, everything in their life came into proper perspective. They now understood why God had taken their lives down the pathway He did. Their failures as well as their successes, their heartaches as well as their joys, finally made sense to them. Their purpose in life came in to focus at last. As a result, these businesspeople are dramatically expanding God's kingdom.

That is my prayer for you. I am keenly aware that I have only one life to live. It is too precious to squander! The same is true for you. As you go deeper in your walk with Christ, He will transform you to think, feel, and act like Him. He will lay His heart over yours. You will readily discern what matters in life, and what does not. You will find yourself drawn to invest in that which is eternal, and you will grow to disdain that which is temporal or carnal.

Hopefully as you have read these devotional thoughts, you have done so with an open mind and heart. A devotional cannot change your life. But the Holy Spirit, who is with you as you read, can. Welcome His involvement into your life. Eagerly respond to His promptings. Trust Him regardless of how impossible His word may appear to you. And obey. Immediately. Your life is too valuable to spend it in any other way than in the center of God's will. Live well, and enjoy your Savior.

ABOUT THE AUTHOR

DR. RICHARD BLACKABY is a prolific author, international speaker, grateful husband to Lisa, and proud father to Mike, Daniel, and Carrie. He invests himself, encouraging people to seek God's best for their lives. He works with Christian business leaders, helping them to be on God's agenda in the marketplace. Richard has a Ph.D. in history and has been a life-long student of leadership. Dr. Blackaby currently serves as the president of Blackaby Ministries International (www.blackaby.org) through which he teaches business, church, and family leaders how to take their leadership to a higher level. You can keep up with him at facebook.com/DrRichardBlackaby and twitter.com/richardblackaby

DR. BLACKABY HAS written numerous books including *Experiencing God, Spiritual Leadership: Moving People on to God's Agenda, God in the Marketplace: 45 Questions Fortune 500 Executives Ask About Faith, Life, and Business; The Seasons of God: How the Shifting Patterns of Your Life Reveals His Purposes for You; Unlimiting God: Increasing Your Capacity to Experience the Divine; Fresh Encounter: God's Pattern for Spiritual Awakening; Putting a Face on Grace: Living a Life Worth Passing On; Hearing God's Voice; Experiencing God: Knowing and Doing the Will of God;* and *Called to Be God's Leader: Lessons from the Life of Joshua.*

CONTRIBUTORS

Jack Alexander, Vice Chairman and Partner,
Rainmaker Group Holdings.

James Barnett, President, DaySpring.

John D. Beckett, Chairman, The Beckett Companies;
Author, *Loving Monday* and *Mastering Monday.*

Jed Burnham, CEO Vectra Bank (retired).

Rich Case, CEO, Benchmark Associates, Inc.

George L. Clark Jr., Managing Director, Freestone Partners, LLC.

Lawrence A. Collett, Chairman of the Board,
Cass Information Systems, Inc.

Jeffrey H. Coors, Chairman, Fiskeby Holdings US, LLC.

Marjorie Dorr, Chief Strategy Officer, Wellpoint Inc. (retired);
CEO, Anthem BCBS Northeast (retired)

David L. Dunkel, Chairman and CEO of KForce, Inc.

Dave Fagin, CEO (retired) Golden Star Mining.

Brent Garrison, Ph.D., Director of CEO Relations,
CEO Forum.

Lou Giuliano, Chairman and CEO, ITT Corp., (retired).
Workforce Ministries.

Steve Hughes, Management Consultant.

Greg King, Principal of GCK Ventures, LLC.

Clyde Lear, Chairman/CEO, and Founder,
Learfield Communications, Inc.

Richard McClure, President, UniGroup, Inc. and CEO, United Van Lines and Mayflower Transit.

Mark Nelson, President, Chevron International Pte Ltd., International Products.

Terry Noetzel, Principal, Deloitte Consulting LLP.

Clarence Otis Jr., Chairman and CEO, Darden Restaurants, Inc.

J. Michael Perry, EVP Business Development, Williams Financial Group.

Lynda Pitts, CEO, Legacy Marketing Group.

David Ratcliff, Chairman/President/CEO, Southern Company.

Cort Randell, President, Corporate Media Services, Inc.

Jeff Reeter, Managing Partner, The Texas Financial Group LP of Northwestern Mutual.

Paul Spence, CEO of The STI Group.

Tom Starnes, Chairman and CEO, Inflexis.

Steve Taylor, Former CEO, Fresh Express

Ron Wagley, Chairman, CEO and President Transamerica Insurance (retired).